EGYPT

AND

TUNIS.

EGYPT

In 1855 and 1856;

TUNIS

In 1857 and 1858.

BY

W. H. GREGORY, M.P.

VOL. I.

LONDON:
PRINTED FOR PRIVATE CIRCULATION,
BY JOHN RUSSELL SMITH,
36, SOHO SQUARE.
M.DCCC.LIX.

PREFACE.

A NEW work of merit needs no explanation of the circumstances of its birth, no apology for being brought into the world. It will be gladly received and welcomed; and if without a preface, so much the better—a valuable acquaintance requires but little introduction. If, however, any book needs a preface, this assuredly does; for the very fact of its being printed for private circulation only, is a proof that the author considers he is not depriving the world of any store of original observation, research, or imagination. It is printed at the request of private friends, as it was intended while being written, for their amusement only; and it professes to be nothing more than an accumulation of random notes and extracts, converted into the continuous Narrative of a Journey from Marseilles to Egypt and Nubia, and a five months' residence in those countries, in 1855 and 1856.

The object of it is to be something more than an itinerary, and something less than a work of imagination—to describe the impressions which those luminous lands have produced on the writer, and which will, perhaps, be reproduced on those readers who may hereafter visit them; and to bring before them as graphically as he can, the grandeur of the Nile-valley monuments, the grandest and the oldest in the world. The author's sole wish, therefore, being to carry home to friendly firesides, Nile scenes painted as vividly and as correctly as it lay in his power, has not scrupled to borrow from other writers such passages as he has considered conducive to that purpose. An amateur, although conscious that his attempts, as works of art, are of no great value, may still like to adorn his walls with his own drawings of spots which bear with them recollections. These he wishes to recall; but if he comes across, and can become possessed of, sketches of these same spots conceived in the very spirit with which he himself viewed them, but executed with a bolder hand and a happier pencil, he will rejoice to secure such masterpieces, and to substitute them for his own; much more then, in the present instance, when the author's object is not merely to please himself, but to give to his friends the best possible idea of Egypt and its scenes, is he justified in borrowing from the descriptions of others, even to a far greater extent than he has done. If he blame himself at all, it is perhaps for having had too little rather than too much recourse to writers who have traversed the same ground.

As much of these volumes was written on the Nile, and the remainder in the country, where the writer was unable to procure the books from which he had selected extracts, in some cases he has forgotten to whom he is indebted, and has merely marked the passage in *italics*, as not being original.

These preliminary observations are intended not for the purpose of deprecating criticism, but to account for the introduction of many trivial observations and unnecessary descriptions, which would certainly have never been introduced had the volumes been intended for a circulation larger than that of a circle of intimate friends.

COOLE PARK, *Oct.* 1857.

EGYPT AND NUBIA

In 1855 and 1856.

At half-past ten o'clock on November 28, 1855, the *Vectis* weighed her anchor, and we left Marseilles with a bright warm sun overhead, and a brisk breeze behind us. Fortunately, as we subsequently discovered, the wind was light, and with us; for a more uneasy, dancing, tumble-about, wet concern than the *Vectis*, even by the confession of the crew, in spite of her sea-going excellencies, could hardly be conceived; so much so, that the purser was heard to pour out his sorrows to a sympathizing lady's-maid, by assuring her that it was the "disagreeablest craft" he had ever sailed in, and that he was destroyed by the "rheumatiz," from the constant wettings he had received, not to mention the loss of five pounds' worth of good clothing, rendered useless by repeated duckings. The company which assembled at breakfast gave one, on the whole, a very good opinion of one's fellow-voyagers, and the fare was unexceptionable; but we were crowded to such an extent, that on my expressing an opinion, that in hot weather such close packing would be unwholesome, a medical gentleman intimated very decidedly, that it would be liable to bring on a great amount of sickness. An idea of the discomfort may be formed from the condition of my cabin, which would have been considered small for two persons in a Holyhead packet, where the crossing is an affair of five hours; yet here I had, in this miserable little hole, to contemplate a six or seven days' voyage with three other persons; to be immured, moreover, in a berth which totally precluded the possibility of stretching one's legs to anything like their natural elongation, and with a space between one's head and the deck-beam above of only six inches—a very pleasant prospect for a restless sleeper or an unquiet conscience.

After once we settled down, and got ourselves and baggage somewhat ship-shape, a good deal of *bonne camaraderie* and amusement prevailed. We lived well, the sea was calm, the sun was bright, and we rose early the following morning to have a good look at Corsica and Sardinia, for we were passing through the Straits of Bonifacio, almost within stone's throw of the Sardinian shore. It seemed, as far as the eye could reach inland, rocky, uncultivated, and uninhabited. There was a pretty good library on board, and reading, talking, and an occasional cigar, consumed the time till the bell announced the solemn hour of four, when dinner was proclaimed. After dinner, some returned to the deck; others beguiled the hours of darkness with the lively backgammon, the less lively draughts, the solemn chess, or the disputatious whist. At cock-crow—and the cocks crew loud and shrill till the third day, when the sacrificial knife cut short their orisons—the faithful Hubert, my Belgian servant, stood by my berth and summoned me to the bath-room. Over the wet plashy deck, one wended one's way for a glorious plunge into sea-water, cold and brisk and fresh, and which the rolling of the vessel rendered an admirable imitation of receding and advancing waves. By breakfast time on Nov. 30 we were opposite Marsala, in Sicily, and its long white walls glistened brightly and cheerily in the sun; while, close in to the shore, the *speronari*, like white sea-birds, seemed chasing each other to and fro, as they tacked and weared. In this manner, during the day, we ran along, coasting the island as far as Girgenti—the ancient Agrigentum; and nothing could be grander than the view. Mountain after mountain receded inland, their peaks now obscured by clouds, and now revealed by the gilding of the mid-day sun. Little wall-surrounded towns were set like brooches on their breasts; an enormous plain, apparently barren, stretched between them and the sea, on the shores of which bright, flat-roofed, white houses shone along uninterruptedly, and gave me the idea of a teeming population. It was altogether one of the most beautiful views that could be well conceived; and one little wondered, even after so slight an insight as this into its beauties, how the fair island has been wooed and won by Punic, Greek, Roman, Saracen, French, Spanish, and Italian lords; and now we hear that all her thoughts are directed to, and her hopes centred in, the red-coated, blue-eyed strangers of an island in the Northern seas, to drive away the Bluebeard under whom her riches and her beauty pine and fade. Daily, the poor captive cries aloud, "Sister Ann, sister Ann, see'st thou the champion coming?"— But sister Ann gives her no response; for as yet from her watch-tower, casting her eyes around her far, she sees neither the red-capped Zouave, nor the purple-plumed Sardinian, nor the tartaned Highlander, pricking across the plain to her relief. Yet, assuredly, all that day (Nov. 30), if they availed her ought, she had the sympathies of the Oriental and Peninsular steamship *Vectis*, and from our hearts we wished that God might speedily send that oppressed and lovely captive a good deliverance.

Next morning, betimes, an unusual clatter on deck announced an event, and the stewards informed us we were in Malta harbour. Notice was posted that we were given a holiday till twelve o'clock, when we were to return again on board. Away we fled, like boys from school, up flights of stone steps, through covered ways, and fortifications where big guns eyed you uglily as you advanced, some ladies, their maid, myself, and Hubert, forming a strong storming party. We breakfasted on a decoction of beans called coffee, and probably caper-leaves called tea, and then proceeded to see the marvels, commencing with the grand old cathedral of St. John, which required, alas! far more time for inspection than we could then afford to give it. The sides of this fine church, parallel to the nave, are divided into chapels of the knights of different countries; and the pavement is formed of the gravestones of these *avant gardes* of Christianity, in every variety of brilliant polished marbles, adorned with traceries and scrolls of many colours. We had but short space to read and mark; but still, as we passed along, we saw the great names of those devoted champions of Christendom which once filled the world with their glory—the Rohan of France, the Doria of Genoa, Gonzalez of Spain.

> The knights are dust,
> Their good swords are rust,
> Their souls are with the saints we trust.

Thence we wandered through the strange, narrow, oriental streets, half African, half Italian in appearance, with *jalousies* and balconies almost touching, and, passing by two or three splendid *auberges* of the different nations, mounted to the Governor's garden. The great harbour, with its men-of-war and transports full of soldiers for the Crimea, lay beneath us, and the eye ranged over the fortifications and much of the apparently barren, rocky, glaring island. After this we visited the Governor's Palace, where there are some wonderful tapestries of ancient date, and quaint old pictures set in the walls, representing the sea combats of the knights with the followers of the " false Mahound," and the triumphs of the Maltese cross over the pale crescent on a blood-red ground. Then came the old armoury—the most remarkable circumstance connected with it being the smallness of the suits that incased such heroes; for assuredly, on board the *Vectis*, out of the sixty or seventy passengers, there were at least twenty who by no process of compression could have been introduced into such limited accommodation; and I may venture to assert that in the whole collection there was not a suit that would have fitted one of our average lifeguardsmen. I remember, on a visit to Warwick Castle, some years ago, being much surprised at the same result, when some of the visitors, rather below than above the middle height, attempted, but in vain, to inclose themselves in the ancient armour. So I presume we must conclude of the knights, as Virgil expresses himself of the bees, that they bore " Ingentes animos in corpore parvo."

But time began to press, and the ladies had to shop, so we bought very fair gloves at a shilling a pair, and straw hats of Tuscan plat for half-a-crown; and cotton coverings for the head against the Sun, into whose dominion we were about to pass, and oil of lavender against the fleas, his liege and ever-faithful subjects; and, having thus protected the outer man and woman, we adjourned to the market and bought mandarin oranges—delicious little fellows, which seemed ready of their own accord to throw off their coats to help you to consume them—and luscious buttery bananas, and juicy insipid prickly pears; and the queen of all good fruits, the custard apple, or chirimoya of South America, which melts in the mouth with savour indescribable; and then, having despatched letters to all good friends at home, we returned to our floating prison, and employed the half-hour of delay before starting in watching the extraordinary and unerring diving feats of half-naked Maltese for sixpences; and then a scream from the steam whistle, and away we went again, wending our way to Africa.

All had been peace and quiet up to this time; but, alas! that night the wind came down on us, and the sea came up on us; and few were the gallant Britons that showed a bold front the morning after, at breakfast—fewer still at dinner. The devil seemed to have possessed the *Vectis*; she plunged and rolled, and then ran through a wave which retaliated by washing over her from stem to stern. Then she seemed to stand still, as if in a fit of obstinacy, and made up for it by performing a series of antics, kicking, prancing, and curveting, to such an extent that no serious person could tolerate it; therefore most of us in disgust retired to our couches. This unhappy state of things continued the whole of the day, the following night, and a good portion of the succeeding morning. It was impossible to remain on deck, from the waves beating over us, although the officers called it only a good steady south-easter. The state cabin was intolerable, from the moans and noises of the wretched victims in the adjacent cribs; so, in despair of peace, quiet, and dry clothes, I had to retire to my little hole, and there snooze and grumble and pester the steward about the time of day, during the weary, weary hours. At last there came a lull; and in the morning, by holding well on by ropes or spars, a few of us contrived to emerge and get a mouthful of fresh air, and an escape from a very good imitation of suffocation. We had, in consequence of the sea running so high, been battened own, as sailors call it—an operation which those who have undergone the same, under an eastern sun and a south wind from the desert, will fully appreciate. About eleven o'clock A.M. the cheering sound of "land in sight" infused much animation among the sufferers. In a short while after, the shores of Africa, lying low, were plainly distinguished, and we steered into the port of Alexandria, having on our left the Raset-Tin (the headland of figs), where the Pharos celebrated of yore was built, with the fine simple inscription—

Σώστρατος Δεξιφανους Κνιδιος
Θεοῖς σωτῆρσι
ὑπὲρ τῶν πλωιζομένων.

Sostratus, the Cnidian, son of Dexiphanes,
To the Saviour Gods
For Mariners.

Assailed and beset by donkey-boys, we fought the best of our way into the Great Square, where the hotels, chief mercantile residences, and consular offices, are built, and found every nook and cranny occupied by the influx of passengers from India, and by the *Ava's* voyagers, who had preceded us by a few hours. After the greatest difficulty and many entreaties, aided by the kindness of the captain of the *Vectis*, who acted as intercessor, we contrived to get a little hole in a garret at one hotel for the ladies, and I was promised that I should have a bed somewhere or other. A very short walk convinced me that a more uninteresting town cannot possibly exist than Alexandria. Dirt, dust, glare, and ruined tumble-down mud hovels, when you leave the Great Square, are its characteristics. Then came the night—the first night in Egypt—and such a night! My dormitory I found already occupied by thirteen other individuals, of all classes and distinctions. Two or three closets, equally closely packed, opened into it. On lying down, in

1*

the fond hope of sleep, the futility of human expectations was soon apparent. First of all arose the trumpeting—not to call it by the gentle term snoring—of two able-bodied seamen; then resounded for another hour or so the uninterrupted howl and barking of dogs engaged in their nocturnal frays; babies in the adjoining closets next took up the din; this was varied by the occasional piercing shriek of some ill-omened bird of night; and lastly, as morning approached, the cocks commenced their challenge in every possible direction. Had even tired nature been able to overcome all these hindrances to repose, there was one still more formidable foe to be encountered, and demanding blood. "Fee—faw—fum!" said the musquito, like the Welsh giant; and, turn which way you might, there he was, buzzing and singing in your ears, and giving those premonitory signals of attack which the swollen faces and punctured foreheads of my companions showed next day to be by no means empty threats. "Ya habeebee!—ya habeebee!"—(O my darling!—O my darling!) is, according to the Arabs, the refrain of the mosquito's love-song; and certainly never lover wooed reluctant object of his devotion with greater assiduity than these wretches pressed their attentions on us, during that *noche triste*—that night of tribulation. Sleepless and unrefreshed, we gladly heard the summons to prepare for the journey to Cairo; and, at a good steady pace by rail, got over two hours and a half of the sixteen hours which we were told was to be the time consumed, but which we found to exceed twenty.

As we left the station, we got a good view of Pompey's Pillar, so called. It stands boldly out upon an eminence; and, though the name may recall recollections of the great triumvir, in reality it has nothing to do with him, having been erected by Publius, prefect of Egypt, in honor of the Emperor Diocletian. Ask, however, an Arab or a dragoman who erected it, and the reply will be, in all probability, that it is the work of Pharaoh. "Everything in Egypt is connected in the popular mind with this marvellous mythological personage, who seems to occupy the same position, as worker of marvels, with Sekunder and Roostam in Persia, and the monkey-god Huneyman in India. The very animals and natural products are somehow connected with him. The ichneumon is his cat; the dirty white phœnicopterous vulture is his hen; the prickly pear is his fig; and the mongrel race of the country are designated in scorn and contempt, by the pure-blooded Bedoueens, as sons of Pharaoh. There seems no lower epithet in their vocabulary than to call the Egyptian 'Ya ibn Firaun!' (thou son of Pharaoh)." The country through which we passed was fertile beyond description—flat, black alluvial deposit, producing maize, sugarcane, wheat, millet, cotton, crop after crop, white or green, in inexhaustible profusion. It was a pleasant daydream, to think of exchanging a few thousand acres of my stony patrimony in Galway, for a similar number of these, were I even forced to take along with my bargain some fifty score dingy looking fellahs, who were lazily breaking up the clods with heavy hoes, together with their blue-shifted veiled spouses and ophthalmious children, their muddy ungainly looking buffaloes, and troops of tawny goats. At the expiration of the two hours and a half aforesaid, we arrived at the present terminus, and came, for the first time, in sight of Nil-el-Mubarek (the Blessed Nile), rolling along its turbid waters.

Without indulging in any sentimental exuberances, there is certainly a deep feeling of interest in approaching, for the first time, the banks of this mighty and mysterious river, of whom, as of its own goddess Isis, it may be said, that none have ever lifted its veil. One cannot help reflecting, that on its shores, in the very earliest ages of mankind, when the rest of the world was plunged in barbarism, this small space between the Lybian and Arabian hills, rendered fertile by its waters, was the seat of civilization, of flourishing cities, of enlightened monarchs, where works were executed of such stupendous dimensions as to have been the marvel and study of nations mighty also in their undertakings, and grand in their conceptions. Here, on the verge of the desert, unharmed by time, and apparently indestructible by the ravages of man, have reared their majestic heads for more than five thousand years, the Pyramids, the purposes of which have been for ages a perplexity to the wise and learned. But modern science has commanded those mute walls to speak, and the strange mysterious characters of the monuments to reveal their purport; and they tell us the history of great conquerors and beneficent rulers, of foreign wars and domestic improvements, and religious rites and daily habits—of a state of vigorous society, though not in its first youth when Abraham came down to Egypt. And when Jacob and his sons, from the black pastoral tents of Palestine, gazed with awe at the magnificence of Memphis, they were, doubtless, told by him who rode in the chariot next to Pharaoh, of the same great avenues of sphinxes, and of obelisks and of portals and mausolea, extending along the banks of the sacred river far away into the south; for Joseph's days were the palmy days of Egyptian dominion, wealth, and intelligence. In other countries, modern philosophical investigations have disallowed long-established claims to very high antiquity; but here, research and science, so far from diminishing the lapse of ages hitherto granted to the infancy of Egyptian art, are, as information increases, extending its history into the very childhood of the human race. As each successive torch is lighted, the deeper do we gaze into the cavernous recesses of old time; and the mind stands aghast at the almost unfathomable gulf it is called upon to traverse, ere it arrives at the dynasties of those early monarchs whose names and titles are graven upon stone in characters as clear, as sharp, and as defined, as when they left the carvers' hands. There is something, too, in Egyptian architecture peculiarly solemn, striking, and mysterious. Its gigantic dimensions, its gloomy severity, its crushing weight—the grand colossal images, ever sitting, mute mourners of gone magnificence—the strange idols, typical of hidden meaning, only known to those learned in all the learning of the Egyptian race—the priestly caste, with whom Herodotus held intercourse, and heard things that he might not tell of—the interminable cities of the dead, which the perpetual ravages of the spoiler for more than eighteen hundred years have as yet rifled but of a portion only of their contents — the embalmed bodies of those who lived and loved three thousand years ago, and which now tell the tale of their sex, of their employments, of their habitations, and of their monarch;—all these changes cannot fail to move one deeply, as one first gazes on the waters of the Nile; yet, with the names of Menes and Shoofoo, and Kephren, and Sesostris, and Rameses, surging upwards in our minds, column-like as the great rebel Jinn in the Arabian tale, can we forget the fair lady that lay at his feet, and not remember, too, that serpent of old Nile—Cleopatra, loved of Ammun.

This digression may well be warranted, for we lay for two hours before starting at the mud village of Kafr-el-Lais, waiting for a special train which was to convey one of our passengers (Mr. Bartle Frere, since distinguished in India), who had been left behind at Alexandria, and without whom the transit officials positively refused to start the steamboat. At last the missing gentleman arrived; and we got under way, steaming onward by the side of high banks, mud villages, pigeon turrets, and sheiks' tombs. There were palm groves ever and anon, and processions of camels paced gravely along the towing-path. Nothing could be more oriental, and the weather was enchanting; but here my commendations cease; and my earnest hope is, that I may never again pass thirteen hours in a Nile steamer *en route* to Cairo. When evening meal-time came, a scene of barbarous confusion arose, more worthy of a gathering of harpies than of—so called by themselves—respectable human beings. The cabin, dimly illuminated by a few blearing tallow candles stuck in bottles, revealed the sight of a thick seething crowd, struggling, clamoring for food, drinking beer out of cups and saucers, and dislocating chickens with teeth and fingers. It was in vain to contend for a spot; so, seizing manfully a whole chicken and some bread, I fought my way up again to the deck, and being gallantly seconded by a young Indian officer, who brought up the rear with one plate and a dish of turnips, we managed to procure a meal for the famishing ladies, and get the pickings for ourselves. But the cup of bitterness was not yet exhausted; and I well may call it the cup, for I believe there were not half-a-dozen glasses in the boat. When darkness came on, the tired wayfarers descended into the cabin. There the horsehair seats were elongated into a kind of couch, and, like the defunct in the Morgue, each man was stretched out on his black slab; thus we lay side by side. The mosquitoes had departed, being driven away by the wind; but in their place came forth a horde of bugs, and they passed over the bodies and faces of the heavy sleepers, and when they awoke, they found that all comeliness had departed from them, and that their likeness was as those who have had a favorable measles. Such, indeed, was the physiognomy of the many whom these insects affectioned; for, capricious wretches that they are, they clove to some, and rejected others. For myself, I soon perceived what was impending, and took refuge on the deck. There a pleasant welcome awaited me from an American friend, Louis C——, who offered me share of a snug retreat he had made on top of the luggage, by the appropriation of every loose shawl and great-coat that had been abandoned by their owners. There he and Captain Flle. beguiled the night with the nigger minstrelsy of Tennessee.

At about one in the morning we arrived at Boulak, the port of Cairo; and in about another hour the vans deposited us on the steps of Shepheard's Hotel. Again we found every hole and crevice full, partly from residents, and partly from the boat that had preceded ours. A most good-natured, charitable woman, however (whom I subsequently found to be Mrs. Walker, a well-known personage at Cairo), contrived to procure for the exhausted ladies a bedroom, I believe, by giving up her own. The divan of the great saloon was reserved for the multitude, myself among the number. And now for night the second. It was pretty much the pendant of night the first, except that, on this occasion, the victims who could get no beds, were obliged to take chance on tables, sofas, and divans; and by wrapping up the head, as the Romans of yore when devoting themselves to the infernal gods, *capite obvoluto*, to defend themselves against the assaults of legions of mosquitoes. But no wrapping could avail against the new foe which had spared us hitherto. The attacks of the bugs anon were the attacks of the heavy armed; but now came forth from the crevices, skirmishing parties of the light and agile flea. "No quarter to the well-fed, sanguine, tender-skinned Howaga!" was their motto. In agony, like poor Strepsiades of old, under similar circumstances, in the thinking shop of Socrates, I cried aloud—

    ἀπόλλυμαι δείλαιος· ἐκ τοῦ σκίμποδος
    δάκνουσί μ' ἐξέρποντες οἱ Κορίνθιοι
      καὶ τᾶς πλευρὰς δαρδάπτουσιν
      καὶ τὴν ψυχὴν ἐκπίνουσιν
      καί με —— διορύττουσιν
      καί μ' ἀπολοῦσιν.

Wretch that I am—beneath this rug
I thought to lie right warm and snug;
But hordes come forth, fierce hordes from river Bug,
    And my flanks they tear and flay,
    And my lifeblood drink away;
    There is not a sound particle
    Left of my whole cuticle;
    And like engineers they bore
    Into my very core
    Incessantly, incessantly:
    Oh! they 'll be the death of me!

The scene should be described. Fancy an immense high room, with sofas long enough for three or four persons at full length, arranged against the sides. Unsightly objects, without form or shape, are tossed upon the said divans; the unhappy ones there huddled up are struggling against mosquitoes. On a table extending down the middle of the room you see similar prostrate forms. A dim lamp is swinging overhead. All is still within: no snore is heard this night, for no one sleeps; outside, however, the same noises rage as did the night before—the howling and contention of dogs, and the shrieks of birds of darkness. Suddenly you hear an energetic slap, and a "D—n you, I've got you at last,"—the triumphant war-cry of some one who has slain an over-obstinate mosquito. At last we heard from the end of the room a loud but melancholy exclamation, "I'm darned if I must n't shove my head into this 'ere boot." We all burst out laughing simultaneously, and, throwing off our coverings, beheld poor Louis C—— sitting cross-legged on the divan, brandishing a boot in each hand, and doing fierce battle with the mosquitoes. Of course all idea of sleep was now at an end. We assembled round our friend, and by a general discharge of pipes, cigars, and cheroots, drove the mosquitoes in disorder to some other spot; and then we laughed and chatted till the "wolf's-tail," as it is called, " rose in the heavens, the first blushes of grey light which appear as the forerunner of dawn." Finding it impossible to get even a hole to one's self for dressing or ablution, I took the sage counsel of one who knew the locality of old, and sallied forth in quest of some retreat.

Many years will pass away before I forget the impressions of that first morning in Cairo. In stepping from the hotel door, one stepped at once into the very heart of oriental life. Alexandria, with its bastard population and European houses, had been utterly dumb, and revealed nothing of the East but glare and dirt. Its "glory and havoc" had yet to come. We came into Cairo by night, and saw but darkness; we had no preparation—

nothing to break this sudden transit into a new life; for Europe is Europe everywhere. The Ezbekieh was being lit up with the first rays of the morning; the sky was soft and creamy, but without the clearness of our own: everything was still, calm, and quiet, save a few turbaned Muslims on their way to their avocations, and the wheeling, whistling kites, that perched on and swept from the fine plane and wild fig trees that fringed the gardens. I did not mark the parched, baked, and unverdant clay that had replaced the greensward of Western city parks; for I was looking at the great mimosa Lebek and its huge pendent pods, and the faint but luscious yellow buds of the Sont acacia and date palms, which were waving over latticed houses, and minarets and mosques. It had all burst upon me at once; nor was there the jar and turmoil of throngs to interrupt the first sensations that can never, while memory lasts, be forgotten, and never be revived.

William's Hotel was our destination; a small establishment in another wing of the Ezbekieh, fitted at the most for about ten or a dozen inmates. We found the doors still closed, and walked about again, till it suited the inhabitants to rise, when we had the good fortune to get a most comfortable, clean, airy room and a breakfast, which made ample amends for the compulsory abstinence on the blessed Nile. As the journey over the desert to Suez was protracted till nightfall, away went the company fluttering in every direction: some to Shoobra; some to the Pyramids, which they never reached; some to the mosques, and others to the citadel. I invited two of the ladies, who were anxious to escape the crowd at Shepheard's, to dine with me, and in the interim we took a carriage and visited the citadel, the mosque of Mohammed Ali, and his palace. The citadel is worth seeing, from its unrivalled view over Cairo and the Nile plain, right to the Pyramids. The minarets of Mohammed Ali's mosque are delicate and beautiful, piercing the sky like burnished needles; but commendation must cease here. The mosque itself is a large tawdry building, on which a great deal of money has been lavished, and, as in all the modern architecture of that country, with very little regard to taste. The palace, so called, is small and unpretending; the garden looks like the front of a citizen's box in a London suburb during dusty August; and with the exception of the view, which is magnificent, and the Memlook's Leap, there is but little inducement to pay a second visit to the citadel. The story of the escape of the single Memlook from the massacre of March 1, 1811, is interesting. It is well known that, on the occasion of the war with the Wahabees, Mohammed Ali invited the body of the Memlook chiefs to confer with him in the citadel. Having entrapped them by specious pretences within its walls, he caused the gates, on a given signal, to be shut, and had the inclosed remorselessly shot down, to the number of four hundred and forty. Among them was one Emin Bey, who, seeing no hope of escape, turned his horse gallantly at the low wall which runs along the most precipitous part of the citadel, and took the fearful leap which has since immortalized the spot. At the present moment, although heaps of rubbish are at the bottom, from the buildings that are being pulled down and repaired, there is at least thirty-five feet of perpendicular descent. The brave horse neither refused nor shirked, and was killed instantly by the fall; but the rider was unhurt, and contrived to reach the tent of an Albanian soldier of the Pacha, who, wonderful to relate, had the generosity to give him shelter. He remained there for some time, and at length escaped to Syria, where he died only a short time since, full of years and honor. Our return from the citadel was likely to have brought my gossipings to a close. The wretched little Arab horses had been toiling all day with similar parties. The way was steep and narrow; the vehicle high and heavy. With great difficulty we got up, by dint of pushing and halting and vociferation. The descent was speedier. Hardly had we got on the verge of the long steep incline when the driver lost all command over the horses; with usual Eastern apathy there was no drag, and away we went as hard as ever the horses could lay legs to ground, swinging and swaying like a ship at sea. There was an abrupt narrow turning towards the conclusion of this break-neck gallop: the odds were six to one in favor of an upset. If so, reduction to what Louis C—— would call "almighty smash" would have been the inevitable result. Somehow or another, with a terrific lurch, we got round it, and were safe. Providentially we met neither camel nor ox cart on the road, or it is most unlikely that I should now be writing the detail of what I cannot help considering a most remarkable escape. The ladies were delightfully unconscious of their danger: I told them it was the custom of the country, and to hold tight. This they did, and were quite reassured, calmly enjoying the oranges they had plucked in the Pacha's garden. Our dragoman muttered "God is great," and sagaciously resolved that there was no use in making a fuss about what could not be helped, as it had no doubt been wisely preordained long ago whether we were to be smashed or not.

But, alas! the inexorable hour-hand was pressing on, and a long and last adieu with the companions of my journey, impending. A pleasant dinner at my hotel, a bottle of champagne, and parting words, consumed the time till the summons was given, and the cressets flaring along the Ezbekieh announced the arrival of the vans for Suez. I believe all the party was sorry at parting. I can answer for myself. Louis C— and I nearly shook our hands off, and I heard him, as his van rumbled away, keeping up his spirits by intoning a cheerful Alabama ditty, much to the edification, no doubt, of a venerable Jesuit missionary, whom ill-assorted fate had selected for his companion through the desert.

The following day we devoted to a general lounge through Cairo, a never-failing source of amusement. Leaving altogether the Muski, as the principal bazaar is called, and which is chiefly occupied by a mixed population of Greeks, Levantines, Jews, Italians, and mongrels of every description, we plunged into the heart of the city, and steered our asses through the dense crowds that incumbered its narrow streets. No city in the East is, they say, more characteristically oriental than this immense Cairo. As soon as you strike away from the Muski, you feel, as it were, totally dissevered from every connection with Europe. Costumes, shops, merchandise, and traffic, are all subjects of incessant interest. We will first go to the Turkish Bazaar, and discuss with a merchant of Anadol the price of carpets—indispensable articles for a Nile trip. We turn off abruptly to the left, and dismounting from our donkeys, owing to the impenetrable crowd, elbow our way through some narrow passages, making the best use of sticks and shoulders; then we dive down another narrow passage, and enter a large courtyard, round which the little box-like shops of the carpet-sellers are established. Our eye is caught by a brilliant pattern, and the grave occupant invites us to a seat on his shopboard, proffers his pipe, which we accept, and treats us to muddy coffee in little cups holding about a thimblefull, and enclosed in a filagree case to protect the hand from the heat of the fluid; for it should be drunk boiling hot, and is very commendable, in spite of the sediment. He then commences to produce his articles, the worst always first; these we treat with contempt, at which he seems surprised and sorrowful. We continue puffing silently and haughtily. He retires again, and produces something better; another look of disdain, and a fresh volley of tobacco smoke, on our part. The old gentleman makes another search, and brings out some really beautiful carpets or, rather, rugs. We inspect them with a little less indifference, and puff again. After a short interval, just as it were for the sake of saying something, we ask the price. Three hundred piastres (about £2. 12s.) is perhaps the reply—delivered in a tone and with a look as much as to say, " Your sympathy ought to be great for the ruinous sacrifice I am making for your sakes." But we, with bosoms insensible to sympathy, look fierce and indignant, and address our dragoman in loud accents of surprise that we should be so unconscionably treated, and sternly bid him to offer one hundred and fifty. The reply to this is the repacking of the carpets, and a kind of mutter that perhaps he might take two hundred and eighty. Then the dragoman waxes energetic, and harsh Arabic gutturals are exchanged between the parties; the bystanders assemble, and assist in the conference, endeavouring to assuage the mutual recriminations. During the wordy war, we jingle money in our hand to the amount of perhaps two hundred and forty piastres. The vociferation continues, but the eye of the carpet man is fixed upon our coin, and he calculates the amount to a nicety. The dragoman takes us by the arm to go away; the merchant clasps the other, and urges us to remain. He makes an expiring effort; "Hamseen" (fifty), he whispers in our ear. "La!" (No!) we exclaim, striking the ground with our staves. "Arbaeen" (forty) is our ultimatum. The battle is over—our friend yields, and sighs forth a gentle "Tayib!" (good!), and the rug becomes our property. The faces of the crowd brighten up—all is again serene—and we retire with the conviction that we have fought a vigorous fight, and have, of course, been cheated both by the dragoman and the merchant. But, after all, we are pretty near the mark, as we discover by submitting our purchases to a resident lady, who very kindly inspects them for us, and gives us generally a preliminary idea as to the point on which we should take our stand.

A pipe is another desideratum; so we mount our asses, and proceed to the Pipe-makers' quarter.

Another battle for a cherry stick—then for the mouthpiece—then for the little wooden tube of the mouthpiece, for all are in separate departments, and to be purchased separately. Then back again to the Muski for tobacco, of which there are various kinds. The dispute here is not on the price, which is pretty well known, but on the change for the golden piece given in payment; and, as the coin in this country daily fluctuates, a good deal of disturbance is occasioned. It is, however, pleasant to watch the recalcitrant shopkeeper disgorging little copper coins like drops of blood, one by one, halting and faltering until the full change has been delivered, of which he professes to be quite ignorant; but try it on, to get one farthing beyond what is legitimate, and the granite statue of Rameses the Great is not more impenetrably obdurate. While filling our calfskin bags with odorous Gebeli and Korauni tobacco—the fragrance of which, alas! must remain for ever unknown to those who stay at home and smoke Cavendish and bird's eye, and such other palsying abominations—we linger fondly about the shops, and accept the proffered pipe of the long-nosed, one-eyed Hassan or Mohammed (for every one is either Hassan or Mohammed), who serves us taciturnly. The blue perfumed vapor curls aloft, it softens the heart and inspires generosity. "On our eyes be it," we cry aloud, and call for El Homar (the donkey), pronouncing it like the French *homard,* or lobster. The Maugrebyn, or West

African Bazaar, is our destination, where we mean to inspect white burnooses of silk and soft camel's hair—gifts for the only ones we have ever really loved in England, and perhaps elsewhere. An old hoary headed, keen-eyed, lantern-jawed Moor produces the treasure. The crowd, as usual, take part, and seem greatly pleased with the costly raiment; but we boggle, and look downcast at the price, our object being to combine economy with munificence; in fact, to do that which is as difficult in Egypt as elsewhere—the handsome on a small outlay. The merchant sees our hesitation. In a moment we are enveloped in the folds of the garment, and the *capuchon* is thrown over our head, with the tassel arranged so as to cover one of our eyes, and give us a rakish, knowing appearance. This ought to have been irresistible, and the vender steps backward as if immensely struck with our extreme beauty; but the generous pipe is now absent from our lips, and we remember sagely the old saying, "It is a far cry to Lochow"—in other words, that we have a two months' journey before getting to the Second Cataract and back again, and that letters of credit may miscarry, and we tell the patient man that at a more convenient season we will talk with him. But we have not half done yet, for my friend's heart is fixed upon a gorgeous dagger of Damascus blade, and green jasper handle; so back we go to the Turkish Bazaar to purchase this indispensable. Again we sit sagely; and while the contention of bargaining progresses from tepid warmth to fever heat, we watch the dense crowds passing to and fro, exhibiting and commending their wares. Here rushes one with a gaudy array of kufeyas (handkerchiefs for the head), second-hand and new; another exhibits a pair of blue baggy inexpressibles, much the worse for wear, but, according to his account, exceeding in merit all inexpressibles, past, present, and to come; another exposes for sale two bottles, which bear a most suspicious look of having in better days contained forbidden cognac; here comes one with outspread fingers brandishing amber mouthpieces, the lemon tinge of which delight the lover of the pipe, but the price of which forbids the rash outlay; a swarthy Bedoueen proffers dates and almonds, compressed into a cheese, from the shores of the Red Sea; and a wild-looking friend of his almost butts one with the horns of an ibex from the same region. We ruminate on these things, and find ourselves plucked by the sleeve; it is a *santon*, or holy man, who, in a state of half nudity and complete sanctity, does not disdain the alms of the unbelieving dog. We refuse not his request, and disburse a charitable halfpenny. We ruminate again, and this time find ourselves gently plucked by the beard. It is only the shopkeeper appealing to that our venerable appendage against the unconscionable parsimony of our friend, who cannot endure to give £5 for the dagger, but who might be tempted to give £4. 10s. All things, however, have an end. The dagger becomes English property. Then two donkey saddles are purchased, with brilliant red leather humps and copper stirrups, and adorned bridle, at the moderate rate of 10s. each. Then another pipe and more coffee, and then homeward; for the early closing movement is fashionable at Cairo, and our turbaned acquaintances are padlocking their little niches, and proceeding to enjoy the society of family and friends. And the soft sunny day is going homeward too, sinking behind the Lybian hills. But ere it declines, like the dying dolphin, it changes ever into fresh tints, opal and crocus coloured, until at last a blaze of glory and vermilion proclaims its euthanasia.

And now dense darkness prevails, and little lights are dancing to and fro: they are the lanterns borne by all respectable persons, and prescribed by law; and now, too, the great Caliph Haroun-al-Rashid, with his Vizier Giafar, sallies forth, and before them the black slave Mesrour bears the lamp. They are disguised as Moosool merchants, for he has come to visit his Egyptian subjects; nor do we doubt that, if he directs his footsteps to the Coptic quarter, but that he will hear the sound of the lute and of feasting, and that he will find noble ladies, as noble as Zobeide, Amina, and Saffia, hospitably entertaining three one-eyed Calendars. Let us hope, as we believe, that the stories he will hear are as pleasant and as strange as those he has heard before. But as we, Christian dogs that we are, cannot be expected to gain admittance to the revels of the Commander of the Faithful, let us wait a few hours, and take a stroll through Cairo by midnight. There are certain scenes that print themselves on memory, and endure as long as memory endures; of this class is such a stroll. When the moon is high in the heavens, with the stars raining light on the world below, there is something not of earth in the view. We wander through the narrow deserted streets, looking upwards for our light and guide. A glimpse at the strip of pale blue sky above, scarcely reveals three ells of breadth. In many places the interval is less. Here the copings meet, and there the outriggings of the houses seem to be interlaced. Now they are parted by what seems but a pencil; then, by a flood of silvery splendour; while under the projecting cornices, the great hanging windows of fantastic woodwork, the gateways huge enough for behemoth to pass under, the blind alleys, and long *cul-de-sacs*, lie patches of dense darkness, made visible by the dimmest of oil lights. The arch is a favorite in Cairo. In one place you see it, a mere skeleton, opening into some vast deserted hall; in another it is full of fretted stones and carved wood, and stalactitic ornament. Not a line is straight. The great dead walls of mosques slope over their massive buttresses, and the thin minarets seem to fall athwart your path. Cornices project crookedly from houses, and vast gables stand merely by force of cohesion. But the lines of beauty are not wanting; for the graceful bending form of the palm—on whose topmost feathers, quivering in the breeze, the moonbeam glistens—springs from a gloomy mound, or from the dark mass of houses almost level with the ground. The whole view is so fantastic, so drear, so ghostlike, that it seems imaginative to believe, that in such places, human beings like ourselves, can be born and live, to carry out the command—" Increase, multiply, and die."[1]

Such is the midnight aspect of this great city, which seems as it were turned by the spell of some enchanter into stone, with nothing to break the deep heavy silence that weighs on you like a millstone, except the occasional fierce jar of dogs, or, in the distance, the discordant mirth of some intoxicated Levantine proceeding from the Frank quarter. You can scarcely credit that it is the site of the gay scenes you witnessed all the morning from your windows; of the seething busy crowd with which you have been jostling and struggling all the afternoon. But the dawn will again peep into your latticed bedroom, and seduce you from your mosquito curtains; and again you will distinguish the swarthy down-looking Copt, with his sombre head gear; the white-turbaned Turk; the green-clad Shereef, descendant of the Prophet; the wild Bedoueen, in striped burnoos of camel's hair, proffering date cheese and ibex horns from Mount

---

[1] Burton's *Mecca and Medineh*.

Sinai; the merry sable slave from Kordofan; the serious, black-robed, square-capped Armenian; the Circassian, like Byron's Assyrian, in raiment of purple and gold; the Levantine population, and nondescripts of all sorts, in red tarboosh and tasselled kufeya; veiled women will spread, with rosy henna-colored fingers, their black sails to the breeze: all forming the gayest confusion of attire the eye ever rested on. We loiter as we dress, for a merry group is before the door, beneath the gigantic evergreen acacias, watching the performances of an Arab's wonderful goat, and still more wonderful asses,—a string of camels, with noiseless velvety tread, defile gravely onwards,—a dashing Bey gallops in golden housings madly by on a milk-white Arab,—dromedaries, with their leopard-skin attirings, swing in briskly, bearing home a party of adventurers from the Pyramids of Saccara,—a carriage, preceded by vociferating blacks of the Soudan, and containing a veiled hareem, trots importantly along, and on ass-back proceed to their different avocations throughout the awakened city: Jew, Turk, and Infidel, slippered, tarbooshed, baggy, red, green, and golden-sleeved, in all solemnity and sedateness.

But we must below to breakfast; and having despatched little eggs somewhat larger than those of pigeons, and butter in appearance rather like

2*

consolidated cold cream, and buffalo milk prepared like Devonshire cream, together with dark-brown Egyptian, best of all marmalades—so good that, after tasting it, no one will be in a hurry to throw up his bonnet for that of bonnie Dundee,—we descend and fight as usual with the donkey-boys. The hotel door is, as it always is, blocked up with them; but we now know the value of long sticks, and are able, without much buffeting, to select the most promising of the herd of asses, and make our way to the Bab-el-Nasr, or Gate of Victory, on our way to Heliopolis. But, before arriving at the ancient On, we pull bridle-rein, and enter the Garden of Matareeh, a little village on the way. In the centre of it there is, widely spreading, an ancient wild fig-tree. It looks as if it had seen the revolution of many ages; and old legends tell how Mary and the infant Jesus used to repose beneath its shade during the dwelling of the Holy Family in Egypt; and how, when the horsemen of Herod were in pursuit and close at hand, it opened and received within its bosom the young child, until the danger was overpast. Like other travellers, we cut some bark from this tree, which is venerated by the churches of the East and of the West, and bears on it the names of innumerable visitors; and we collected sweet blossoms from the pink jasmine that was trailed around it. Another production of the garden too we possessed ourselves of, but one hardly as fraught with such pleasing associations, being nothing less than a vigorous and well-grown scorpion. My companion—whose thoughts were ever running on noxious reptiles of all descriptions, and who fancied them lurking about his divan, under his matting, haunting every stone, and even invading the sacred precincts of the bed—inspired me with a somewhat morbid curiosity to see some of the wretches whose malignity, he confidently predicted, I should have soon and serious cause to rue. Although the dragoman insisted that in winter such creatures were invisible, we offered the large *buckshish* of a piastre to any boy who should bring us a scorpion. Several Arab volunteers bounded incontinently to the chase, and, after kicking down a portion of an old mud wall, almost immediately returned with a fine light-colored specimen, about five inches long from stem to stern, wriggling viciously between two stones, and poking with his tail at everything that approached. An uglier, more cantankerous-looking brute could not be imagined; our own crabs and lobsters, which are not particularly pleasant in appearance in their uncooked state, are lambs in comparison; and I fear we were not as ready to rebuke the Arabs as we ought to have been, who subjected him to harsh treatment in order to excite his resentment, and finished him at last, as far as his scorpion-hood was concerned, by lopping off the last joint of his tail. After this operation was concluded, they made a playmate of him, much in the manner that English boys do of cockchafers. Not quite half a mile further off are the mounds that encircle the once famous Heliopolis, or On; and in an orange garden stands erect the great obelisk of Sesortesen III. The inscriptions on it are as clear and as well defined as if it had only recently left the workman's hands, save in parts, where it looks as if boys had been pelting it with mud. The unsightly additions thus conferred are the result of the diligence of wild bees, who have chosen the crevices of the engravings to deposit their habitations. There has been much discussion as to the antiquity of this remarkable and solitary pillar. Bunsen places its date as low as 2801 B.C., Lipsius at or about 2330 B.C. "Of this Sesortesen we possess many interesting records, enlightening us on events unknown to, and unchronicled by, any ancient writer; and it is the pride of modern hierology of the last quarter of a century, to have brought to light some annals of a monarch whose existence and name were omitted by all historians, and yet whose deeds place him among the greatest of kings. The monuments of Sesortesen begin at Nubia, near the Second Cataract, where he erected a temple; and a tablet, exhumed from this spot by the French and Tuscan commissioners, and now at Florence, records his victories over the Lybians and other African nations, some of whom must now be sought for towards the mysterious sources of the Nile. He built the sanctuary of the temple at Karnak, where an enormous statue representing him once stood, cut out of crystallized sulphate of lime. One of his generals lay buried in a tomb at Benihassan. An obelisk at Fayoom, as well as this at Heliopolis, records his name and title. Scattered fragments bearing his legend are still found in the window-sills of mosques, and thresholds of doors, at Cairo, which Mahometan desecration has taken from Heliopolis and Memphis; and we possess monuments which bear the several dates of the 9th, 13th, 17th, 25th, 42nd, 43rd, and 44th years of his reign. The summary of deductions to be drawn from these records, is that Sesortesen was a great and wise monarch, who ruled the land of Egypt with much regard to the welfare of his subjects. He repulsed the wandering tribes of the Lybian deserts. In his reign religion was protected; and the arts of painting and sculpture reached a bold purity of style, unsurpassed in execution by the more florid characteristics of a later period." In this extract from Mr. Gliddon's work on *Egyptian Archæology*, I have substituted, for his reading of this king's name Osirtesen, the name Sesortesen, which recent Egyptologists are, I believe, unanimous in maintaining. Bunsen's opinion is that this monarch Sesortesen is identical with the Sesostris of the Greeks, and the wise beneficent Pharaoh of the days of Joseph. Independently of the great similarity of name, and the dissimilarity of that of Rameses, hitherto generally considered to be Sesostris, an argument by no means to be overlooked, there are other circumstances appealed to by Bunsen, which strongly confirm his opinion. For instance, Strabo mentions that Eratosthenes speaks of a monument at the southernmost point of Arabia, the Bab-el-Mandeb, of Sesostris the Egyptian, and adds, "he was clearly the first who subjugated the land of Ethiopia, and that of the Troglodytes. From thence he crossed over to Arabia, and thence overran the whole of Asia." Now, this statement cannot refer to Rameses, for the Thothmes Pharaohs, his predecessors, had already conquered Ethiopia, and have left behind them monuments, still existing, attesting their conquests and permanent rule. But we have Thothmes IV. in the temple of Amada, in Nubia, offering homage to Sesortesen; and in another Nubian temple he is addressed as "God, the great Lord of Nubia." Besides this, we have actually his own great works, before alluded to, still extant to attest his supremacy in Ethiopia. At the narrow pass of Samneh, some distance above the Second Cataract, there are to this day remaining in preservation, the massive cyclopean walls of the fortress erected to command the passage of the river; and a temple yet stands upon these fortifications. He was the great warrior-hero of the old dynasty. The Greeks hearing of the subsequent achievements of Rameses, the magnitude and the comparatively recent epoch of which threw into the shade the exploits of the older conqueror, applied to Rameses the historical name of Sesostris, which the extention of Egyptian domination had familiarised throughout Asia. If Bunsen be correct—and there is no doubt but that his reasons are strongly put, and carry the greatest weight—then it follows that Sesortesen is the Pharaoh of Joseph; for all tradition assigns to Sesostris the arrangement and settlement of the land-tax; and the accounts in the Bible and Herodotus show such marked coincidence, that we cannot hesitate to ascribe to that monarch the proceedings, during the seven years' famine narrated in Genesis, in which Joseph plays so prominent a part. It is not, therefore, too much to affirm that there is a strong probability, that in this very garden, Joseph, the vizier of Sesostris, stood, and superintended the erection of this very obelisk, which stood with its fellow, now buried or destroyed, before the portals of the Temple of the Sun.

The height of this obelisk is 61 feet, and its base $6\frac{1}{2}$ feet. It is a beautiful single shaft of red granite, and has been transported from the quarries of Syene, a distance of 640 miles from its present site, which fact gives some idea of the resources and gigantic undertakings of the ancient monarchs of Egypt. Its characters have been thus translated:—"The Horus; living of men; Pharaoh; sun offered to the world; lord of Upper and Lower Egypt; the living of men; son of the sun; Sesortesen; beloved of the spirits in the region of Poné; ever living; life of mankind; resplendent Horus; beneficent deity; sun offered to the world; who has begun the celebration of two great religious festivals to him who makes him, vivifier for ever." It is dedicated to Phré, the sun-god, to whom was also dedicated the city, on the ruins of which this obelisk stands, termed in hieroglyphics, the city of Phré. This name it has preserved in every language. In Greek it is called Heliopolis, the city of the sun; in Hebrew, On, and Beth Shemmin, or house of the sun; in Saracenic Arabic, Ain-es-Shems, or fountain of the sun. Having made use of the term of Pharaoh in the translation of this inscription, it may be well to explain, that the meaning of the word, which was the title of the kings of Egypt, as Cæsar of the Roman emperors, or Shah of the Persia king, is derived from Phré or Phra, the sun-god. The king was the image of the sun on earth—an incarnation of dominion and benevolence; and in the Bible, the Hebrew letters composing this word strictly spell Phràh, rendered Pharaoh in our version. Every Pharaoh was the sun of Egypt; and, as the sun was Phra, so each king was Phra in common parlance. Each monarch, by law, inherited his father's throne, so that the incumbent was Phra, son of Phra—literally, son of the sun; and Phra itself is the compound of Pi, the article *the*, and Ra Re, the sun. I am aware that Bunsen objects to this interpretation of Pharaoh, from this very fact, the Pi Ra would mean, in Egyptian, the sun—not the son of the sun. He derives the word Pharaoh from the old Egyptian word "erro" or "uro," signifying king, from whence the word "uræus," or royal serpent, is derived.

But one must avoid these archæological surmises, far too deep and erudite for a mere transitory visitor, a stranger in the land of Ham, and with no knowledge of oriental languages; but, whether this monument be anterior or posterior to the days of Abraham, it, nevertheless, seemed strange to touch a work of art on which the patriarchs had laid their hands; to wander in an orange garden, once the site of a great temple, with its statues and avenues, through whose portals Joseph and his wife, the daughter of its high priest, had often passed, and then to reflect, that within the short space of a mile are, calmly gazing on each other, the obelisk of Sesortesen and Phré, the fig-tree of Jesus and Mary, the minaret of Mahommed. Verily, verily, naught may endure save mutability.

But who that has a soft thought left, can gain his home again without halting by the field-sides, and watching the snow-white *Ibis*,[1] so called wrongly by travellers, the loveliest of all birds, that so confidingly look up, and scarcely move out of your way, knowing that your heart can never be so out of tune as to injure things so gentle. "If there be

---

[1] This bird is not of the Ibis species. It is the *Ardea bubulous*, a small white kind of heron. The Arabs call it Abon Girdan, the father of apes, for what reason I know not.

metempsychosis, surely," said I, to my companion, "these can only be the souls of children who have died without sin, spotless, unstained, and snowy now, as they were spotless, unstained, and snowy then; or perhaps," I added, in compliment to my companion's faith, "here is the vexed question solved of what has become of those little ones who have died before obtaining baptism." "A pretty thought," he replied, "but hardly so pretty as the fancy in your own country, that in another world there are clear fountains ever playing, and by them little children ever drawing water in golden vessels, so perforated that their labor is ever vain, without pain and murmuring, but also without the happiness of those admitted to nearer communion with the blessed. That," said he, "is the fate attributed in some parts of Ireland to those who, by accident or neglect, have lost the saving benefit of baptism."

Some days after this we received, through a mutual friend, an invitation to visit Il'hamy Pacha, son of the late Viceroy of Egypt, Abbas Pacha. According to ordinary rules of succession, this young gentleman would have been the reigning Viceroy; but by the treaty between Mohammed Ali and the Porte, the reversion to the government devolves upon the eldest member of the family of Mohammed Ali. This wretched system is contrived with more than usual Turkish stupidity, although sanctioned by the European powers, to render, if possible, this rich but unhappy country more ill governed than it would be naturally under Mahommedan rule. The result of it is, that each successive viceroy knowing, that after his death his family depends solely on the amount of the accumulations he may contrive to amass, is chiefly occupied, while time and opportunity permit, in providing for that inevitable catastrophe. Everything he can lay hands on is set aside; and works that would conduce to the benefit of the country are ignored, unless the immediate profits are likely to repay him for the outlay. He can have no interest in improving communications, constructing roads, opening irrigations, or ameliorating the condition of the wretched fellahs and peasants; by doing so, he would only be injuring his own family, for the benefit of a successor, whom he has the best reasons to dislike, and who is, in all probability, plotting to encompass his death. As for public spirit, it is a quality perfectly unknown.

Mohammed Ali was succeeded by his son Ibrahim; Ibrahim by Abbas, son of Toosoom, another son of Mohammed Ali; and the present ruler is a third son of Mohammed Ali, and will be succeeded by Achmet, son of Ibrahim. It is notorious that Abbas was murdered by his Memlook slaves; and it is generally hinted that Saïd, the present Viceroy, was not ignorant of the plot. He was an object of great suspicion to his nephew, and was himself convinced, whatever other persons may have supposed, that his life was in considerable danger, and was, perhaps, of opinion that the old saying, "Aide-toi et le ciel t'aidera," was applicable to his precarious position. However, be that as it may, Abbas was, like John Gilpin, a man of prudent mind, and contrived, during his short time of power, to accumulate for his son, Il'hamy, an income of at least £160,000 per annum, and by some asserted to be considerably more, besides ready money to an amount unknown, but enormous. Had the succession devolved on his son, there is no doubt that Abbas, who was a man of great determination, and some ability, seeing that his family were thus provided for, would have devoted his attention more to the general improvement, and less to the general squeezing of the country; but there is an ingenuity in the stupidity and retrogression of the Turks that renders everything they attempt a failure, and themselves a hopeless and incurable incubus over any unfortunate land that Providence may have inflicted by subjecting to their rule.

The palace in which Il'hamy was living (for he has got about twenty), was about a mile from Cairo, at a place called the Abbassia, where Abbas had laid the foundations of a new town, but which, as a matter of course, has been neglected and abandoned since his death, and is going rapidly to ruin. The palace is a fine large building, surrounded by a high wall, and without any pretensions to architecture. It is magnificently fitted up, as we were informed, for we only entered the large reception saloon on the ground floor: this is an immense room, without furniture, paved with white marble, and having a fountain in the middle, from whence canals are cut through the marble, and streams of water run coolly and clearly along, forming a delicious retreat in summer. In a large recess by the window we took our seats, leaving the corner, or place of honor, for his Highness. He kept us waiting but a very short time, and was extremely courteous in his reception. His age is about twenty-two, and his appearance most prepossessing; he is extremely fat for so young a man, with a remarkably open, good-tempered countenance; and we heard that his character by no means belied the outward man. The conversation was through an interpreter, although the Pacha speaks and thoroughly understands English, but is nervous and somewhat shy at attempting it before strangers. The *Times* and *Illustrated London News* come regularly each mail to the Abbassia. Camels and horses and dogs and sporting were the topics of discourse, and then his Highness proposed for our edification to step out and see a camel-fight in the court-yard, which was at that moment being organized. Having finished our most incomparable pipes, we readily acceded to the invitation. A small female camel was first let out, and followed by two males, in a state, judging by their foaming and noise, of the greatest indignation with each other. The female remained present, to encourage the combatants by the smile of beauty. One of the male camels was a beast of great size, and white in color; the other was dark brown, and considerably smaller; but the Pacha informed us that he had already fought with one hundred and nine of his own species, and had never been worsted in an encounter. The battle that ensued was extremely amusing, and, unlike other fights, perfectly bloodless, and unaccompanied with the least cruelty; it was, in fact, a trial of skill and dexterity. The object of the camel in fighting is to get his antagonist's head under him, when he immediately kneels on the neck, and, if not driven off, remains there till, as they say in Ireland, he has squeezed the life out of him.

At a signal the combatants were let loose, and at it they went, not tooth and nail, for they have no nails to speak of, and their teeth were muzzled, but neck and legs, and legs and neck, most vigorously. No Westmoreland wrestler could have shown greater skill, in tripping, parrying, shifting, and dodging of every tactic, although the strife was certainly conducted in rather a heavy, sedate manner, as befits such grave, unwieldy quadrupeds. The Pacha was in ecstasy, the slaves grinned from ear to ear, and I ran down the steps into the courtyard, to have a nearer view of the belligerents, but was quickly warned back, for fear of accidents. At first matters seemed to go all in favor of the white knight; his great size and weight told terribly. The brown champion was driven to and fro, and the gentry of the Newmarket betting-ring would have laid considerable odds "that they named the winner." But these odds shortly varied. Although a novice in the encounters of these animals, I soon perceived the great science of the smaller camel. He was pushed about, and knocked about, but he never gave a chance when his legs were concerned; they were always just where they should be, and he as firm as a rock upon them, except when he shifted them to avoid a trip, or when he retaliated on his adversary. The battle had now raged about twenty minutes; at last the white camel gave an opening: as quick as thought the brown one got his leg between those of the other; in an instant the huge animal was upset, and the little hero had his knee on his neck, and was proceeding to strangle him, in a majestic, calm, camel-like manner, when he was driven off by the attendants, having added the one hundred and tenth laurel to his brow.

Thus ended the tournament; and we returned to compose our minds, after this exciting scene, with fresh coffee and pipes. The conversation naturally turned upon camels and dromedaries, which bear the same relation to one another as cart-horses to racers: the dromedary being of course the high-mettled thorough bred. It may be as well, as we are on the subject, to remark, that Europeans, on first coming to the East, form some erroneous ideas as to the difference that exists between the two, and have a notion that they differ from one another by the dromedary having one and the camel two humps. This is altogether incorrect. The dromedary, as I said above, is the swift steed, the camel the slow beast of burden. The dromedary is nothing more than a light-limbed, active, slim, high-bred-looking camel, used almost exclusively for riding purposes; and in Egypt and Arabia it is a rare circumstance to meet with either camel or dromedary having two humps. In Central Asia, on the contrary, the one-humped animal is rare. There is, therefore, no distinction made between them, nor has Nature, in her bountiful distribution of two instead of one hump of fat, given the fortunate possessor of the double appendage the slightest advantage; neither is the rider in any way better off, by having the comfortable support fore and aft, that is imagined, by reason of the two humps, for the saddle is raised equally over the two as over the one. In short, dromedaries and camels are precisely the same in kind, although differing, as we may say, in degree; and the two-humped are merely a local variety from the one-humped breed. The dromedary, called Heggin from his carrying pilgrims, is a much more valuable animal than the dull working camel, used as a beast of burden, and called

Gemel. A good dromedary, of the Mecca breed, would cost as much as £40, while a camel's ordinary price is about £7 or £8; and a Bedoueen would feel as much affronted if his swift favorite were called Gemel by some ignorant Frank, as Lord Jersey, if some utilitarian carrier were to remark on the ill aptitude of his magnificent Bay Middleton to drag a luggage van.

But to return from this digression. His Highness informed us that dromedaries were much more vicious and treacherous than camels; for, independently of using their teeth in a most formidable manner, they sometimes, if out of humour with their groom or master, take the opportunity of rolling on them when they find them sleeping, and thus reduce them to the appearance of a pancake. He mentioned that one of his best dromedaries obtained from Mecca, was a most unconscionable brute, and had already committed two premeditated murders. Inadvertently I happened to say that I had never seen, and consequently never mounted a dromedary. The Pacha laughed, and said something to a black attendant, which I did not comprehend, but which seemed to create general amusement. A little afterwards we rose to go, the Pacha accompanying us; and my horror can well be conceived when, grunting and growling at the steps of the palace, lay three dromedaries magnificently caparisoned. My friend and myself were invited to mount. In vain we protested: no excuse could be taken. After some clumsy efforts, which greatly pleased the assembly, we took our seats, held on manfully and grimly while the brutes rose, and went forth swinging out into the desert, with an Arab for our guide, perfectly ignorant where we were going, or what was to be the end of it all.

By the way, this mounting and descending from camels and dromedaries causes at first a considerable inconvenience to the uninitiated. The beast lies growling and testifying his displeasure, and one imagines that there is nothing to be done more than to get your legs on top of him as soon as possible, and to cross them one over the other as the Arabs do, the mode of which one takes care to ascertain beforehand. There is a narrow round iron bar in front for pummel, and a similar one behind for cantle; so the novice considers himself pretty fairly fixed between the two when he has once got his seat; but, as the dromedary rises with both hind feet simultaneously, the violent jerk propels you forward, and the bar of the pommel in the pit of your stomach brings you up by no means agreeably. The fore legs rise similarly; so back you go, and are again brought up by the cantle-bar just in your lower vertebræ. These shocks are not gentle; but you soon learn by rough experience to lean well back, and push against the pommel at motion No. 1, and to lean well forward and hold tight at motion No. 2; and similarly in dismounting. Sometimes, however, if your attendant is at all careless, the brute jumps up before you have even your legs crossed, and then the safety of your bones depends pretty much on the part you land on, or the softness of the soil you fall on; for the odds are considerably against your having the slightest power of maintaining your position, until you have gained some practice in this kind of desert riding. So much for what, I suppose, I must call dromedary-ship.

During the ride that ensued there was but little sociability; for we remembered the misdeeds of the Mecca dromedary and carefully avoided each other, and the friendly advances of the Arab, not knowing which of us might be perched upon the homicide. The day was a real hot one; and as, to do honor to the Pacha, I was in Sunday best, with a European hat, I was by no means as cool as I could have wished, and at last insisted on returning, which we were fortunately able to effect, by steering our course to Mr. A—'s phaeton, which just then appeared in sight on the Suez road. The motion of the dromedary was pleasant enough, especially when in full pace, far easier and softer than that of the camel; in fact the Arabs boast, that you may drink a cup of coffee while going full trot without spilling a drop. On arriving at the phaeton, the attendant pronounced the command to kneel, making a noise in his throat resembling a gargle, and we were soon in cooler quarters, being reconducted to Cairo by Mr. A— in his covered carriage, having much enjoyed our visit and the hospitality of the good-natured Pacha. Poor fellow! He is a lucky man to have for his friend and adviser Mr. A—n, to whom Abbas his father, with discrimination unusual for a Turk, entrusted him. This gentleman was an English lawyer; but, having settled at Cairo, became acquainted with Abbas, and has remained with his son who is greatly attached to him, and has placed in his hands the very intricate management of his affairs. Unlike the generality of adventurers who fix themselves on the wretched Turkish grandees with the sole view of plunder and embezzlement, Mr. A— has behaved in his relations towards Il'hamy, as an honorable English gentleman; and is, consequently, detested by the gang of mongrels who infest Cairo, to whom his integrity is a reproach, and who long to step into his shoes, as Il'hamy would be a good milch cow. His enormous wealth has naturally made him a mark for spoliation, and were it not for the dauntless and determined manner in which Mr. A— has fought his battles, to use the expression of another Englishman high in authority there, this helpless young man, utterly inexperienced in business, and without a single protector, would long since have been left without a feather in his tail. One feels pleasure at this, for there is certainly a good humour and kindness in his manner which is taking, and he is, as his father was before him, a known and staunch friend of the English nation, being always happy to receive our countrymen whenever presented to him. When our light cavalry regiments passed through Egypt, on their way to the Crimea, he was the only one of the viceregal family, except the Viceroy himself, who showed them attention, and the entertainment he gave the officers is said to have been magnificent.

Our next expedition was to Shoobra, a palace built by Mohammed Ali on the banks of the Nile, to the north of Cairo. The ride on a hot day is agreeable, under the pleasant shade of wild fig-trees and oriental planes, which are growing grandly on each side of the fine high road—or, rather, avenue —about two miles long, leading to it. Its chief renown is derived from its gardens, which are, or were under the supervision of a Scotch horticulturist. I can say but little in favor of their extreme beauty; orange and lemon trees laden with fruit, and very dusty, as is every garden in Egypt, seemed the predominant vegetation. Of course, this being the month of December, one could hardly expect brilliancy of coloring; but I imagine that at no period of the year is Egypt remarkable for its flowers. The fierce heat and dryness of the atmosphere, without showers to cool and invigorate the plants, is ill supplied by irrigation. There is, however, a very pretty little kiosque well worth seeing.

It consists of a large square court built of marble, with a colonnade running round it, and handsome rooms at each corner. The middle space forms a good-sized reservoir for water; and a fountain rises from the centre, supported by marble crocodiles, who spout forth water when called upon to do so. Old Mohammed Ali used to amuse himself here occasionally with his harem. The boat is still shown which he propelled himself by the help of a wheel; and there are also sundry small rickety-looking skiffs, in which the ladies used to take their pleasure. These the merry old gentleman, by a sign, caused now and again to be upset, and took infinite delight in seeing the drenched and discomfited fair ones scrambling about, and shuffling out of the water as fast as their baggy integuments would permit. As we leave the gardens, the garden boy our attendant, looks furtively round, and pulls forth from the capacious bosom of his shirt some half score of delicious mandarin oranges, expecting *buckshish*. We discussed them very gratefully trotting home; but we beg others who are less drouthy and more rigid than ourselves, to bear rigidly in mind, that they were stolen property, and that the donor, had he been discovered, would in a few seconds have found his heels in the air, and the soles of his feet subjected to the bastinado. But what Arab fears contingent bastinado with immediate *buckshish* before his eyes! The palace, which we did not approach, belongs to Haleem Pacha, brother of Said. He is described as a particularly agreeable, gentlemanly young fellow educated in France. He is well known as a first-rate shot, and is a *chasseur determiné*. There is a rumour that he has applied to be appointed Governor of the Soudan, and has received the office. Conjecture is naturally rife as to the causes that have induced him to leave pleasant Cairo, and betake himself to such unwholesome climates far removed from civilization. His friends assert that it is from pure love of sporting; his enemies, from anxiety to escape his creditors. I believe there is truth in both assertions, and that his departure for the south is to enable his brother the Viceroy, to put his somewhat disorganized financial affairs on a somewhat better footing.[1]

During the remainder of the stay of my companion, Mr. A—, we devoted our time incessantly to the inspection of everything supposed to be worth seeing in the neighbourhood and interior of Cairo; and as he was a good deal interested, and particularly well informed, in Eastern and Mahommedan lore, his society, besides being very agreeable, was valuable from the inquiries he was able to make, and the activity he enforced in our expeditions. Our guide, the dragoman, a most devoted

---

[1] I hear he has already returned. Dec. 1856.

follower of Islam, was very communicative during these excursions, from the admiration which my friend's assertion, that he had read the Koran no less than six times through, inspired. He gave, moreover, such proof of the understanding and digesting of his reading, that he quite overcame any scruples that Mahommedans entertain of speaking on their religious tenets before Nazarenes. Indeed, the old dragoman seemed to think there remained only a slight ceremony to qualify him for Islam. Unfortunately we had not the services of that cicerone, and the benefit of his information, which was marvellous for an Egyptian and a dragoman, in our visits to some of the mosques, and to the tombs of the Baharite and Memlook sultans, having on those occasions fallen into the hands of a stupid lout, who thought he spoke English, and who had, on my first coming, somehow or another connected himself with me. Under the auspices of this worthy, we took one of the most beautiful rides in the environs of Cairo. Going through the great bazaar and the heart of the town, until arriving at the foot of the acclivity leading to the citadel, you strike away to the right under the Mokattam range of hills, and shortly find yourself among the undisputed precincts of the dead. You wander along by tomb after tomb, with its square highly ornamented tower and graceful dome; for tombs in eastern countries are not the cabined, cribbed, confined receptacles which utilitarian England grants to the useless dead, but large and spacious buildings, of rich and curious decoration, with towers and domes, which even now, in their decay, would cause an artist's heart to leap for joy. Of course, I draw a distinction between the graves of the lower orders and the tombs of the rich. The former approach to our English ideas of a tomb, they being merely raised above the ground, with a stone at the head and feet, the top of which is carved into the form of a turban; but persons of even ordinary means have enclosed places of sepulture of considerable dimensions, and surrounded each of them by its own walls. We can thus readily understand how often in Arabian stories, the benighted traveller, unable to enter the city gates which close at sunset, selects a tomb for his hostelry; and in the Gospels we read of one who made them his usual residence. Indeed, I am by no no means sure that, in the course of my wanderings, I shall not have to select a similar spot for repose, with a confident hope there may be nothing worse than ghouls to disturb nocturnal quiet. I purposely omit any account of the particular tombs we visited: partly because they contain the remains of a dynasty which has left but little behind to interest posterity, but chiefly because our guide so jumbled up one with another, that a fresh visit will be required to clear up the confusion. There was, however, one tomb in particular, which, as it contained a mosque, was in somewhat better condition than the others, and on our inquiry as to its owner, the learned guide informed us that it was the mausoleum of the great Saladin—Salah-Ed-deen. We, of course, expressed much satisfaction at being within the precinct of the last resting-place of this gallant warrior Sultan, the type of oriental generosity, daring, and chivalry, so my friend carried off a small tesselated slab as a memento. A little reflection, however, brought with it the recollection that Saladin is buried at Damascus; consequently, all the enthusiasm went for nothing.

Under the care of the same enlightened cicerone, we, the same afternoon, entered the famous mosque of Sultan Hassan. This is the only mosque really worth seeing of the three or four hundred which are said to be in preservation in Cairo. There are two other mosques, which are shut to all disbelievers, without a special order from the governor, but which, as trouble and a chance of being insulted are involved, travellers generally are desirous of visiting. These are the Hassaneen and El Azar. The latter is so far worth going to, from the fact of its being the great Mahommedan collegiate institution of the East. It was founded about the year 970; and even at the present time, although stripped of its former wealth and importance, is supposed to contain from two thousand to three thousand students from every country where orthodox Islamism is professed. Originally it was enabled by the munificence of Mahommedan princes, by lands belonging to it, and mortuary bequests, to maintain a large staff of learned professors, and to keep its students in comfort and respectability; but at present the salaries of the teachers are barely sufficient to keep them from starving, and the students subsist, as best they can, on distributions of bread and of articles of cheap clothing on great occasions. Once a year, as a particular treat, a few peaches constitute what we called "gaudy day" at Oxford, when we grumbled because, with salmon, lamb, and other delicacies, we only got sherry, and were most discreditably and niggardly denied champagne. As far as the mosque itself goes, there is little to recommend it. It is in the shape of a large parallelogramical hall, twice too long for its height; the much-talked-of forest of pillars, which the Cairenes swagger about, are a rambling assemblage of thin, poor-looking, woe-begone, crooked marble columns. A few ill-trimmed oil lamps are suspended dimly through the building. A colonnade runs round the interior, and off this colonnade are the apartments of the students divided into *rishaks*, or halls; or, as the Maltese knights would have them, *auberges* for the different nationalities. These halls are in number twenty-four, one for each recognized nation of Islam; but many of them are closed, and the best furnished contain nothing but dirty and dusty boxes, and dirtier and dustier matting, where the fleas make sad havoc among the aspirants to collegiate honors and reputation.

This mosque is naturally the resort of the most ignorant and bigoted Mahommedans: men from countries where the name of an unbeliever is an abomination, and who have not been sufficiently long in Cairo to learn the mild doctrines of universal toleration, under the persuasive eloquence of the bastinado. The result is, that they regard with considerable impatience the intrusion of those whom they style "howling dogs of Nazarenes"—in other words, Christians—into its venerated precincts; and take every opportunity by stormy language, which is fortunately not understood, but sometimes by stones, the sermons from which are better comprehended to testify how little they appreciate the honor of a visit.

A couple of years before my arrival in Cairo, in the winter of 1853, a strong party mustered to visit the mosque, consisting of several gentlemen and three ladies, all three, strange to say, more or less afflicted with deafness. A couple of Janissaries, so called, were sent with them by the governor of Cairo. The ladies, not being aware of the habits and manners of its inmates, instead of keeping, like sheep among wolves, pretty close to their shepherds, wandered to and fro through the mosque, to the dismay and horror of the Janissaries, two of whom, according to arithmetic, could not accompany three straying females. Being, as I said, somewhat deaf, they asked their questions and made their remarks in a loud tone of voice. They wondered very much why the people knocked their heads on the ground; the people were earnestly praying; and, as they thought the proceeding strange, they stood before the persons so praying, and eyed them with all eyes and eyeglasses. They wondered next, what song it was that an old fellow was singing; the old fellow was the Moollah, and the song was the Koran. They thought that still more funny, and laughed at it. The result was, that the hornets ever ready to sting, became perfectly furious and uncontrollable; they surrounded them, jostled them, called them names that it would make me blush to repeat, and then proceeded to pick up stones to enforce the epithets, by treating the female dogs as male dogs are usually treated. The deaf ladies were terrified at the outbreak; they were separated from their friends, and called in accents loud and despairing for assistance against the horrid men. Christian and Frankish wail resounded through the colonnades—Arab and Maugrebyn execrations responded; nor was it without a liberal laying-on of sticks by the Pacha's soldiers or Janissaries, aided by the efforts of the Cairenes connected with the establishment, who knew, if anything happened, what would be the condition of their feet the following day, that the unfortunate fair ones were got safely into the street.

My informant declared with an emphasis, which bore the stamp of earnestness, that it was the last time he would ever enter El Azar in company with ladies, whether they were easy or hard of hearing.

After all, it is not to be wondered at that intrusions of this description should cause the greatest indignation. Let us always in such cases apply to ourselves the simple rule of doing unto others as you would they should do unto you. Let us fancy a number of veiled Turkish women accompanied by their turbaned, baggy-breeched husbands, entering one of our own churches, and passing lively remarks on the comical appearance of a gentleman in his shirt, meaning the surpliced clergyman, or even venturing to comment aloud on the funereal toggery of the pew-opener. I do not at all say that we should apply to the ladies precisely the same language as the Azar students made use of; or that we should assert publicly ought affecting the fair fame of their grandmothers; or that we should run out to that portion of the street lately macadamized, and collect a pocketfull of stones to pelt them with; but we should, in high and majestic dudgeon, summon policeman of division A, and, after giving the offenders into custody, have the satisfaction the following day of hearing the worthy magistrate deliver a stern and suitable lecture to these disturbers of a quiet congregation. And yet we wonder at, and apply the terms of barbarian, savage, and bigot to a set of wild uneducated men, collected from the rudest and most ignorant countries of the East—men who, from their earliest childhood, are taught along with the profoundest reverence for their own creed, loathing and contempt for all that is alien from it, because they testify their indignation, and I term it just indignation, at the unjustifiable levity of strangers within the precincts of places rendered venerable and sacred by the traditions of their fathers, and the religion to which they cling with the most conscientious tenacity.

To revert, however, to the mosque of Sultan Hassan—the only mosque, after all, that is worth a visit within Cairo. It stands below the citadel, towering over all other buildings by its size. From afar you have already wondered at the massive grandeur of its lofty minarets; and when you reach it, after removing the shoes from your feet, you pass through a gateway constructed, as it were, by the hands of Titans, and grand enough for Titanic heads unbowed to enter. The interior differs from ordinary mosques, as it consists, first, of a large hypœthral court, with a fountain for ablution in the middle. On each side is a square recess covered in by a fine arch, beneath which the believers pray. Behind this, and surmounted by a noble and majestic dome, is the tomb of the founder. But, alas! the beautiful wood carvings and stalactitic ornaments which adorn its summit, are falling into rapid and lamentable decay, although a small expenditure would be sufficient to restore them. But such is eastern apathy—even in the case of objects of the greatest sanctity and veneration. The good old days of ginns and enchanters and wonderful lamps, when mighty works were completed in the twinkling of an eye, by the muttering of a cabalistic word, must return again, if we are to expect the preservation of works of art, which require either trouble or expense. Like our good friends the Irish, they mumble here, "In the name of God," and leave things to take care of and mend themselves; and shrug their shoulders, if asked why a trifle should not be laid out for the preservation of monuments towards which they profess such inordinate attachment. But we must not expect anything from the present race of rulers, save useless barrages that obstruct, and do not benefit; standing armies to resist invaders, which the same armies would welcome as rescuers and friends; factories that do not pay; and men-of-war that neither sail nor float; and enormous straggling palaces fitted up at ruinous expense, and with the worst of taste; these, in their turn, at their builders' death, to be abandoned to fleas, dogs, and dervishes.

Fortunately, in Egypt, there are few modern buildings to evoke these reflections, and of the few, this noble monument is the greatest. Not knowing much about the founder, some of the party endeavoured to obtain a few statistics from the guide; and the following conversation will give some idea of his and the literary capacities of dragomen in general:—Visitor: Pray, when did this Sultan Hassan live?—Dragoman: O, great time since! He, old Sultan, he very old!—Pertinacious Visitor: But when?—Dragoman: O, he very old: time of Lateens, Greeks.—Puzzled Visitor: Indeed! Latins, Greeks; perhaps you mean the Greek and Latin Churches.—Dragoman: No, sar; he build mosque, no church: he not Nazarene; he like Mohammed.—Distracted Visitor: Never mind what he built, or what he liked: when did he live?—Dragoman (getting sulky): He live here, in Cairo.—Obstinate Visitor: Yes, yes; we know well enough that he lived here—but when? —Dragoman: Long time back, sar: he very old. You see, sar, large round thing up in wall,[1]—bread loaf dat large, and sell for one piastre when he live; bread dear, sar, now in Cairo; my family large one, sar; pay much for bread.—Jocose Visitor: Yes, I see, you explain remarkably well; I suppose he lived about the time of Firaun (Pharaoh)?—Dragoman: Yes, sar, 'bout den. He fight Firaun; make Firaun build for him.—Visitor: So he made Firaun build for him, did he? Perhaps he knew Mousa (Moses) too, and Nooh (Noah). Were they living at Cairo in his time?—Dragoman: Not think so, sar. Mousa great prophet; Nooh great prophet. Cairo very cheap then: very dear

[1] This dragomanic observation refers to a large disc, fixed in or modelled on the wall; and it is the tradition, that in Sultan Hassan's time, a loaf of that size could be procured for the same amount as the somewhat diminutive loaves cost at the present day.

now. My family large one sar; pay much for bread.—Sarcastic Visitor: Thank you for the information you have given us; you explain remarkably well. I suppose you learn a great deal, in order to explain to visitors.—Dragoman: Yes, sar; me learn very much; me very good dragoman; English shentlemen always take me. Me know well all the atiques up Nile; should like to go with you, sar, if you go up. Bread very dear now, sar, in Cairo.

This may seem too ridiculous a version of our conversation; and, though I do not vouch for its verbal accuracy, yet in the main it greatly resembles the discussion we had with our erudite cicerone that same morning. I was so amused, that I took the heads down in my pocket-book; and travellers may rest assured that, if they seek for information from native guides who call themselves professors of Frank languages, they will be often edified in a similar manner. The ignorance of these men is very conceivable. Many of them originally started in life as donkey-boys, and, having picked up a few phrases and more piastres, they emerge from their rags in gorgeous costumes, and offer their services to conduct families to Timbuktoo, and further still, if required. And yet we hear of travellers gravely giving heed to, and publishing to the world accounts emanating solely from these worthies! But travellers are not all of them particular as to the accuracy of the information they receive. They ask a question, and any answer will do well enough. Lieutenant Burton mentions, that "in the map drawn by some learned eastern investigator, a village in the Euphrates is set down as M'adri—which means 'Don't know.' A very common reply, but which in this case answered, to the full satisfaction of the enquirer, the purpose of a proper name."

As far as I have seen of dragomen, I certainly prefer a native of the country and a Mahommedan. Curtis, in his *Nile Notes,* as truly as wittily divides the whole great family of dragomen into four categories:—There is, the Maltese, or the cunning knave; the Syrian, or the active knave; the Greek, or the able knave; and the Egyptian, or the stupid knave. No doubt but that they are rogues, all of them; but you have a chance with the Egyptian, which you have not with the others. In the first and main place, he is not, like the Maltese, under British protection, and, consequently, perfectly indifferent to your threats, or the nature of your certificate, as he can and will readily forge others; avoid him as you would a pestilence. In the next place, you are pretty well able as far as intellect is concerned, to strive with and overcome the Egyptian; but you vastly overrate your Macchiavelian proficiency, if you imagine you have the slightest chance of coping with Greek or Maltese. In the third place, a Mahommedan attendant is always preferable to a Christian; he is looked upon with much more respect by your crew, and can exercise an authority and despotism which would be resisted in a Christian; and, last but not least, if he misbehaves himself, he is perfectly aware that you have nothing to do but to complain to the police of Cairo, and that bastinado, or extensive bribery to avoid it, which is quite as bad, will be the penalty of your denunciation. The result of valuable information and some experience, having made several experiments and failures in trying to get a suitable attendant, is to this effect:—First of all: Eschew Greeks and Maltese as you would malignant spirits; as for Syrians, I have never tried their services, and know nothing of them; but they are not so immediately under Egyptian law, and can escape the consequences of their misdeeds by slipping back quietly to their own country. Secondly: Take a Mahommedan of the country, and if he appears intelligent, and, above all things, determined, so much the better. And thirdly, and lastly: Do nothing in a hurry. You would not buy a hack without riding him; why then tie yourself to a dragoman for better or worse, during two or three months, for which period, if ignorant of Arabic, you can hardly call your soul your own, without giving him also a preliminary canter. As to his intelligence, a few minutes' conversation will satisfy you on that point; and then, by way of proving his trustworthiness, take him out shopping. But, before you go, get a general idea of the value of the article you require, such as a burnoos, or carpet, or kufeya; and on your return home, ascertain what others have paid, and what you ought to have paid for the purchases you have made. This is an excellent test; for the Egyptian rogue is essentially a stupid and shortsighted rogue. No hopes of future plunder on a grand scale can divert him from a present larceny. The "bird in hand" is his motto; and a few piastres to be realized on the nail will overcome every dictate of prudence, and every prospect of two months undisputed cheating. I believe the best and most conscientious of the genus dragoman obtain about five per cent. upon all the purchases you make, which is added to the price you pay; but this you must consider as a matter of course, and be satisfied that every day of your life, you have experienced from your London tradesmen, and your London servants, precisely the same treatment.

But all this time that we have been lounging through bazaars, visiting mosques and gardens and palaces, and wandering among tombs, we felt that we had left unseen the great sight of all Egyptian sights,—the Pyramids of Ghizeh; and yet, day after day, we had watched their summits mistily in the noontide heat overtopping the palm groves on the opposite Nile bank, and then they seemed afar; but when evening came, they advanced nearer and nearer to us, bathed in rosy light, and seemed to convey to us dumb but eloquent reproach for our indifference. No longer could we stand these mute upbraidings. So the order issued for Mahommed the dragoman and donkeys four, for the following break of day.

At half-past eight next morning we were in marching order—crossed the Nile at the Ghizeh ferry, and found that, as the waters of the inundation had not sufficiently diminished, we should have to make a considerable detour, by adopting the high and winding causeway as our road. We were immediately joined by some Bedoueens of the Pyramids, who are generally on the look out for victims at the ferry, with a view of disposing of, without the competition of the whole tribe, their curiosities in the shape of copper coins of the later Roman emperors, images, beads, &c., found in the tombs and excavations made in the great sepulchral fields of Ghizeh and Sakara.

As soon as we left the villages and palm groves, the two Pyramids emerged before us in all their grandeur; but a view of these monuments from a distance cannot give the slightest idea of their enormous magnitude; you must approach and literally lay your hand upon them, climb unaided some of the immense blocks of which they are composed, and gaze upwards at their summits, before you can have a sense of their gigantic dimensions. After a gentle ride of about three hours, we reached the foot of the largest Pyramid, and there completed the necessary arrangements with the shekh, to secure us from the annoyances of his insatiably greedy flock. We were to give him a dollar apiece for the ascent and visit to the interior; and it was distinctly stipulated that none but the number of Arabs absolutely necessary should accompany us, and that the word *buckshish* should not be pronounced until the conclusion of the affair. The first operation was the mounting to the summit of the Pyramid. Each of us was provided with three Arabs—one to haul at each arm, and a third to push from behind; a boy was also in active attendance with the water-bottle. The day was unfortunately intensely warm—one of the hottest we had hitherto felt, so much so, that after having been dragged and shoved up half way, I determined, for my own part, to go no farther, but to sit calmly with my pipe under the shadow of a huge block, and await the return of my companion. In about ten minutes a shout of triumph announced his arrival at the summit, where he and his assistants seemed scarcely larger than long-legged birds. His descent, however, was so protracted that the delay became unaccountable; and when he did return, he informed us that, whether from the heat and exertion or from vertigo, he had fainted twice, and was obliged to rest for some time at the different halting stations. Although the ascent is not in the least dangerous, still the blocks of stone to be surmounted are so large, that it requires some labor to surmount them;

but that it is by no means even a great effort, is sufficiently proved by the number of ladies who annually record their visit to the apex. The view is, doubtless, extremely fine; but perhaps, as I refrained from reaching the top myself, I was disposed to undervalue it, and to imagine that from my perch I had very nearly the same thing,—the valley of the Nile under me; and Cairo spread out with its domes and mosques beneath the Mokattam range; the site of ancient royal Memphis, clearly visible, with its palm forest surrounding it; and the rival but inferior pyramids of Sakara, Abouseer, and Dashoor, standing along the Lybian tableland.

The exterior of the Pyramid having thus been accomplished, the interior remained to be explored. You mount, before arriving at the entrance, to a considerable height on the northern side, and on sliding down a block of smooth granite, you can pass into the black cavernous hole, through which you enter stooping. So admirably are the granite stones which case this passage, connected together, and so skilful the masonry, that you cannot pass the point of a thin penknife between them; and so polished are their surfaces, that it would be difficult to mount the steep ascent without some assistance. But away we went, at first on hands and knees, and then slipping and struggling, pulled and hauled. The Arabs, bound down by their agreement, refrained from their invariably direct howl for *buckshish*; but they made it the indirect burden of the song with which they accompanied the hauling and dragging of the unhappy Howadgi. It ran pretty much in this manner:—

>Lah-il-lah, La-il-lah;
>Very good shentlemān,
>Give good *buckshish;*
>Very good shentlemān;
>Lah-il-lah, Lah-il-lah;
>Give good *buckshish.*
>Shekh keep all;
>Him very bad man;
>Poor Arab get nothing;
>Very good shentlemān
>Will give poor Arab *buckshish;*
>Lah-il-lah, Lah-il-lah.

Such was the wording of the song, to the tune of which we were lugged into the dark funereal chamber, where lies the sarcophagus of the mighty Cheops, or Shoofoo. We were silly enough to comply with the poetical request; and, by being very good shentlemān, and giving poor Arab *buckshish,* we were tormented, annoyed, shouted at, importuned, and nearly worried to distraction for similar favors, the whole time we remained at the Pyramid. Half-a-dozen would at one moment thrust their objects of curiosity on us, and ask unconscionable prices for articles obtainable in Cairo for a few piastres. If we attempted to move off to see anything by ourselves, we found ourselves intercepted by some skirmisher whom we had lately repulsed, but who was in hopes of doing better business by catching us alone; others bothered us to give them half-a-crown, to run up to the top of the Pyramid and down again, in ten minutes; every boy who had a water-bottle considered himself entitled to *buckshish*, and clamored accordingly. Other minor vermin, who had lit some person's pipe or cigar with some unodoriferous substance, pressed loudly for payment; and when, after visiting some tombs and the Sphinx, we made ready to depart, every hand without exception was protruded, and every tongue yelled, growled, and hissed out *buckshish;* and when far, far away, we heard the hated word still lingering in the distance.

In spite of all the heat and bother, which considerably put us out, we both were delighted with our visit; for, although previous reading and drawings had given us a good idea of the objects and scenery we were to visit, yet nothing but personal inspection could enable one to form a correct conception of these enormous piles of masonry. The visit to the interior is perfectly unnecessary. When you are in what is called the King's Chamber, you can see nothing but darkness; for in fact there is nothing else to see; and the same emptiness exists in the other chambers subsequently discovered. Here are none of the gravings and sculptures and decorations, which render some of the other Egyptian monuments of such intense interest. These great mausolea of kings are remarkable for being altogether devoid of such ornaments, although some of the tombs of their ministers and servants, in the immediate neighbourhood, are richly adorned. Neither are there any of the names and titles which subsequent Pharaohs so liberally scattered over the land, to be found on these Pyramids. The inferior personages of the same date are much more profuse of self-commemoration; so much so, that Dr. Lepsius boasts in a passage which I shall subsequently quote at length, that he could almost compose a calendar of the court of King Shoofoo, from the adjacent monuments. The group of pyramids extending to Sakara are the oldest remains of human labor in the world; and modern investigation, according as fresh light is thrown upon their history, instead of diminishing their antiquity, extends their origin to the very earliest epoch of the post-diluvial race. In number the Pyramids of Ghizeh are three, and are called those of Cheops, Cephren, and Mycerinus; or, as the Egyptian inscriptions are read, of Kings Shoofoo, Shafra, and Menkere— or Remenka. The height of the largest pyramid (that of Shoofoo) is 460 feet; of the second, that of Shafra, 447; and the third, or small pyramid of Menkere or Mycerinus, 203. In the time of Pliny, it is supposed that the Pyramids presented a smooth exterior surface, part of which, on the Pyramid of Shafra, is still uninjured. It is to the Caliphs that one may, in all probability, attribute the spoliation that has since taken place. We are informed by historical accounts derived, most likely, from old Egyptian annals, that King Shoofoo employed 100,000 men for twenty years in the construction of his prodigious sepulchre; and that the ten years preceding the commencement of the undertaking were occupied merely in preparing the materials, and the causeway whereon the stone was to be transported. Nor need this assertion be a matter of wonder, when we know that the base of the Pyramid occupies a space about the size of Lincoln's Inn Fields, and that the structure itself contains six million eight hundred and forty-eight thousand tons of stone. But this is not the only proof of the great power of the ancient monarchs of the fourth dynasty, whose sway is placed by Bunsen at 3200 B.C., and by Lepsius at 3400 B.C., —five thousand years before our period; for even in the peninsula of Mount Sinai, the name and tablet of Shoofoo show that in those dim ages his dominion extended over these Arabian districts, where copper-mines were worked for him; moreover, this great mausoleum is lined, as I before remarked, internally with beautifully polished and massive blocks of red granite, not one particle of which exists below the country of the Cataract of Assouan, or 640 miles from the quarry to the Pyramid. In the year 1837, Colonel Vyse made a remarkable discovery in this Pyramid: he opened for the first time a chamber above that which is called the King's Chamber, where the sarcophagus remains, and there found the king's name, Shoofoo, written in hieroglyphical characters in red ochre on the rough stone. These characters had, without doubt, been scored by some of the workmen or overseers at the time the building was going on. A signet ring, bearing upon it the name of the same king, in massive gold, was discovered a few years since in the tomb of one of his ministers. The whole of the surrounding neighbourhood is one great place of sepulture; but the tombs are not like the rock grottoes we shall subsequently explore, cut into the face of the hill, but buried deep in the rock which forms the basis of the Pyramid. A great deal of attention of late has been paid to these most early and interesting monuments of Egyptian power, particularly by Dr. Lepsius, sent by the munificence of the King of Prussia, in the year 1843, to investigate the antiquities of the valley of the Nile. He thus speaks of some of his excavations in the vicinity of, and amongst monuments coeval with, the Pyramids:—"The painting, on a very fine coating of lime, is often beautiful beyond conception, and is sometimes preserved as fresh and perfect as if it had been done yesterday. The representations on the walls chiefly contain scenes from the life of the deceased, and we thus become familiar with all the details of his private history. The numerous inscriptions describe or designate these scenes, or they exhibit the often widely branching family of the deceased, and all his titles and offices; so that I could almost compose a court and state calendar of King Cheops or Cephren. The most splendid tombs belonged principally to the royal princes, their relatives, or the highest official personages under the kings, beside whose pyramid they are laid; and not unfrequently I have found the tomb of father, son, and grandson, even great-grandson, so that whole pedigrees of those distinguished Egyptians who, above five thousand years ago, formed the nobility of the land, are brought to light. The most beautiful of the tombs which I myself discovered, with many others beneath the sand which here buries all things, belongs to a prince of the family of King Cheops."

It is perfectly absurd the amount of laborious nonsense that has been written by learned men, as to the origin and intention of the Pyramids. Some of the theories assign to them an origin earlier than the deluge, although two of the most ancient of Memphis are built of sun-dried brick, which would not have endured the influx of water for a month; others have considered them as vast temples for the purposes of fire-worship; while others have contended that they were erected for astronomical purposes. We have, however, abundance of evidence, besides the actual testimony of the monuments themselves, *to know* that they were built for purposes of sepulture, and for nothing else. Nor is it in the least wonderful, that with unlimited power, and with their peculiar religious tenets, the mighty monarchs of early Egypt should have erected these imperishable tombs. When we have arrived at our explorings of the rock grottoes in Upper Egypt, I shall take the opportunity of remarking on the reasons which induced the peculiar anxiety, on the part of the former inhabitants of this country, to maintain the inviolability of their last resting-places:—"The early kings seem, from the very commencement of their reigns, to have set to work at the preparation for their sepulture. As soon as he ascended the throne, each monarch began the building of his pyramid. At first he only designed a small one, to ensure himself a complete tomb, in case he were destined to be but a few years on the throne; but with the advancing years of his life, he increased it by successive layers, till he thought he was near the termination of his life. If he died during the erection, then the external covering was alone completed, and the monument of death finally remained proportionate to the life of the king. Thus the whole building proceeded from a small pyramid, which was erected in stages, and then increased and heightened by superimposed coverings of stone, from fifteen to twenty feet in breadth, till at length the great steps were filled up, so as to form one common flat side, giving the usual pyramidical form to the whole. This gradual growth explains the enormous magnitude of some pyramids, and the smallness of others." The learned Lepsius, whose theory I am adopting, and whose words I am almost quoting, goes so far as to be of opinion, that if the Pyramids had remained uninjured, we might even now have been able to calculate the years of the reigns of their particular kings, just as one is able to determine the age of a tree by its successive rings.

I have omitted, for the present, doing more than merely to mention the name of the Sphinx; for the day was so hot, and we ourselves so exhausted, that we confined our visit to this most remarkable and mysterious monument, only to a rest under its shadow. Hereafter, on returning down the river, I hope to have a longer time to examine this wonder—no less a wonder than the Pyramids themselves.

We returned home weary and jaded—Hubert, my Belgian servant, gallantly leading the way in a full suit of blue pilot cloth, selected for its heat and thickness, with a view to a bivouac before Sebastopol. He wore it like a hero, and asserted stoutly that it was a suit far better for extreme heat than our lighter garments, being more impervious to the fierce sun of Africa. My friend Mr. A. rather maliciously informed Mahommed the dragoman, that Hubert thinks there is a good deal in Mahommedanism. He is consequently so occupied in the work of conversion, that he will hardly attend to his other business. Hubert apparently likes the brilliant offers of beautiful ladies, both in this and the next world; of Gebeli tobacco, and perhaps of high official rank, to which his old seducer tempts him to aspire; but he boggles altogether at certain initiatory ceremonies, indispensable to Judaism and Islam, to which Sidney Herbert pleasantly alluded in the House of Commons in a recent debate on the Jew Bill.

The sultry day of yesterday was the precursor of a perfect infliction, namely, a burning, violent wind from the S.W., or great desert, the Sahara. We are all ill—Egyptians, Turks, Franks, Infidels, and Believers. I am parched up and feverish and unhappy. This annoyance endured nearly a week, and, finding myself really the worse for it, I took the advice of an old hand, and passed the best part of a day in the Arabian desert: the wonderfully pure, dry, fresh air, which pervades it, is peculiarly bracing and invigorating, after the sultry and damper atmosphere of the alluvial region near the Nile. The spot I selected for the day's bivouac was six or seven miles from Cairo, where the extraordinary remains of a petrified forest extend for miles and miles. This great expanse of ground is completely covered with fossilized trees of the thorn, palm, and bamboo species; none are now standing, and most are lying about broken in pieces; but every here and there you meet, half-embedded in the sand

4*

large trunks of trees, stretched out as they fell. I myself actually measured one of the length of forty feet. Many of them are perfectly complete, except being shattered at the joints; nor is it difficult to discover where the branches were originally connected. Geologists are of opinion that formerly the Red Sea and the Mediterranean were connected between Suez, to the east of the Nile embouchures, and that these trees covered the low land of the water's edge. Thin slices of this petrified wood have been submitted to the microscope; and their dicotyledonous structure is found as strongly developed as in oak and chestnut. These deposits are of a comparatively recent date; not only do they belong to the tertiary division, but to the most modern formations of that division.

This excursion is most delightful for an invalid, and many persons are in the habit of pitching their tent in the desert, and remaining there for several days, as an infallible remedy for all disease. In the summer it seems almost as if the feast of tabernacles was held there, so many, dotting it with white patches, are the tents of those who leave the stifling heat of Cairo to woo its singing breezes. Mr. Bayard Taylor writes with eloquence and enthusiasm of his experience of the desert, a more terrible one too than this,—the Great Nubian Desert. He says:—

"I found an unspeakable fascination in the sublime solitude of the desert. I often beheld the sun rising, when within the wide ring of the horizon there was no other living being to be seen. He came up like a god, in awful glare; and it would have been a natural act, had I cast myself on the sand and worshipped him. The sudden change in the coloring of the landscape on his appearance—the lighting up of the dull sand into a warm golden hue, and the tintings of purple and violet on the distant porphyry hills—was a morning miracle which I never beheld without awe. The richness of this coloring made the desert beautiful; it was too brilliant for desolation. The scenery, so far from depressing, inspired and exhilarated me. I never felt the sensation of physical health and strength in such perfection, and was ready to shout from morning to night, from the overflow of happy spirits. The air is an elixir of life—as sweet and pure and refreshing as that which the first man breathed on the morning of creation. You inhale the unadulterated elements of the atmosphere; for there are no exhalations from moist earth, vegetable matter, or the smoke and steams which arise from the abodes of men, to stain its purity. This air, even more than its silence and solitude, is the secret of one's attachment to the desert. It is a beautiful illustration of the compensating care of that Providence, which leaves none of the waste places of the earth without some atoning glory. Where all the pleasant aspects of Nature are wanting—where there is no green thing—no fount for the thirsty lip—scarcely the shadow of a rock to shield the wanderer in the blazing noon—God has breathed upon the wilderness his sweetest and tenderest breath, giving clearness to the eye, strength to the frame, and the most joyous exhilaration to the spirits."

There is no doubt whatever but that the most inveterate cases of ophthalmia are speedily and effectually cured by a short sojourn in this mighty wilderness of sand; and that fact completely controverts the opinion, which has attributed this distressing and too common disease to floating particles of minute sand, which in certain winds it is impossible to exclude. Sir G. Wilkinson says:—

"After many years' experience, and repeated attacks, I am persuaded that ophthalmia arises in the transition from excessive dryness to damp; and, though Egypt is perhaps the driest climate in the world, the difference between the generally dry atmosphere, and the damp exhalations on the river or in the streets of Cairo and other towns (which are not only narrow, but are watered to keep them cool), is so great, that the eye is readily affected by it, particularly when in that susceptible state caused by the sensible and insensible perspiration, to which the skin is then subject. Hence it is that during the inundation, when the exhalations are the greatest, ophthalmia is most prevalent. The fact of its non-existence in, and speedy cure if a patient goes into, the desert, sufficiently substantiate this opinion; and this is further corroborated by the comparative comfort the eye receives there, by the dryness of the air."

Be this as it may, I certainly returned from my excursion quite a new man; the languor had disappeared, so much so, that on the way back I took a constitutional tour of several miles, much to the astonishment of the donkey-boys, who never see any one walk who can possibly ride, and to the annoyance of my guide Mohammed, who considered himself in honor bound to go shuffling along after me in his red slippers, in spite of my request that he should continue to avail himself of our stalwart asses. Besides the other indispositions which I carried with me, and sent forth like scape-goats into the wilderness, I had also a very bad cold, which disappeared shortly with the rest, and which I caught from taking a Turkish bath at a late period of the day, and exposure to the evening air in going home after it—an error which the natives always avoid, by performing their ablutions early.

Although so many persons have now been in the East, and enjoyed this so-called luxury, it may be as well to give one's experience as to how they manage these things in Egypt. If you wish to be particular, you should pay some 7s. or 8s. for your bath, and order it exclusively for yourself, at about midday, by which time the good Muslims have retired. You should bring your own towels, order the water to be completely poured out, and the bath filled in your presence, to prevent the unpleasantness of being submerged in the abstersions of the previous comers. On arriving at the street-door of the bath-house, you pass into a long dark passage, and then find yourself in a large anteroom, with raised divans around, on which is spread palm-matting. This may be called the House of Commons, where the poorer classes squat and smoke when their bath is over. Next comes a much smarter chamber, for the more select, with comfortable sofas, where smart folks recline, drink coffee, enjoy their Gebeli tobacco, and take a nap, if so disposed. Here you undress, and being shod with high wooden pattens, are led sliding and stumbling about into another room, from which there are small recesses, the uses of which you will shortly experience. After traversing this, you mount some steps, and find yourself in a low small chamber dimly lighted by a few little panes of glass in the dome which surmounts it. In the middle of this is a reservoir, supposed to be filled with extremely hot water, the vapour of which is to be a sudorific ere you take your plunge. As a preliminary, you are laid down like a fish on a slab upon the tesselated floor, with a twisted towel put under your head as a support. In this posture you remain till your attendant considers you to be sufficiently sodden, when he seizes you by the arm, cracks all your fingers and joints, turns you over with a jerk, and performs the same operation on the vertebræ of your back, and last of all nearly dislocates your stubborn English legs. At each crack he expresses his extreme satisfaction, and appeals to you for your opinion of his performance. You are then left for a few minutes to recover yourself, when he returns, armed with an implement intended for a flesh-brush, but which, from the Mahommedan horror of anything appertaining to the unclean beast, the pig, is not constructed of bristles, but of the rough interior of a kind of water cucumber. With this he rubs you vigorously over, and sedulously collects the long rounded particles of skin of which you are denuded, and accompanies this flaying-alive proceeding, by holding up before your eyes these spoils of that which was lately part of your constituting substance. After this you are invited to plunge into the hot-water reservoir, where you remain, dangling your legs into it, until you are supposed to have sufficiently perspired. At that period of the ceremony, a sheet is wrapped round you, and you are conducted from the bath into one of the little recesses I alluded to, and are seated on a wooden stool. While you wonder what possible annoyance can come next, you ascertain the fact, by two or three buckets of what seems uncommonly cold water, but which I hear is tepid, being thrown over your head. Half drowned, and altogether furious, you splutter out exclamations, which in England would be considered energetic. But here your torments come to an end. You are led back into the smart chamber, swathed in warm garments, and left to your coffee and repose. In the instance to which I allude, our solemnity was not concluded till past six o'clock; and, as that was dinner hour, we had to hurry forth, with open pores, into the evening chill, which inflicted so bad a cold, that it caused the remembrance of the *hamam* to be anything but agreeable, and for which I had to call in the aid of the desert air, as the only effectual restorative.

The last few days of my residence in Cairo, I was unusually busy in preparing for the voyage to the south; but I did not leave unvisited the Coptic churches in Old Cairo, nor the Friday performance of the dancing dervishes. Although there is a quarter of New Cairo almost exclusively occupied by Copts, yet their main residence and most ancient sanctuaries are in Old Cairo, which is a ride of about two or three miles from our sojourn. It is completely separated from the present town, and surrounded by a very high and lofty wall. On arriving at the foot of this circumvallation, we were at a loss how to enter, as there was neither gate nor visible opening for thoroughfare; but, seeing a blue-turbaned Copt emerging on a donkey from what seemed literally a hole in the wall, we entered by the same narrow inlet, which hardly afforded room for a single passenger. It really reminded one of Sidney Smith's reasons for continuing the iron bar which divides the little gate at the back of Spring Gardens, leading into St. James's Park—" If it were not for it, such very fat fellows would get through." The streets were as confined as the entrance; and the town seemed deserted, until we reached what apparently was a stable, but which turned out to be the main door of the old church. There was little of interest in it, except its extreme antiquity, and a subterraneous grotto, appropriated by the Latins, as being an especial holy spot, from having been the hiding-place of the Virgin and Holy Infant on their first arrival in Egypt, where, as the legends narrate, our Lady supported herself by mantua-making.

"The church itself is divided into four or five compartments, as all Coptic churches are. The *heykel*, or chancel, containing the altar, occupies the chief and central portion of the compartment at the upper end; which is screened from the rest of the church by a partition of wooden panel-work, in this instance curiously colored and inlaid with pretty ivory arabesques; before the door which leads into this, is suspended a curtain, with a large cross worked upon it.[1]" The compartment to the right of this is appropriated to the priests who read the lesson; and we had the benefit of a Coptic evening

[1] Sir G. Wilkinson.

service. The prayers and scriptures were intoned by a priest and two acolytes, in a sing-song protracted drawl, and without the slightest reverence. Indeed, on several occasions, the service was interrupted by an animated conversation with the dragoman, and then resumed with the utmost coolness. This is not to be wondered at, as very few of the Coptic priests comprehend one word of what they read. The women occupy a partition completely screened from the men by lattice-work; and on the walls were gaudy pictures of saints, among which our own St. George, in busy encounter with the dragon, was pre-eminent. At the extreme end of the church there is a tank, where, to commemorate the baptism of Jesus, men and boys plunge on a particular day, and the Muslims declare, that as the Coptic votaries take their spring, they shout to each other, "Plunge as thy father and grandfather plunged, and remove Islam from thy heart." I believe, however, that this custom is but little practised in Cairo, but it is almost invariable up the country, in the Coptic districts of the Thebaid. There is in the gallery leading to this church a curious old inscription in Greek characters, set up by the early Christians. I could still make out many of the letters, and I hear it has been deciphered; but I have not seen any interpretation given of it. It is on wood: a singular proof of the dryness of the climate.

If the streets were deserted on our arrival, we

had to tell a very different tale on our departure, for we were literally beset with beggars, who would take no denial, but clung to our donkeys, seized them by the tails, and insisted upon alms. We fought vigorously with sticks; but mine, although a stout one, was broken in twain on the back of a stalwart mendicant at the very commencement of the affray. 'Twas then our dragoman opposed to the attack a strategy worthy of the Great Duke and the retreat on the lines of Torres Vedras. Fixing firmly his donkey across the street, he bade us make good speed to the exit from the town; and, as we hurried off on our asses, we watched him giving thrust and point to the clamorous rabble, with the skill, energy, and gallantry of a life-guardsman. *Sic nos servavit Apollo.*

On our way back to Cairo, we visited the old mosque which Amr, the famous general of the Caliph Omar, founded in the year 638 A.D., when he conquered Egypt. The immense number of columns composing the building, and the fact of its being the earliest temple of Islamism in Egypt, render it, in spite of its abandoned and decaying appearance, well worthy of a visit. The building is a large square, open except under the colonnades, and going rapidly to ruin. At the west end, the pillars of these colonnades are in a single line; at the east end, six deep; and they are curious, owing to the variety of their capitals, which are of every description of architecture—Doric, Ionic, Corinthian, Composite, and many borrowed, like the old Egyptian, from water-plants. They are in number 230, and seem a perfect forest.

The legends connected with this mosque are nearly as numerous as its columns. When Amr was about to commence it, he selected a large extent of ground, part of which was the property of a Jewish widow. His strict ideas of justice forbade him from forcibly taking possession of that which belonged to another, though that other was not a Mahommedan, and one of the conquered race. He offered, therefore, to buy the land, which she, to his surprise and annoyance, obstinately refused to part with, in spite of ever increasing offers to an extent far exceeding its value. In this dilemma he resolved on consulting the Caliph Omar, who was then at Yambu, a port of Arabia; and he sent a messenger to detail the circumstances. When the messenger arrived, he found the Caliph walking in the outskirts of the town, and he laid before him the difficulty of the victorious general. The Caliph, having listened attentively to the story, picked up a sheep's skull which was lying on the ground, and dipping his finger in the inkhorn hanging from his belt, drew two lines on the blanched white bone— one straight, the other crooked; and merely observed, " Return and bear this to Amr, the servant of the one God."

When Amr received the sheep's skull, he pondered long on the mysterious signification of the two lines; but at last, suddenly comprehending their import, he cried out—"Thou art right, O Caliph; men should follow the straight line, which is of God, and avoid the crooked one, which is of the devil, whose name be accursed." From this has arisen the Arab saying, "Remember the sheep's skull."

In spite, however, of Amr's recognition of the principles of going straight, he seems to have acted with rather sharp and crooked practice towards the Jewess; for though he refrained from taking her land by force, or compelling her to sell it, he seems to have been aware of the trick played by the Phœnicians at the founding of Carthage, and to have done the Israelitish widow out of her land in the same way as Dido treated her admirer, Iarbas. He sent for her, and requested permission to buy at a high price only so much of her field as a bull's hide would cover. She gladly accepted the terms; but, to her astonishment found, that by cutting the hide into narrow strips, it surrounded as much of the land as sufficed for the site of the present mosque, with its large square, galleries, and walls.

Neglected, abandoned, and falling into ruin as is this mosque, yet when the Nile refuses to fulfil its usual functions, and the insufficiency of its rising alarms the country with the prospect of famine, its sanctity is then remembered, and ulemas and imaums and moollahs proceed in state, escorted by soldiers, and the old galleries are again filled with worshippers. Prayers are daily said before a particular *kebla,* or point, called the *kebla* of the rise of the Nile; and Allah is requested no longer to delay the wished-for inundation. This ceremony is supposed to be always efficacious, and immediately after it, the Nile commences gradually to increase.

But these are not the only miracles connected with this poor, old, unfashionable mosque. In the south-west corner there is a small well, the source of which is supposed to communicate with the famous Zem Zem of Mecca. It was only lately that a Maugrebyn pilgrim, returning from the Hejaz, found in it his copper cup, which he had accidentally dropped into Zem Zem. If you venture to remark, that it is difficult for a little trickling stream like this to have crossed the desert and the Red Sea, you are instantly stopped by the reply, that "God is great." The greater the impossibility, the stronger the belief.

One of the columns too, is the subject of a mighty miracle. It does not belong to the locality, but was conveyed thither. At the time that Amr was building this mosque, the same Caliph we have alluded to, was pacing to and fro beneath the galleries of the mosque at Mecca. His thoughts were on Amr and the holy building that was then being raised by him at Cairo. By the power given him from heaven, he perceived his Lieutenant, Amr, in the act of giving orders to the workmen, to erect a column for the support of the roof in the very place where the present one stands. Omar, by his supernatural intelligence, perceived that the column was made of faulty stone, and that it endangered the stability of the whole edifice. He turned therefore at once, and addressing one of the innumerable pillars of the mosque of Mecca, desired it instantly to remove to Cairo, and take the place of the faulty column there. The pillar trembled, but did not stir. Omar again repeated his order, and slapped it with the palm of his hand. The pillar shook violently, and turned round on its base, but still lingered. Striking it furiously with his *kurbash* (or whip of hide), Omar cried out—" In the name of God, the most clement and most merciful, away with you!"—" Why did'st thou forget to invoke the name of God before?" said the now obedient pillar; and, taking flight, it immediately placed itself where it now is; and whence no human force can dislodge it, till it be the will of Allah; but when that time comes, the whole mosque will crumble into ruin.

Mahommed showed us on the marble the mark of the fierce blow of the Caliph's scourge; but he refrained from showing us the site of another miracle, which is not in such repute, however, at present. In some part of the building there are two columns placed close together, through which Mahommedans declare no Christian can pass, although to do so, is a feat easily performed by themselves. So many slim unbelievers have of late passed through, and so many fat believers have stuck fast, that the Muslims have been scandalized, and somewhat shaken in their belief in this puzzle-Christian. Our guide, therefore, old Mohammed, being highly orthodox, thought it better not to give us a chance of a successful trial, and said nothing on the subject till we were well away. On our subsequently touching on the subject of the ancient tale, the old gentleman got out of the perplexity by assuring us, that the difficulty was not for a Christian to get through, but for a person of evil life. On that principle we may presume there is excellence in thinness, and corresponding iniquity in what tailors call stoutness; and we have a certain confirmation of this theory, by remembering what happened to Jeshuron—that "he waxed fat and kicked."

The performance of the dancing dervishes, which takes place every Friday, the Mahommedan sabbath, is one of the lions of Cairo, and which few Europeans miss seeing. There is not the slightest objection on the part of these vagabonds (which is the best epithet to apply to this useless and vicious community) to their ceremonies being witnessed by the public. Indeed, any person that chooses can join, and many persons do so, in this extraordinary exhibition.

These dervishes, or, at least, dervishes in general,

enjoy by no means an enviable reputation in the East: gluttony, drunkenness, theft, profligacy, hypocrisy, and insubordination, being the characteristics generally attributed to them. In fact their numbers are composed of idle, dissolute fellows, unwilling to work, and desirous of covering every evil propensity under the cloak of sanctity. The Arabs say that the father of evil, hearing so good an account of these folks, once joined their body for a week; but at the end of that time was so appalled by their wickedness, that he left them without bidding good-bye, and returned whence he came for peace and quiet.

This mosque is some distance from the town, near Boulak, the port of Cairo, and is a domed building, remarkably clean, and ornamented with drums, tamburines, and other implements of the trade. We went a strong party, ladies included, set ourselves down on mats by the wall, and found the proceedings already begun. The *corps dramatique* consisted of about twenty-five persons, the greater portion being what, I suppose, I may call the laity; the rest were the dervishes, distinguished by long flowing unkempt locks, and high, conical, peaked caps. The dancing portion of the fraternity wore a felt hat, uncommonly like a whitey-brown flower-pot, and a long flowing garb like a dressing-gown. At first the ceremony consisted of one of the party reciting from the Koran, to whom at stated periods the main body responded in chorus.

After this had lasted some time, they all sat down, and commenced repeating the word Allah (God) in a low deep tone, bowing their heads gently in tune. One of the whitey-brown flower-pots here stepped into the middle of the circle, and, with hands extended and fingers bent downwards, began to wheel round and round. Another shortly followed; and, as the rotatory motion continued, it increased in violence, until the dress floated out like an extended parachute. The sitting performers in the meanwhile were by no means idle: they gradually increased the loudness and depth of the intonation of the word Allah, and in such perfect accordance, that at last I can only liken the sound to the deep sough of a regularly moving steam-engine—Al-lah-Al-lah, laying a stress on each syllable, and bowing till the head nearly touched the floor. At length, at a given signal, they all sprang upon their feet, and many divested themselves of their upper garments; for the fun was now getting "fast and furious." One of the party blew a low-toned flute as accompaniment, and the same bowing and repeating the word Al-lah was continued; but the chant grew louder and louder gradually, and the bending and swaying of the body more violent—all, however, still maintaining both in voice and action, the most perfect accordance. The shekh, or chief of the dervishes, one of the handsomest men I ever saw, and richly dressed in fur-edged pelisse, was perambulating the circle, and beating time with his hands, bowing to, and encouraging with benevolent smiles, the more energetic performers. The sight had now become a very extraordinary one: the low clear notes of the flute, the deep hoarse cry of Al-lah, the violent swaying of the bodies, the long hair of the performers sweeping backwards and forwards and touching the ground, and the flower-pots continuing within this strange circle their interminable whirl, all formed a spectacle of which it is really impossible to describe the impression it conveyed. But at once the most horrible shrieks proceeded from one of the performers, an old, grey-headed, grey-bearded dervish, who reeled out of the ranks in a state apparently of epilepsy. Two or three others followed, similarly affected, uttering the same piercing cries, foaming at the mouth, and reeling as if under the influence of violent convulsions. They were obliged to be held down with all the strength of their associates. This is considered the culminating point of the performance, when any of the party become thus *melboos*, as they term it, or inspired; and there is no doubt whatever that this frenzy is not feigned, but the result of extreme physical and mental excitement.

The ceremony was over, and we departed; but I could not help reflecting, while homeward bound, how astonished and horrified Mohammed the Prophet would have been at such an exhibition. The one God, Allah, whose unity had been infringed by the superstitions of mankind, and whose simple worship it had been his object and mission to re-establish, is evidently far less thought of in these barbarous ceremonies than the crazy, half-maddened performers themselves. Nor is it only the poor and ignorant, but even people of condition, and comparative education, who contemplate these weekly exhibitions with veneration, and even at times take part in them themselves. It is precisely the same feeling which makes the barbarous Indian bow in terror and submission, erect altars, and proffer deprecatory gifts to the irregular powers of nature—the thunder, the lightning, the storm, and the whirlwind—that influences the Orientals in their reverence for these physical outbursts, that convulse the human frame, or for the aberration of intellect in lunatics and idiots. The barbarian sees unreflectingly the daily revolutions of the heavenly bodies, which give light and heat, and the annual succession of seasons, which bear with them their various gifts; but they are regular, and move him not. It is the violence of the hurricane, or the peal of the thunder shock, that rouses his insensibility and prompts his adoration. So, too, the Eastern sees with little emotion the ordinary functions of the human mind; he deals not in abstract inquiry, nor resorts to metaphysics; but when he perceives that something is astray—that the reason wanders, and the thinking faculty is obscured, he reverences the power, preternatural to him, that has willed this mental aberration, and, believing that the soul has been reft from the body, and translated to the regions of the blest, he is deeply affected by a crazy epileptic dervish, and looks on a madman as the especial favorite of Heaven.

After all, before condemning the Mahommedan religion as the cause of these extravagancies, let us remember that the same evil tendencies may result from unchecked fanaticism and superstition, even in the purest and simplest creed. These wretched epileptic dervishes are not one whit worse than members of the Greek Church, the creed of Imperial Russia and Christian Greece. What can be more horribly revolting, more profane, than the conduct of the devotees in the presence of the tomb of their Saviour, running round it with frantic cries, half naked, howling, jumping on the shoulders of one another, trampling each other under foot? Is not the description by Jerome of the proceedings of some of the early Christians, who performed similar antics before the supposed tombs of John the Baptist and Elisha, in Samaria, almost an exact narration of what we witnessed this day? " Ululare more luporum—vocibus latrare canum—alios rotare caput et post tergum terram vertice tangere."—"Some of them went howling like wolves, some barked like dogs, some rolled their heads about and bent backwards till they struck them on the ground." Such are the excrescences of a goodly tree.

But at last the end of December arrived, and with

it letters from Constantinople, announcing the fact that the friend on whose society I had calculated, although having actually taken his place to Alexandria, was obliged, by news suddenly received, to return to England. This, of course, upset every arrangement; but as George Selwyn, on the death of an old and valued friend, went down to the club and took another, so was I also obliged to go to Shepheard's Hotel, and proffer my society to some one in want of a Nile companion. There was little difficulty about finding a fellow-traveller, but much in finding a suitable one; and I was driven to many shifts and expedients not to wound the susceptibility of those with whom I had commenced negotiations, as a few minutes of their society convinced me that a few days of it would see the bonds of union severed, and one or other of us returning whence we came. To one whose time I knew was precious, I pretended an absolute necessity to reach the Mountains of the Moon; to another who was determined, as he said, to *do all* the Nile, I invented imperative business, which would render Thebes the furthest possible limit of my journey. At last, however, I was fortunate enough to meet a gentleman who seemed to be of kindred tastes, and we at once, as time pressed, energetically set to work to select and furnish our *dahabieh*, or Nile boat. A very excellent honest Arab, Hassaneen by name, the superintendent of the dockyard, had a small boat, somewhat cramped for room it is true, but the more adapted thereby for ascending the cataracts, and we accordingly engaged it.

A description of that which was to be our residence for the next few months may give some idea of life on the Nile. Figure to yourself a craft in dimensions about the size of an ordinary canal-boat, very low in the water, with a lofty raised stern about one-third of the length of the whole, containing our apartments. You enter by a small door into the saloon, so magnificently designated, but which is in reality not more than about ten or twelve feet long and eight feet high, with sofas or divans on each side of it in gorgeous chintz. Beyond this are two small recesses for bath and other conveniences, and after them the sleeping-room. It was originally composed of two divans, opposite each other, horseshoe-wise, with a passage down the middle, but for the sake of privacy we had it divided into two compartments boarded off, and as the smaller division fell to my lot we threw down the partition which separated it from the bath. Being provided with indiarubber tubs, we abolished, or rather converted that institution into a cellar, over which my carpet was spread, thus forming an excellent divan for dressing at the foot of the bed. So much for the interior. At our stern-pole flew the union-jack of England; and as every boat carries a private signal, which is duly inscribed for the recognition of fellow-travellers in a book kept at Shepheard's Hotel, ours purported to be—A flea sable couchant on gules field. The bark itself was entitled El Berghoot, or the *Flea*—a name originally intended to represent her smartness and activity, as well as to allude to one of the most peculiar of Egyptian productions, as others had called their vessels the Ibis, the Lotus, and such-like. All our predecessors had been sentimental; we were forced, in order to keep up the allusion to the Nile and its progeny, to be somewhat satirical; but indeed, as it subsequently turned out, we found that a more suitable appellation could not possibly have been selected; for if, as they say, Nazareth be the abode of the King of the Fleas, our boat seemed really the receptacle of the Queen of that race, and of the rest of the royal family. Our first night convinced us of that sad fact:—they literally swarmed; they bit and crawled and skipped over us, as if holding a flea festivity on the joyous occasion of our arrival. Our old dragoman took it very coolly. He merely advised us to commence a *chasse*, and that each day's *chasse* would diminish their numbers; and here, as I write, we have been *chassé*-ing with a vengeance for a whole week, with wonderful steadiness; but still the exclamation from both sofas, oft repeated, of " Confound the fleas," shows that a good deal remains to be done. I proposed to keep a game-book, so great has been the *battue*, not to mention the diversity of game in the way of bugs and mosquitoes; but of late it is a real happiness to say that our efforts have been crowned with success, and that our average of captured fleas has dwindled down to one or two of a night. A pair of silk drawers (which should be very baggy and sewn up at the feet), bought at Cairo, has been, I really believe, my salvation from their first bloodthirsty onslaught. We were provided with mosquito nets, but found that enemy to be of very much less importance. At first they sounded their trumpets in defiance, but the curtains prevented all attacks; the fleas had a complete monopoly. But after a few days, by practising the same steady system, we completely extirpated this detachment of enemies, and now, the eighth day since our departure, we have got rid altogether of their society, and discarded our gauze defences.

We must, however, return to the other preliminaries, the most important of which was the provisioning. Great were the bags of rice and mishmish (dried apricots); great the influx of potatoes, flour, bread, biscuits, gingerbread nuts, marmalade, oranges, candles in profusion, sauces without end; and last, but not least, "O word of fear, unpleasing to a Muslim ear," were two gigantic Yorkshire hams. Then came sherry and marsala, to dilute Nile water, in spite of the fact of Ptolemy Philadelphus sending it weekly to his daughter Berenice into Syria; and champagne for very great festivities; and gin, whose punch delighteth the soul of man; and arraki which undiluted, delighteth the soul of Egyptian women; and brandy, for heroes and for medicine; and beer without end, for drouthy souls. All these things and many more, were borne by patient oxen in carts; and the decks of the *Berghoot* assumed the appearance of a fortress victualled for a siege. But this was not all. Old Mohammed's department next deployed, with mighty junks of beef, and the half of a sheep; and cages of palm wood containing innumerable cocks and hens, and others with turkeys, and others with pigeons, and others with eggs, and others with vegetables—the fragrant cabbage, and still more fragrant onion, and *fines herbes* for omelettes, and tomatoes for cutlet sauce, and gourds for other abominations. Thus the poor *Berghoot* seemed a vast menagerie of birds, a butcher's stall, and a green-grocer's establishment; and in despair we hid ourselves in the cabin, and wondered where all these things could be stowed away, and how standing room on deck could ever become obtainable.

The last formality now remained, which was the binding of the reis, or captain of the boat, and crew, to our good will and pleasure during our expedition up the river. We proceeded to the consul's, and there, for the sum of 12*s.*, an indenture was drawn out, purporting that we had engaged our boat for two months certain, from Hassaneen Effendi, at a certain rate per month; that he had agreed, in consequence, to furnish us with all necessaries for the journey—linen, crockery, cutlery, &c.; that our ship's crew were to consist of reis, steersman, six sailors, and loblolly-boy; that they were to obey us in all things; that they were to demand no *buckshish;* that one should always hold the main-sheet for fear of gusts of wind; and that, the wind failing, we should be entitled to call on them to track, or haul the boat from sunrise to sunset; and that, if we ascended the cataracts, we were to do so at our own expense.

All these formulas having been duly read, and the reis having been warned as to the duty of passive obedience, and as to the results of insubordination, nothing more remained than to select that most indispensable official, the cook. Our dragoman informed us that he had one in his eye— an undoubted *artiste*, whose name was Hassaneen, or the " Doubly Beautiful." This Doubly Beautiful was introduced, and a more ugly, toothless, torrefied, half-naked, old rascal, can hardly be imagined. But we were assured of his abilities; and it was agreed that, if they proved equal to the representations of the dragoman, we were to secure his valuable services at the rate of £3. 10s. per month, with an additional *buckshish,* if at end of our wanderings, we had nothing to allege against his conduct and *cordon blue.* We were, moreover, as we thought, very wary, and resolved not to take the word of any man, much less of a dragoman, in a selection so important; so we invited friends, and gave a lunch, to criticise the abilities of the Doubly Beautiful. In due time an Irish stew, worthy of

M—e H—l, a fowl split and broiled, cutlets by no means discreditable, and an omelette that would not have been disowned by the *Trois Frères*, made us believe that we had got the right man in the right place; and the Doubly Beautiful became our own. Time, alas! proved that it was Hubert made the omelette, and that the Irish stew was the supreme, almost I may say, the only effort of Hassaneen's intelligence. Were it not for the failure of our potatoes, I should never be able again to look on that savory condiment without dismay, so often would it have our *pièce de resistance*, without a hope of change or novelty.

Our crew were now summoned and inspected, and we were pleased with their appearance. They were all Berberi, or Nubians, fine-looking young fellows, and preferable to Arabs, being much less inclined to rascality, and more subordinate. The reis was a tall, slight, handsome man, very dark, but with none of the Negro characteristics of some of the sailors. We were quite taken with his mild, gentle voice, and equally gentle expression of countenance; and, as far as we have yet seen, his conduct has not belied his appearance. (It must be remembered that I am writing on the ninth day of the voyage; a little later, I might have expressed very different opinions.) This is pleasant enough, as it would be a sad pang to see the mild eye of the reis raised in deprecation of the bastinado that follows the least misconduct. I feel as if I should hardly have the heart to order the execution, although examples at times are necessary, *pour encourager les autres*. It was only the other day that we met a merry party of our countrymen returning from the citadel, where they had been officiating at the festivity of administering a *quantum suff.* of *kurbash* to the soles of their reis's feet, as the preliminary to starting. It appeared from their account, that he had refused to obey orders, and been otherwise recalcitrant. An Arab, however, who was telling me all about it, considers the affair to have been altogether a mistake on the part of the unfortunate reis; but added, that, after all, it was much better, mistake or not, that it occurred; for that it would convey a valuable lesson, not only to the sufferer, but be particularly serviceable to others.

It is probable, as the word "crew" is mentioned in conjunction with our pleasure-boat, that European imagination may imagine the aforesaid crew to resemble that of a fashionable yacht. They may suppose them to be, perhaps, somewhat dingy in complexion, and somewhat woolly about the upper regions, but no doubt well clothed, smart, able-bodied seamen—or, rather, river-men—with, possibly, blue jackets and brass buttons, and neat straw-hats, with bands round them, bearing the yacht's name, the *Flea*, in large and legible characters. They must, however, dispel these imaginings, by being informed the strict truth, that from the captain to the cabin-boy, there was not a single coat, jacket, or pair of trousers; and that the sole integuments of our gallant ship's company, except on very great occasions, such as visiting their relations at Assouan, consisted of a loose blue calico shirt, and a somewhat dirty rag, by way of turban, round the head.

Every object being now accomplished, on the afternoon of the 2nd of January, the lively *Berghoot* was shoved away from the Boulak shore, and we started on our voyage. The breeze blew fair from the north; but that night, like young birds, we only tried our strength preparatory to migration. We advanced a few miles, and, having found some indispensables still wanting, halted at Old Cairo. The following day the wind was again vigorous and propitious; we soon bade farewell to our friends the Pyramids of Ghizeh; and the rival Pyramids of Sakára, Abouseer, and Dashoor, with the Arab village, Mitrahenny, the ancient royal Memphis, were successively passed, and faded from the view. For the next week we slowly advanced on our flight southward; the wind fell, and our poor crew were obliged to track at times the inert *Berghoot*, under a sun which, although a wintry one, sent the thermometer up from 95 to 106. They seemed cheerful enough under the infliction, and it was amusing to listen to their boat-song, as they poled along in places where bends in the river or the low water prevented them from tracking. One of them gave the word, naming first the Prophet, then some member of the Prophet's family, and the rest struck up the chorus, "May his name be blessed"—"Sall ala Mahommed"—"Bless the Prophet." "Allah humma sally alyk"—"O, Allah, bless thee"—laying a fine stress on the first syllable of "humma." Thus they went on till their genealogical knowledge was exhausted, then back again to Mahommed. Fancy a boat manned by Mormons, and the boatswain giving time as he named the relatives and successors of that illustrious and holy man, Joe Smith:—"O, Joe Smith! O, let us bless him!" "O, Brigham Young! O, let us bless him!" "O, Bill Tomkins! O, let us bless him!" and so on through all the relatives and successors of the prophet of Nauvoo.

For the next week there was but little variety. I was attacked with violent diarrhœa, almost approaching to dysentery; and having with true improvidence laid in sauces enough to poison a synagogue, but no medicine for any complaints likely to arise in Egypt, although an ample stock for those of South America or Sierra Leone, I found much difficulty in stopping it; the least infringement on abstemiousness, or indulgence in any food except rice, tea, and chicken broth, producing immediately a return of the ailment. To travel in Egypt one should be provided with medicines for this disease, for ophthalmia, and colds. It is needless to go beyond this very short catalogue of disease in making up one's medicine-chest; provided always that the trip is to be up the Nile; for in parts of the lower country, at Damietta to wit, fever is very prevalent.

The 6th of January was, however, to a sportsman a memorable day, and to be noted with a white stone. Old Mohammed gravely announced as we were reading in our saloon, that, according to his belief, a *timsah*, or crocodile, was on the opposite bank. Out went our glasses, and there in truth lay the monster—not a very large one, but a very green one (at least in color), in his armour of verdigris hue, basking at the foot of some high rocks. Not a moment was lost; the *sandal*, or small boat, was disengaged, and we dropped slowly down upon him. At about sixty yards we poured in the contents of two rifles; the result was, that the reptile wagged his tail, and waddled leisurely into the water. This was our first and last interview with that individual. Although common some hundred miles higher up, crocodiles are rarely seen as low as Benisoaef; and therefore one is bound to commemorate this first and very unusual meeting. Sir G. Wilkinson asserts that they are not seen more northwards than

Benihassan, from which we were still at a distance of ninety miles.

But if we missed securing the *timsah*, we had our revenge on the pigeons. Our old dragoman, when we were laying in shot, remonstrated with us on our extravagance; for with thoughts solely intent on kitchen pot, he assured us that one discharge of a double gun would kill quite sufficient for a day's provender. We however, with souls above provisions, and altogether disbelieving a travelled dragoman's tales, purchased the shot; and rejected the statistics he gave us of pigeon shooting, believing them to be a clear case of " long bow." On the 9th, therefore, seeing sundry pigeons flying to and fro, we determined to test the accuracy of the information.

On landing, we tried a 'prentice hand on sundry hawks, which are inconveniently numerous and impudent, on an owl or two, some doves for breakfast, and a hoopoe for our collection of natural history. The hoopoe is a wonderfully busy, pretty little fellow. From his speckled body, and saucy erect crest, he is easily discovered, and seems to be of a most active, fussy temperament—hunting ever about after insects, and sticking his long curved bill into every hole and corner. He is, among the birds, the best representative of what the armadillo is among the beasts. This restless, bustling disposition of his, has immortalized him in Aristophanes' famous comedy of the *Birds*, where Epops or Hoopoe plays a distinguished part, as the alert merry slave in Cuckoo-Cloud-city of Bird kingdom. After some amusement and practice in this way, in the long palm grove, all at once our sable attendant made a significant gesture, and, with his hand on my arm, whispered cautiously, "Shoof," "look!" We "shoofed" accordingly, and saw nothing but a good deal of dust, a few hundred yards off, just outside the grove; but confiding in our guide, philosopher, and friend, we directed our steps to the dust, and found that it was kicked up by an inconceivable quantity of pigeons, into whom incontinently, at about thirty yards, we blew four barrels. The carnage was astonishing: the dead lay thick, and the wounded were hopping and fluttering off in every direction. The great mass of pigeons were so astonished at the attack, that instead of avoiding the fate of their comrades, they flew round and round us to ascertain what could be the meaning of such a hubbub; and not until by sad experience of some more discharges, did they ascertain how dangerous at times may be over-curiosity.

That evening was a festive one to the crew of the *Berghoot*, who, gorged with pigeons, sang the praises of the beneficent Howadgi; and the Howadgi themselves rejoiced not a little at the happiness they inspired, and which they themselves participated in, when Hubert placed before them for their evening meal a succulent *salmi* of turtledoves. Let us unselfishly admonish the Nile traveller when he sees a grove of mimosa, to get ready his fowling-piece, and explore the recesses of the grove; for there it is that turtledoves continually resort. Abstractedly his heart may recoil from the massacre of these cooing innocents; but he that has fed on them as we have done, in *salmi,* in pie, in currie, or in simple spatchcock, will shut the door on pity, and bang away as long as a single individual flutters among the trees, until, indeed, he becomes as heartily tired of them as we were. By way of comment on pigeons, let me add, that a vast collection of their livers in a pillau of rice makes a very commendable contrast to the interminable toughness of tough mutton and tough fowl.

Having used the word Howadgi, it may be as well to explain, that it is the generic appellation of Europeans in this country, and that its real meaning is merchant. Some persons assert that it is the pride of the Mahommedan, who refuses to give to a Christian the title of Effendi, which is the word used when you address a Mussulman well dressed, or apparently well to do. In reality, however, there is no foundation as to this latent contemptuous intention. In the East no one ever dreams of travelling except for trade or on official business; and the natural impression of the natives is to address foreigners as traders or merchants, knowing them not to be officials. Nor, again, does the term trader or merchant convey a derogatory impression, as the word shopkeeper would to some supercilious ears at home. The Easterns all engage in trade, and it is most honorable to be so engaged. Gentlemen at large are varieties of the human species quite unknown here. But as a proof that no disrespect is meant, when passing Gebel et Tayr, or the Mountain of the Bird, our boat was beset by Coptic Christian monks from the convent which is situated on the summit of that mountain. They swam like Newfoundland dogs round the boat, begging eagerly for charity, or anything they could see; and their continual cry was, "Ana Christian, Howadgi" (I am a Christian, O foreigner). Of course they would never think of employing a term conveying contumely towards persons of their own religion, and of whom they were requesting alms; so that the contemptuous meaning of the word attributed to it by several writers, appears to me to be quite unsubstantiated. By the way, a sad set of rascals these same Coptic monks seemed to be. After pestering for money, and receiving a few piastres, they then begged a few empty bottles to store their oil in; and having obtained them, they next requested a few full bottles of rum, to drink our healths on the spot; and implored us by the Holy Trinity not to refuse the supplication. This last demand quite outraged the teetotal majority of the crew, who cursed them in no measured terms, and sent all sorts of naughty messages to their lady relatives. The old "Doubly Beautiful" waxed positively furious; and to him we are indebted for our deliverance from these vociferous importunates, for in the plenitude of his anger he swore strong guttural oaths, and these failing, he rushed to the crew's kitchen and hurled the fire-bricks at the Coptic heads which were bobbing about the boat. The manœuvre was successful, and drove them howling, but still begging, to the shore.

Our first week, but for the episode of the crocodile, was singularly devoid of interest. The wind fell, and we made but little way. Our poor Berberi tracked and lugged and poled, and seemed ever in good spirits, especially since the advent of the pigeons. These Nubians or Berberi are, by the way, the Paddies of this part of the world, and Cairene story-tellers amuse their audiences by tales of their simplicity. A favorite mode of irritating them, and causing much amusement to jokers in Lower Egypt, is to say to them—"We have eaten the clean, we have eaten the unclean," to intimate that they are by no means acute in their powers of discrimination. Lieutenant Burton tells the story of the origin of this expression. A Berberi, says Mansfield Parkyns, had been carefully fattening a fine sheep for a feast, when his cottage was burnt by an accident. In the ashes he found roasted meat, which looked tempting to a hungry man. He called his neighbors about him, and all sat down to make merry over the mishap. Presently they came to the head, which proved to be that of a dog; some enemy having doubtless stolen the sheep, and placed this most impure animal in its stead. Sadly perplexed at this, the Berberi went to their priest, and dolefully narrated the circumstance, expecting absolution, as the offence was involuntary. "You have eaten filth," said the man of Allah. "Well," replied the Berberi, falling on him with their fists, "filth or not, we have eaten it." Our crew pretended to be much amused whenever we alluded to this little bit of scandal; but they are not all of them, nor always equally well pleased with jokes at their expense. Pigeons *in esse,* and *buckshish in posse,* made them think us extremely pleasant, and our jocosities worthy of applause.

It has always been a subject of annoyance to me, not to have had some intelligent person, thoroughly understanding Arabic, in my perambulations through Cairo. You see groups sitting down around the story-teller, with earnest eyes fixed on every gesture; sometimes moved almost to tears, at other times convulsed with laughter. For the tragic parts of the tale I did not care much; but as nothing can be more awkward than to be seriously contemplating a merry throng without the slightest comprehension of the fun, one looks and feels rather silly. These stories, they say, although generally by no means proper, are at times extremely entertaining and very witty, sometimes just as in the strain of our own *Arabian Nights* (which are only translations of these tales of the market-place), full of wonderful adventures, and telling of ginns and talismans and fairies and deeds of fell enchanters; but anon becoming satirical, and leaning by no means lightly on constituted authorities, exposing in the broadest comedy the avarice of the cadi and the hypocrisy of the dervish.

A gentleman long resident in Cairo told me a few of these stories, which amused me at the time, and as a sample I may give the following:—

A robber one night, in the exercise of his calling, broke into the house of an honest man, a weaver. The room was dark, and the robber eager for spoil, but in his hurry he knocked his head against some of the weaver's implements, and put his eye out. The following morning he presented himself before the cadi, haling with him the weaver; and appealing to the law of the Prophet, insisted on the compensation prescribed in that immutable code. An eye for an eye is the letter of the law. The poor weaver in vain alleged the involuntary nature of the accident, in vain insisted on the sanctity of his house, which the robber had violated, and thereby brought punishment on himself. The cadi was inflexible. The Koran had declared an eye for an eye, and the weaver must prepare himself for mutilation. As the operation was about to be performed, he begged a private interview with the cadi, and having employed the well-known means of persuasion, he added, " I am aware that the law is inviolable which demands an eye for an eye, but it does not specify whose eye it is to be. Now, there lives next door to me a man who gains his living by fowling. He has one eye too many, for in shooting he is always obliged to close one eye ere he fires. Take his eye therefore, which is rather in his way than otherwise, and spare mine, which is necessary to me." The cadi acceded, and, sending for the sportsman, vindicated the majesty of the law, while the weaver regained his home uninjured.

Another story was to this effect:—" There was a man living in Cairo, Ravendi by name, who openly boasted of his religious scepticism, and had no scruples in even indulging in sarcasms, not overt of course, but perfectly comprehensible, about the peccadilloes of the Prophet—whom may Allah preserve! Some of the Hadgis, returning from their pilgrimage to the Western Country, related among their Maugrebyn friends (the Maugrebyns are Western Africans from Tunis, Morocco, Algiers, &c.) these unparalleled enormities. One of the listeners determined to do Allah good service, an to rid the world of a character so detestable. He embarked accordingly, and after many troubles and adversities by land and water, reached Boulak, the port of Cairo, in safety. Here he was accosted civilly by a man, who, seeing him to be a stranger, offered to be his guide, and informed him, moreover, in strict confidence that he had come from Upper Eygpt, to put to death one Ravendi, a noted scoffer. The Maugrebyn opened his heart, and told the stranger that he too was from a far country, for precisely the same purpose. The civil friend was, however, no other than Ravendi himself, who had been duly informed of the Maugrebyn's pious intentions. The simple Western was flattered with the courtesy of his more polished acquaintance, and gladly acceded to the proposal that they should hunt in couples. As the Egyptian professed to know the scoffer by sight, it was agreed they should devote the following day to hunting him. When the first grey dawn appeared, away they started through streets and lanes, bazaar and mosque, backwards and forwards, but no Ravendi was to be found. At last night came on, and hungry and exhausted they took refuge in a mosque. Here they asked for a little food in the name of Allah and his Prophet, but curses and kicks were the reply to their impertinent request, from the pious officials of the institution. The next day again at dawn they started on their expedition—again the same weary wanderings to and fro, through the whole livelong day; but instead of retiring to a mosque in the evening, they went into the Jews' quarter, and knocking at a house where they perceived lights, were most hospitably entertained with the best of suppers and downiest of beds by their Israelitish host. The poor Maugrebyn thought the contrast strange between the churlishness of the faithful and the liberality of the impure. He said nothing, but ruminated the more. On the following morning they renewed their weary search, but as may be supposed, without much success, and being utterly knocked up, the Maugrebyn proposed to enter a bath, which they were chancing to pass. Hardly had they begun the preliminaries of the refreshment, when a loud noise was heard, and the master of the bath informed them and others that they must instantly clear out, as the rooms were required by one of the black eunuchs of the Sultan. The rest bundled off, but the Maugrebyn and Ravendi had only just time to get behind the door as the eunuch appeared. This important personage muttered the usual formula on his entrance, of 'God is great, and Mahommed is his Prophet;' but being a barbarian, and neither well understanding the language, nor the subject on which he was talking, his words sounded like 'God has flown away, and carried off Mahommed on his back.' When they got safe into the street, Ravendi burst out laughing, and asked his friend what he now thought of the estimation in which Muslims held their religion and fellow-believers in Islam—whether they had not been abused and treated like dogs in a mosque, but were well and hospitably received by a Jew—whether, though good Mahommedans, they had not been kicked out of a bath to make way for a barbarian, who talked nonsense of God and his Prophet—and, to sum up all, whether it was worth while to hunt Ravendi any longer, who only laughed at hypocrites and fanatics, which was the cause of his bad name and unpopularity? The Maugrebyn replied, 'I now know that you are no other than Ravendi himself; but fear not, your life is safe, as far as I am concerned; my only object is now to get back to the West again, for after the specimens I have seen, I fear if I remain in Cairo, that I shall be more free in my expressions and opinions than even you are said to be yourself.'"

The word Maugrebyn, or Western, is applied to the Mahommedan countries to the west of Africa; and from it is derived our word Moor—Maurus-Moro, Moor. The word Saracen, about which there has been such controversy, is, after all, nothing more than Sharkeyin, or Eastern.[1] The Greeks had no letter, nor combination to express *Sh*, therefore they used the simple hard *S*, and pronounced the word Sarkeyin—whence Saracen. In the same manner the word Hashshasheyin, by the rejection of the *Sh*, became formed into the word Assassin. It only expressed originally "a drinker of hemp";

[1] Lieutenant Burton's *Mecca*.

but as this was the decoction with which the satellites of the Old Man of the Mountain inflamed themselves before executing his bloody behests, the word subsequently obtained the meaning of "deliberate murderer."

The dead calm, and the consequent monotony of our slow onward progress, has I presume led me into this gossiping. The wind has totally failed, and here we are on the eighth day of our journey only 150 miles from our starting-post, having taken seven days to accomplish that which with a smart breeze should have been completed in three or four. This is the more vexatious as it militates against all our plans, which were to proceed as fast as possible to the utmost limits of our journey in Nubia, but should the wind fall, to visit everything interesting while the calm prevailed. We are now at Minieh, and as bad fortune will have it, from Memphis hitherto there has been nothing to repay the trouble of a hot walk on the mainland. We should not have reason to complain could we but advance fifteen miles higher up; for at Benihassan the glories of old Egyptian art commence, and continue far into Ethiopia.

In spite, however, of our grumbling, there is not much reason to complain. There is certainly monotony in the scenery, and but little to excite a man of busy temperament. Everywhere the same mud square-walled villages and round mud-domed tombs, looking like deserted beaver-lodges; everywhere the same clumps of palms; everywhere the same drowsy groaning of the shadoof irrigating the rich black alluvial fields. But there is a calm enjoyment of existence on the bosom of this great tranquil river, known nowhere else. It is what the Arabs define by a word that could only be understood and realized by an Eastern, and which we are forced to express by a periphrasis. They call this dream-life, *keff*, the pleasant languor of tranquillity, " the airy castle-building of imagination, in contradistinction to the vigorous, intensive, passionate energy of Europe."

But the sunsets have a character and an individuality peculiar to themselves alone; nor are they always similar. They are ever like the Egyptian winter's day, soft and gentle; but some have indelibly painted themselves upon my recollection. On one of these occasions the Lybian hills, Egypt's western guardians, had receded far out of sight, and the great unbounded plain was spread before us. From the mound by the Nile's bank, beneath which our bark was moored, we looked forth upon the fading day. In the whole vault of heaven there was not a cloud-speck; but upon the western horizon there seemed to fall a great arch of fire, the gateway as it were of some immortal palace. There it stood, and throughout the firmament there was neither shade nor coloring to divert the eye from the majestic portal, into which gorgeously streaming, the imagination might conceive the cohorts of the celestial hosts in radiant armour and with diamond-pointed spears. Again on our fourth evening we were approaching Samalood. Behind us many *dahabiehs*, like flocks of river-birds, spread their long white wings to catch the last puff of the expiring breeze; but in vain—for the river was like glass, and two Arab fires on the eastern bank rose straight in a slender pyramid of flame upwards, without a flicker; and behind them a fringe of palms, distinct against a pure grey-blue, unclouded sky. This was eastward; but westward came forth cloud streaks of carmine, and the whole vault of heaven was suddenly laced with streamers of ruby and chrysolite and opal, and then far away in front there appeared to us to emerge from the water a glorious city with minarets and steeples and palaces, from whose burnished pinnacles the fading rays were projected sparkling and dancing onward to our boat; and then while we were looking the brilliancy passed away, and a great fulvous light—a kind of ruddy smoke as from some mighty conflagration surrounded our fictitious city; and then the moon came out in her silver boat, and showed us that our fairy minarets and steeples were palms, and our palaces acacias.

At Minieh, on the 10th of January, we halted for culinary purposes. But in vain did the crafty Mohammed perambulate the town in his white gloves, which always denoted a solemn mission; no meat could be obtained, and as we had been now for some days on what our American friends would call chicken fixings, this was a considerable blow. He attributed the scarcity of provisions to the presence of a body of Arnaoots, or Albanian soldiers, who were literally, in school-boy phrase, making hay of the town. A more ill-conditioned gang of cold-blooded desperadoes I have not yet had the misfortune to witness. I imagine they must bear a close resemblance to those efficacious troops the Bashi Bazouks, under their efficacious General Beatson. They were so completely masters of the place, that no one dared call his soul his own; and though it was early when Mohammed went forth marketing, he returned quickly quite appalled, saying that they were in a large body drinking in a coffee-house, insulting every one that passed, and firing their pistols through the roof. We had occasion to go ourselves into the town, and saw several of them, surly-looking vagabonds, armed to the teeth; but they kept their observations to themselves, as from experience they have discovered that Europeans are handier with revolvers than they are with their whole armoury of long silver-hilted pistols stuck into their sashes. *A-propos* to the pistols, it is a point of honor with these worthies, if they once pull them out of their sashes not to return them without firing. They may place their hand in anger on the hilt, and no mischief will ensue; but if they are drawn, it is time to look out—if a spectator, for shelter; if an actor in the fray, for first shot.

Wherever these troops are quartered they are a perfect curse; they take what they please, and pay what they please for it; and of course the wretched peasant prefers to keep his produce unsold, rather than to be despoiled by these ruffians. They are now providentially for Egypt but few in number, and not particularly appreciated even by the Viceroy; but the district rulers like to keep a few in their service, knowing them to be faithful and as brave as lions, and only too ready to strike terror among such malcontents as misgovernment or evil propensities may have driven into revolt. We however cursed them by all our gods, as every hope of a mutton-chop was extinguished by their presence, and tough chickens and pigeons continued to be, as they were before, our *pièces de résistance*.

From Minieh to the village of New Benihassan, we occupied two days more, with little of interest intervening. We paid a visit to some old tombs cut in the rock at Kom Amar; but they were badly preserved and not extensive. We were, however, well repaid for our trouble by climbing up to the summit of the highest hill, where a telegraph was situated. From this, as far as the eye could extend eastward, we had a view of the Arabian Desert. It was truly desert—such as we had not before conceived, very different from that in the neighbourhood of Cairo. For leagues the view wandered over grey arid heights and grey arid valleys, and the deep shade thrown by the hills into these gloomy defiles awed and saddened. They seemed indeed to be, as the Arabs believe, the abode of accursed and rebellious spirits; and to us they fully conveyed that fearful Hebrew expression, "valleys of the shadow of death." But the rich land of Egypt, there not one hundred yards in breadth, ran like a bright green fringe, hemming this garment of desolation.

The calm still continuing, it was not till the 12th that we slept at the little village of New Benihassan. The old town, a few miles off, was utterly destroyed by Ibrahim Pacha in consequence of the thievish propensities of its inhabitants. This punishment was inflicted some thirty-eight years ago, and if report speak true, even this example has not brought the rising generation to a sense of its situation. We hired their asses nevertheless, and handselled our new Cairene saddles.

The rock tombs which we visited were about two miles from our halting-place, cut out of the solid rock on the side of the hill, and were originally the burial-places of the inhabitants of a town called Nus, as we learn from the hieroglyphical inscriptions. This town lay on the opposite side of the Nile; and it is supposed that its destruction was effected at a very early period, during the time of the Hyksos, or Shepherd King invasion, as there is no mention of it by Greek or Roman geographers. It must, although not a royal residence, have been a place of considerable importance, from the size of its rock necropolis, and the costliness of its tombs, the extent and decoration of which it is difficult, with our European ideas of a tomb, rightly to conceive. It has always seemed most strange to me, with our fixed and unalterable belief in a future state, for which this life is but a period of probation, that we should characterize our last resting-places on earth with all the panoply of woe that a gloomy imagination can conceive. Were the dissolution of our mortal frames to be, according to our conviction, the end of what we term life, it would then be comprehensible that mourning friends might wish to invest the last resting-places of those they loved with the symbols of affliction. But as all our hopes and fears, all our deepest aspirations, have reference not to this short sojourn upon earth, but to that immortal state into which we shall soon pass every one away, and in which even the most unthinking of us all fondly hope for that peace denied to us below, how strangely out of place are the sombre and mysterious rites with which we pay the last offices to those whose spirit has departed from us! What connection have the gloomy pall, the hired mourners, the black paraphernalia of sepulture, the graved skeleton on the stone, and the fearful decorations of the cemetery, with that magnificent triumphal strain which accompanies the body, that poor husk, the prison-house of all that is immortal in us, to the grave? Never was song of victory more grand, never trumpet-blast more inspiring, than those majestic words, which all of us have heard, and which none can ever listen to unmoved:—" For if the dead rise not, then is not Christ raised. If in this life only we have hope in Christ, we are of all men most miserable. But some man will say, How are the dead raised up! and with what body do they come? Thou fool, that which thou sowest is not quickened, except it die! It is sown in corruption; it is raised in incorruption: It is sown in dishonour; it is raised in glory: it is sown in weakness; it is raised in power. As we have borne the image of the earthy, we shall also bear the image of the heavenly. For this corruptible must put on incorruption, and this mortal must put on immortality. So when this corruptible shall have put on incorruption, and this mortal shall have put on immortality, then shall be brought to pass the saying that is written, Death is swallowed up in victory. O death, where is thy sting? O grave, where is thy victory?" Were I asked which in my opinion is the sublimest passage, ancient or modern, ever penned by mortal hand, I should turn to these verses of the fifteenth chapter of St. Paul's First Epistle to the Corinthians.

But the Egyptians acted differently from us. They too believed in a future state; and believed that in the body each man was to be tried by the Judge of the dead, previous to his entry into Amenti, or the land of spirits. On a mummy case which I saw at Cairo, there is a strange and impressive delineation of this judicial scene. On a throne is seated Osiris, clothed with the emblems of judgment, and before him stands the mummy containing the body of the deceased. Facing this body is a small human figure with a hawk's head, signifying "truth"; and this represents the soul, confronting it, and bearing witness to the deeds done in the past life. A fearful thought to those old Egyptians, as well as to ourselves, that they bore within them, and we within us, an unerring chronicle of every act and thought, one that cannot lie, that is inaccessible to anger or compassion, and that stands in the hour of judgment in presence of the body, to lay bare before an inexorable Judge all the evil as well as the good—all that the mind has conceived, or the hand executed. This fixed belief in a life after death, and of a relation subsisting between soul and body, accounts for the extraordinary care and attention paid by this remarkable people to their dead. The embalming and swathing of the bodies, and enclosing them in double and triple sarcophagi of the strongest wood or of the hardest stone, were the first offices paid to the deceased. They were then, if of the lower orders, committed to deep pits; or if of the higher, these laboriously excavated rock chambers became their splendid mausolea. "Even in their most prosperous times of peace, and of extended dominion, this nation seems to have anticipated the possibility of future hostile invasions, and of the spoliations of fierce barbarian conquerors; for that reason they ingeniously closed the large granite sarcophagi by means of metal rods, which only fell into the holes prepared for them in the sides, at the last thrust of the cover, which was driven drawer-like in, so that the sarcophagus could only be opened by the determined destruction of these great masses of stone. They also endeavoured to guard even the passage which led to the sepulchral chamber by heavy stone trapdoors, and by ingeniously building up the walls, so as to divert attention, and to protect them in every other possible way from inroad and desecration." Even in the Great Pyramids, the same precaution seems to have been systematically adopted by the powerful kings who reared these mighty edifices, to guard intact their remains until the final hour of trial. In the midst of their grandeur they foresaw the vicissitudes of dynasties. In the great Pyramid of Shoofoo at Ghizeh, in order the more effectually to deceive those who should violate his tomb, that monarch had placed the entrance passage twenty-three feet from the centre. In the year 820 A.D., the Caliph Mamoon, under the impression that a deposit of treasure might be found within, endeavoured to force a way into the interior. He commenced, as was natural, in the centre, but in vain tried to pierce the solid masonry on the face. With extreme labor his workmen at length advanced about one hundred feet, and were despairing of success, when a hollow sound directed them to the real passage some fifteen feet to the left, and by this means they gained access to the sepulchral chamber of the great gallery. They found however that others, in all probability the Persians who were aware of the real entrance, had been before them, and had plundered the royal chamber of its contents.

A desire to construct imperishable depositories for the dead seems to have been a fixed sentiment not merely in pagan nations, but among the Jews, and subsequently among the early Christians. Probably the influence of the original tradition of the resurrection of the body pervaded all the Adamite races; and to date its origin merely from Egyptian belief and ceremonies would be affixing too restricted a limit. It is true that the earliest records of the importance of burial are in the cases of Abraham and Jacob, both of whom had been dwellers in Egypt, and may have carried away with them impressions derived from that country; but the minute account of the purchase of the cave of Machpelah, which was "made sure to Abraham for the possession of a burying-place by the sons of Heth," the dying charge of Jacob, in which he so emphatically signifies his last wishes—"I am to be gathered unto my people; bury me with my fathers in the cave that is in the field of Ephron the Hittite, in the cave that is in the field of Machpelah, which is before Mamre, in the land of Canaan, which Abraham bought with the field of Ephron the Hittite for a possession of a burying-place. There they buried Abraham and Sarah his wife; there they buried Isaac and Rebekah his wife; and there I buried Leah. The purchase of the field and of the cave that is therein was from the children of Heth": all point to a stronger and deeper feeling than that likely to be derived from the customs of an alien and idolatrous people. The early patriarchs wished to lie apart, in a cave or rock grotto, where their remains would rest undisturbed until the hour when they should be awakened and rise again in their own bodies, and in the words of the Arab Job uttered at least sixteen centuries before the Christian revelation, "in their flesh see God"; and in the days of Isaiah, "The kings of the nations, even all of them, lay in glory each in his own house." To bury after the manner of the Jews was thus to bury after the manner of the Egyptians; and, if the Jews did not originally borrow their mode of sepulture from that ancient people, we may presume they were influenced by the same primitive idea of the resurrection of the body, which, though not declared in the Mosaic writings, is proclaimed by so early a writer as the author of the Book of Job. The predominance of the doctrine of temporal retribution for offences, which so pervades the mind of Moses in his dealings with the stiffnecked people he had to mould into that peculiar religious organization he perceived to be necessary for their character, may have induced him to appeal to their immediate fears and hopes far more than to loftier and less direct aspirations. The impression of a jealous God avenging backslidings from His ordinances, and requiting, either in themselves or their offspring, the observance of them, he knew to be far more potent with the race he had to deal with, than the more abstract and remote ideas of punishments and rewards in a future life. Still the practical effects of the old idea remained; and even among the early Christians the maintenance of the body after death in an integral state was carefully observed. It was endeared to them by the treatment of the body of their Lord, whose disciples wound it in linen cloths and in spices, as the manner of the Jews is to bury; nor did all the horrors of the imperial persecutions prevent them from endeavouring to secure Christian burial for the Martyr's body. This belief in the resurrection of the body induced the early Christians to adopt the most exclusive precautions to remain separate and apart; as they were a separate community when living, so they desired to sleep a separate community—the wheat apart from the tares—till the sound of the archangel's trumpet should rouse them from their rest. In that vast city of the dead, the catacombs of Rome, Padre Marchi mentions that lately, in his explorings, he reached a gallery of Christian tombs abruptly terminated by a wall. On further examination it was found that the *fossores* or gravediggers had come upon a pagan *columbarium*, or family tomb. The Christians immediately closed the gallery and walled it up: a remarkable proof of their repugnance to suffer the presence of the unconverted heathen in their cemeteries. When, therefore, a High-Church Anglican bishop refuses to consecrate a burial-place without a wall of demarcation being placed between the holy ground in which the orthodox are to lie, and the unholy ground in which their dissenting brethren are stretched in death so near,—when Spanish fanaticism denies a place of interment for the heretical bodies of Jews or Protestants,—we can trace back these ideas of separation in death as in life, to the early Christians, from them to the Jews, and if not to them from the Egyptians, to at least a common tradition, which we who believe in the enlightenment by their Creator of the first settlers on this earth, must suppose to have been delivered to the ancestors of these early races—

> Imperial Cæsar, dead and turned to clay,
> May stop a bung.

And so, too, from the grand primitive tradition of the resurrection of the body may, in course of time, have sprung up an offshoot of sentiment which has grown into doctrine; and the Spanish ecclesiastic, by whose mandate the heretical carcase is thrown on the seashore, and his English High-Church brother, who walls out the dead dissenter from the benefits of consecrated ground, both may ground their intolerance on the practices of the early Christians.

In spite of the extraordinary care and attention evinced for their dead, the Egyptians did not attempt to invest their sepulture with those gloomy terrors and repulsive associations which the mere expression "graveyard" awakens in European minds. The conducting of the corpse to its last resting-place does not appear to have been accompanied (with the exception of the hired mourners) by any of our paraphernalia of woe; for the Egyptians, if charity or affection induced them to believe in the virtues of the deceased, were induced also to believe, that this severance was but the preliminary to the reuniting of the departed spirit with the divine essence and eternal bliss, from which during its association with the body it was temporarily dissociated. The tombs too were gay and bright, both in their coloring and in the representations with which the walls were covered; and a slight description of these remarkable dwellings of the dead at Benihassan will give a general idea of the nature of the Egyptian rock tombs, with which our future excursions will be much connected. The whole side of the hill at this spot seems to have been excavated into pits or grottoes, and the grottoes differ very much from each other in size and decoration. Some of them are mere excavations, without ornament or space; others are large roomy chambers, with grand columns cut out of the solid rock: of these columns some are in the simple fluted style, resembling the Doric; others are highly ornamented, and as they approach the roof, represent the stalks of four water-plants bound together and surmounted by a capital in form of a lotus-bud.

These tombs are of a very early period of Egyptian art. They were, according to the opinion of the learned in such subjects, excavated during the second flourishing period of the old monarchy, at the time of the powerful twelfth dynasty. This brings their construction, as Lepsius calculates, to about 2200 years B.C. Bunsen goes still further back; but it is enough to attribute to these tomb decorations, with their gay and brilliant coloring, an existence of four thousand years. Some of them are contemporaneous with our old friend the Obelisk of Heliopolis; for they bear the royal ring of Sesortesen.

It is impossible of course, from the mere cursory

view that we were enabled to take, to give any detailed account of the decorations of these tombs; but, in spite of the desecrating hand of fanatic Mussulman, cross-inscribing Copt, and name-scribbling American and European, enough remains to excite the wonder and delight even of the most indifferent visitor.

If you had crossed the Nile from the town of Nus some four thousand years ago, you would have left your painted *baris* or bark on the river's strand, and advanced from it by a spacious road, and up a spacious rock stair, gently ascending to the tomb of your departed friend, Nehera-si-Numhotep. You would have seen other staircases along the mountain-side leading from the plain to give to visitors easy access to other tombs. Of these roads the outline still remains perfect, flanked as they are on each side by immense calcareous boulders dug out of the adjacent hills. After bending the knee, and offering the votive lotus-flower to the goddess Pasht, or to Osiris, judge of the dead, which may have once been represented by the shattered mutilated block which meets your eye in the niche of the interior, and was clearly the deity of the spot, you would then have turned round, and have pointed out by your attendant, the friend perhaps of the deceased, the history that the walls narrated, then hardly more vividly than they do now, of his circumstances, his wealth, and his employment. You would be shown, as you are now, his secretary,

Nefruhotep, introducing to his benevolent master, strangers anxious to become sojourners under his paternal sway—a light-colored race, with their families and asses and baggage and instruments of music, the forerunners probably of those fierce barbarian hordes from Palestine, the Hyksos, under whose cruel tyranny Egypt groaned for five hundred years. In this and other adjacent grottoes you would have a full account of all the doings of Egypt at that period; but your account, had your papyrus survived, could not have narrated as distinctly these doings as the walls continue still to do to us. We find in one part a complete natural history of the birds and animals of the country; and lest, as we foreigners may come to admire his handiwork, they may be unknown to us, the decorator has inscribed the name of each specimen beneath it, in hieroglyphical characters. Here we see the peasants busily collecting grapes for the vintage; monkeys are helping them to gather in the fruit, and also, on the sly, helping them to consume it. Beyond is the wine-press, and the inspiring juice flowing from it. Then comes the sequel in the shape of festive scenes; dancers performing *pirouettes* worthy of Perrot; tumblers going on their heads and over their heads; single-stick players laying on with a will; wrestlers in every possible and conceivable attitude; gentlemen enjoying their after-dinner cups; and, alas! that I should have to mention it, some of them carried home in a state of "How came you thus?" Then there are hunting scenes for sporting characters; shooting ibexes with arrows; killing geese with throwing sticks; and lassoing wild cattle by the head and legs. In another part the scientific inquirer may obtain a full knowledge of the arts of these good old times. There are women spinning, and others weaving; some are preparing flax, others converting it into ropes; another party is engaged in the fabrication of different articles of pottery; here is a group busily employed in glass-blowing; another is in the various stages of the bread-making department. In short, there are few trades into every branch of which one may not obtain a full insight. But, although the manufacturing interest is well represented, the agricultural is not forgotten. Here come in files herds of cattle and flocks of sheep, driven before their lord, and, like Burns' laird,

> The auld gudeman delights to view
> His sheep and kine thrive bonnie, O.

A little further on, the fat beeves are seen struggling in the water, having been caught by the inundation, and the farm servants in boats are hauling them on to *terra firma*. Then follow busy scenes of hoeing, tilling, reaping, and storing up the grain, with a scribe standing by to take note of the produce, and see that his prudent master shall not be pilfered.

To show how light-hearted and joyous were the

Egyptian mortuary associations, I may mention, that on a tomb at El Kab, the ancient Eilythyas, there is a representation of bullocks threshing corn, with (if Champollion be right in his translation) this simple rustic song in hieroglyphics underneath :—

"Thresh for yourselves,
Thresh for yourselves,
   O Oxen;
Thresh for yourselves,
Thresh for yourselves;
Measures for yourselves,
Measures for your masters."

Throughout the whole of these tombs, amid the infinity of decoration embracing every sort of scene, serious and merry, there is not one object calculated to offend the most scrupulous sense of decency; and the more that investigation has extended its researches, the more highly do we estimate the deeply moral, and even gentle tone adopted by the Egyptians in their innumerable representations. Besides their high intellectual and material attainments, they seem, from the record of their own monuments, apart from the character given them by historians, to have been a mild, just, and moral people. Although a strong sense of irrepressible humor pervades many of their compositions, there is no descent into indecency; nor are even their battle scenes and pageants of victory disfigured by the barbarous cruelty represented on Assyrian and Indian monuments.[1] In the tombs we have just visited, some culprits are receiving the award of justice in the shape of the bastinado on the most prominent part of their prostrate figures; but lady delinquents are treated with more respect, and are punished, although with the rod, yet sitting, and with their garments on.

In short, we have left these most interesting records with the very best opinion of this wonderful race of men; and however hitherto we may have shared in the Turkish contempt of the wretched, sullen, down-looking, intriguing Copts, yet we must bear in mind, that these are the Epigoni, the most genuine unmixed descendants of the old Pharaonic nation, that once conquered Asia and Ethiopia, that led its prisoners from the north and south into the great hall of Karnak, that reared pyramids for its dead monarchs, and excavated and adorned mountains for its dead citizens; whose hieroglyphics still seem to yearn to tell their tale of former dominion and magnificence; whose art inspired the chisel of Phidias, and the pencil of Apelles; in whose wisdom Moses was educated, whose philosophy dictated the mystic sentences of Pythagoras, and still lives in the noble words and eloquence of Plato.

[1] The representation at Medinet Abou, of the King receiving the hands of his enemies from the soldiers, does not give any intimation of cruelty, but of the numbers killed in battle.

After leaving the grottoes we went on about a couple of miles to the south, to visit a rock temple called Speos Artemidos, or Cave of Artemis, the Greek name for the goddess Pasht, to whom it was dedicated by King Sesortesen. Near to it is a rock tomb of a very late period, about 300 B.C., in the time of Ptolemy Lagus. The coloring and representations on it offer a marked distinction from the earlier and higher style of Egyptian art; but unfortunately the universal spirit of spoliation has dealt so heavily with it, that it is difficult even to make out the decorations.

The Persians originally commenced this work of desecration, but their demolitions were only continued for a short period. The Copts, or natives, next took it up; and certainly we must give them credit of great success in the pious occupation of defacing the monuments of their ancestors. Fortunately the erasure of the hieroglyphics and figures was a job that required time and trouble, so to spare both, they often covered the emblems of paganism with Nile mud, and on it delineated their clumsy representations of monkish legends. In time this Coptic loam fell off, and the ancient paintings came out once more with a brilliancy and freshness which they would hardly have retained on uncovered walls exposed to the air and sun. Lepsius writes in one of his letters that in the niche of an ancient cellar he found St. Peter in the old Byzantine style, holding the keys and raising his finger; but beneath the half-decayed Christian casing the cow's horns of the goddess Athor, the Egyptian Venus, peeped forth from behind the glory of the saint, much like, I presume, the cow's horns behind the city gentleman's head in Hogarth's "Evening Walk." To her was originally given the incense and sacrifice by the King, who is standing by her side, and which are now offered by him rather comically to the venerable apostle.

But that which the Copts spared, the Arabs have subsequently destroyed. Independently of the private persecution waged by honest Muslims against every graven image representing an object in the heavens above, or in the earth beneath, it is supposed that Mohammed Ali, during his government alone, has broken up and utterly annihilated more objects of ancient art than the whole united efforts of Vandalism since the Christian era. In too many cases, whenever a column, pillar, or colossal image existed in proximity to any of his ill-paying intended factories, it was instantly, to save the labour of quarrying, broken into pieces and converted either into building stones or lime. Too many interesting remains of antiquity, mentioned by travellers and archæologists of recent date, have utterly disappeared; and rock tombs and temples have been despoiled of their supporting pillars because it was more easy to utilise them, than to quarry materials from as fine and as easily worked quarries as the world can supply. Last of all, and most to be blamed, as being actuated neither by a feeling of religion nor of utility, have descended on the unfortunate monuments whole gangs of vulgar wretches, who have endeavored to perpetuate their own vulgar and insignificant appellations by painting, pencilling, and scraping them over in general the most interesting and prominent figures.

At Speos Artemidos are some pits of cats' mummies; and we find a good number of poor mutilated pussies lying about in their sepulchral cerements. The cause of this is owing to an odd superstition prevalent in the Fellah village of Benihassan. When a female has been for a long time cursed with sterility, that reproach of women in the East, she adopts a very efficacious remedy in order to become the mother of a happy family. She arms herself with two earthenware jars of Nile water, and proceeds to the cat mummy pits in question. Having then extracted some preserved mouser from its resting-place, she places it upon a certain stone hard by, and then divesting herself of her garments, performs a complete ablution of her person over the stone so selected. At the expiration of the proper period she is duly rewarded by the favor of the king of the cats, for her confidence, by the birth of the long-attended baby.

On returning to the ship, we found one of our Berberi suffering from ophthalmia, and a smart feverish attack. The poor fellow's pulse was galloping, and his skin burning. I gave him some sulphate of zinc for his eyes, and a powder for his body; shortly afterwards, in consequence of the administration of the drugs being in public, I found myself with the whole of the ophthalmic sufferers of Benihassan on my hands. I now deeply regret that I had neither medicine chest nor book; for at a little expense and trouble I might on several occasions have been the means of relieving much suffering; and certainly one ingredient of cure would never have been wanting, that greatest auxiliary to every doctor—unlimited confidence both in the drug and the practitioner.

The next day, the 14th, was only remarkable from our vain attempts to put rifle-bullets into pelicans, the first time we had seen those huge, ungainly, but most wary birds. But on the 15th a change came over the spirit of our tranquil dream.

The morning dawned cloudy and overshadowed, looking, in short, remarkably like rain; instead, however, of a shower, out of the clouds came a heavy gale, and the hitherto inert *Flea* went hopping and curvetting through the really high sea that was running. The air was a dense mass of brown sand, through which the sun looked small, silvery, and malicious. Old Mahommed grew alarmed, and Hubert as he could not swim, began to speculate whether he might not bind an inflated india-rubber bath to his person, and thereby reach the land in case of a capsize. The reis descended from the quarter-deck and implored the Howadgi to allow him to furl sail beneath the high banks of a hospitable village; but the Howadgi had experienced a week's calm, and were bored and irritable, and they told the reis that come what might, "forwards" was their motto. They had had no mutton, moreover, for some days, and felt carnivorous. The meek reis agreed to go on, observing sagely, that he had but his shirt, while the Howadgi had goods and chattels. He then went through a whole pantomime describing the eccentric conduct of the winds among the notorious heights of Aboufoda, the "*infames scopulos, Acroceraunios,*" the most dangerous passage of Nile navigation, through which we daringly in this weather talked of forcing our frail, top-heavy little *dahabieh*. The Howadgi for answer, scoffingly pointed to a large bark running free before the wind; but the reis shook his head, and foreboded; and lo! and behold! in another half-hour, when they had surmounted an interposing point of land, they saw a vessel with divers flags streaming from her yard; but the sand-whirls prevented them from making out her nationality, until on coming closer they discovered that the apparent flags were but the remaining shreds of the large white sail they had been so lately admiring, and which was now literally blown into streamers. 'Twas then that prudence took the place of daring, and the reis, who before was accused of "*timides avis,*" was now extolléd as an experienced and sagacious mariner; therefore, with some difficulty and much water shipped, the *Flea* was got over to the opposite bank at Kosseyr,[1] where she lay till the afternoon, bumping, thumping, and doing her best to tear away the palm-trees to which she was firmly bound. In the afternoon the storm lulled a little, and the impatient Howadgi spirit again manifested itself. Again the reis protested and pointed to the fleet of barks, which were cowering and huddled together like a covey of frightened partridges, around; but no remonstrance this time availed, and it was a proud moment when the union-jack and the broad pennon of the *Flea* went forth from among the shrinking Egyptians to do battle with the devil-driven gust of Aboufoda; and now, as I write, we are passing the dread defile. The boy Nesnas has mounted the yard, and is gathering in the sail, and we watch his little black "mug" swaying and shaking on the spar, and hear his shrill voice high up aloft, like a chummy's on a London smmmer morn. On the deck a man is sitting holding the sheet ready to let go at the first summons. The mountain looks black and ugly. Hubert thinks, that without any joking, it is time for the bath to be tied to him. Letters of credit are wrapped up in whatever appears most waterproof, and stowed away in our pockets. It is for the first time intensely cold, and we are intensely hungry;

---

[1] The village, not the town of Kosseyr.

but the cook is watching through the darkness the gloomy heights over us, and is forgetful of his cookery. One squall just to give us a sample which nearly lays us over, and then we sail pleasantly along beneath the great frowning arid mountain, rising perpendicularly from the water like a wall; and we drink the old grim monarch's health in a glass of hot gin-punch, and give him a salvo of pistol-shots to hear his echo, and to astonish crocodiles and hyenas. We speculated much on poor Hubert's probable fate, had the catastrophe of an upset occurred; we who could swim would have made a protracted struggle and been drowned at last, or eaten up by crocodiles; but Hubert must have met with a singular end, as he proposed to have the bath attached behind him. Of course, after the first plunge, that part of his person which had the buoyant inflated indiarubber affixed to it, would have emerged from the water, while the head would have remained under. In that guise, head downwards, he would have floated on towards Cairo; and as birds of prey are many and watchful, ascending travellers would have noted in their journals the strange phenomenon of seeing vultures descending the Nile upon an indiarubber tub.

Our success this evening has made us all merry, masters and men, and we have given an outlet to our mirth by nearly frightening the old cook to death. He is particularly fond of a warm, stuffy sleeping berth, and we had watched him in the morning reeking forth from the hold where we store our provisions, and where it certainly seemed impossible that any living being except a rat could have wished to stow himself away. The night being very cold, the old gentleman had made himself snugger than ever, by actually fastening the boards over him, although nearly touching his head, at the risk, one would suppose of positive suffocation. On this hint we spake. Assembling the reis and crew, we disclosed to them in hushed accents our fell design. As they had all of them been more or less abused by this irritable old porcupine, they accepted our ideas with delight. This was the programme:—At a given signal we were silently to lift the heavy cantine on top of the hold, and one of us was to sit on it. The crew were to set up a most diabolical howling, intimating that the vessel was about to be capsized. The reis was in accents loud to call on them to save the "Doubly Beautiful," and to shout to him to come out of his hole, while my office was to thunder on deck with the monstrous ship's mallet, to denote the shocks under which the unfortunate vessel was too soon to founder. Nothing could be more successful. The crew uttered cries and shrieks that would have waked the dead. The reis called on them to save poor Hassaneen. My friend sitting on the cantine resisted all his violent efforts to emerge; and I nearly in reality stove in the deck with my mighty implement.

Hubert, moreover, added his contribution to the general din, by beating a heavy wooden table over the unfortunate man's head, in accordance with my mallet. Then arose from the hold shrieks and lamentations; the unhappy cook, in his despair, called first on Allah, then on the Prophet, and on his successors, Abubekr, Omar, and Ali; but, finding heavenly interposition to fail, he resorted to mortal aid, and supplicated each of the crew by name to save him from a watery grave. The last act of the comedy remained: the crew, at the word of command, silently retired, wrapped themselves up, and simulated sleep; we gently regained our cabin, and Hubert removed the cantine. Then we saw the terrified cook emerge, gaze wildly around, mutter a prayer, and evidently consider himself the sport of the ginns and afreets which haunt this ill-famed spot. The "chaffing," however, that ensued the following morning, must we fear, have induced the belief that human agency had much to do with the phenomenon, and that European devils were more to be dreaded than the spirits of the mountain.

For the first time we had a wind during the night, and took such advantage of it, that before noon of the following day the 16th, we found ourselves at Osioot, the capital of Upper Egypt, which we had calculated on barely reaching the same evening. Here a rest of twenty-four hours, for baking bread and provisioning, was granted to the crew; but considerably more time was consumed by an accident to our rudder, which the dilatory, dawdling carpentry of the Arabs rendered a formidable job. It is not easy for any man to manage his axe or saw deftly, and to hold together at the same time a most heterogeneous combination of shreds and rags. But we took time by the forelock, and visited some old rock tombs in the Lybian mountains, which here for the first time approach the Nile. The town of Osioot is about two miles from the river, beautifully situated, with its minarets and domes rising aloft from gardens of palms, evergreen fig-trees, and acacias. The donkey-boys here gave us regular battle, and threw into the shade their fraternity of Cairo, by their determination and importunity. In vain did we select a comely looking animal; hardly had we raised foot to stirrup when an opposition ass was driven in between our legs, and we were fairly swimming on a mass of donkeys. We plied our sticks with vigor, but with dexterity an ass was invariably interposed to receive the descending blow. At last I could stand it no longer, but unbuttoned my leather case, and I do believe, my indignation was so great, that in another minute I should have pulled out and levelled a pair of opera-glasses against the most hardened offenders; but the effect was electrical. The hubbub subsided in a moment, they begged for quarter, and allowed us to depart in peace. We had famous asses here, the best in Egypt by far, and soon gained the town, where we made a few purchases, chiefly of pipe-bowls and ornamental earthenware, for which the place is famous. Thence we mounted the hills. The excavations here are much the same as at Benihassan, but are by no means in the same preservation. The proximity to the large town has made spoliation rampant, and Ibrahim Pacha employed the columns of the tombs, which he blew up with gunpowder, for some of his improvements. His successor, however, Abbas Pacha, to his credit, issued the most severe injunctions to stop these ravages; but it is impossible to estimate the amount of mischief that has been done. In one of the tombs we visited there are drawings of soldiers carrying shields of enormous size; the soldiers are at present thirty-nine in number, in rows of three, and are so far remarkable, as being similar to those which Xenophon mentions in his description of the Egyptian troops employed by Crœsus. He says they amounted to 120,000 men, carrying shields which covered them from head to foot. It was from the protection of these bucklers, supported as they were by a thong from the shoulders, and from their compact order of battle, that they remained impervious to the Persian attack, when the rest of the Lydian army was routed. They obtained honorable terms from Cyrus, and an abode in the cities of Larissa and Cyllene, in the neighborhood of Cuma, near the sea, which were still called the Egyptian cities, and inhabited by their descendants in the time of Xenophon.

Osioot was the Lycopolis of old days; and as Benihassan has its mummied cats, so has Lycopolis its mummied wolves and jackals. The whole side of the hill seems one vast mortuary deposit of these animals and of men. My friend picked up the foot of a mummied wolf in as perfect preservation as if only cut off a few days before, and purposes to make it the handle of a paper-knife; and I obtained some mummy cloth and a human finger, but have not decided to what useful or ornamental purpose it can be devoted. Some of the inscriptions in the great tomb, called Stabl Antar by the natives, are still clear and unmutilated; the only ones we deciphered were those of W. Lyon and Castlereagh, but without a date. The cartouches of some extremely ancient kings are mentioned by Sir Gardner Wilkinson as still existing on its walls; but as our knowledge of these symbols was at the time of our visit very low indeed, I am unable to record them, which I regret, as it might be interesting to know, from monumental history, at what period of Egyptian history the heavy armour above mentioned was in employment, and which of the Pharaohs were the monarchs favoring this town.

The day was most enchanting, a cool breeze accompanying us all the way, and meeting us coming back. The thermometer stood no higher than 74:

very different in its behavior from the day of our ride to Benihassan, when it rose to 109. The view from the Lybian hills over the country at our feet was extremely beautiful, in fact the only landscape of real champaign beauty that I can recall in Egypt, except from the citadel of Cairo, and from Gebel Assass at Thebes. Just below us, to the right, were the gay white crenelated tombs of the modern Arabs, set as it were in a fringe of palms; a little further on, and relieving their intense whiteness, was the brown square-built town, with its elegant and numerous minarets; around it on each side was the great Nile plain, one rich sheet of verdure, intersected by the now placid river, with the Arabian chain bounding it horseshoe-wise, and far off in the distance rose up facing us, not in gloom and blackness, but struck with the sun's gentle light, our dreaded enemy of last night, Gebel Aboufoda. It is from this town that the trading caravan proceeds to the kingdoms of Darfur and Wady, the King of those districts refusing, from fear of Egyptian encroachment, to have any communication by way of Kordofan, the nearest point of approach to his dominions. A large number of slaves used to be imported by this route, and 'twas here that the manufactory of eunuchs was conducted, shame to say, not by Mahommedans, but by Christians, by Copts. I believe the calculation to be, that one in four survives the operation. That graveyard we look over this morning extends far away into the palm groves of Osioot; and no wonder, if the poor mutilated corpses of these unhappy Negroes are considered worthy of burial.

In the evening, as there was no sign of the completion of the rudder, we gave ourselves up for the first time to the society of ladies. From the accounts of former travellers, we had heard much of the wonderful dancing achievements of a female who rejoiced in the name of Kushuk Hanem, and with whom we expected to become better acquainted on reaching Esneh; but our surprise was great as we were shopping in the bazaar, to see a very grandly attired and somewhat stout dame, accompanied by two well-dressed servant girls, accost our dragoman, and draw him aside mysteriously from the crowd. On his return he informed us that the lady was no other than the renowned Kushuk Hanem, and that her interview with him was touching a letter of great importance, which she was anxious to have conveyed to us, and she requested him to call on her while she indited it. This missive was of course to have been the card of invitation, and we were highly rejoiced at the prospect of witnessing her feats; but, as Mohammed informed us that at least £5 would be the cost of the evening's entertainment, it struck us forcibly that "non cuivis hominum contingit adire Corinthum;" in other words, that we must decline her acquaintance, and form that of other members of the Ghawazi, or dancing profession, just as original, and less expensive. A crafty donkey-boy, the ordinary Mercury on such occasions, was sent forth to organize the preliminaries; and it was soon arranged, that we should leave the boat immediately after dinner, return to the town, and there find the performers and orchestra prepared, and a room swept and garnished, to the exclusion of fleas and other abominations.

At about eight in the evening we started, and by the aid of a beautiful moonlight soon reached the town gates, which were instantly thrown back to receive the owners and dispensers of piastres. We proceeded through the winding and now completely deserted streets, till at the other end of the town we saw a single light glimmering through a window. This was the abode of these charmers of Egyptian hours of idleness. We were ushered into a room somewhat, as it appeared to us, limited in its proportions for a dance in the usual acceptation of the word, but for the performance that ensued it was amply spacious. Except a small part near the door, and devoted to the orchestra, the rest was spread with mattresses, and some tolerably smart and cleanish chintz was thrown over them as a covering. We took our seats very seriously, said nothing, but smoked vigorously. The orchestra immediately struck up: it consisted of an old lady beating a large instrument, half drum, half tamburine; a young Negro followed suit on a similar instrument, only rather smaller; but an elderly gentleman, with a beard considerably whiter than his turban, seemed to be the chief and fugleman, and led the strain on a kind of extremely squeaking double-bass, which produced at times the most astonishing and ear-piercing discords. The performers now entered the arena; in other words, mounted on the elevation of the mattresses at the opposite end of which we were enthroned. They were in number two: the *coryphée*, a lady somewhat in the decline of years and beauty, dressed in a speckled *robe de chambre*; and a younger *artiste* in full attire of scarlet. I could not help remembering the costume of the wicked woman of Babylon that sitteth upon seven hills, the theme of many a weary dreary Irish sermon. Both of them were decorated profusely with gold ornaments, and their long plaited lovelocks were intertwined with strings of coin apparently of the same precious metal. The tunes, as may be supposed, were simple, and more noisy than harmonious. The dance consisted of some very extraordinary contortions, first of all from the waist downwards, the remainder of the body remaining perfectly still; then the same tremulous motion pervaded the upper part of the body, the lower remaining unmoved. This stationary performance was varied by waving the arms to and fro above the head, jingling brass castanettes to keep time with the musicians, and a few slow turns, for *pirouettes* they could hardly be called. Since that first representation I have seen many others, and never could comprehend the unspeakable delight with which orientals gaze, perhaps for a whole night, at these proceedings. All of them are more or less indecorous—all, in my opinion, more or less dull; and as I have seen some of the most celebrated dancers of the day—among many others Serafia and Kuskuk Hanem, the Duvernay and Fanny Elsler of Egypt—if I am wrong in my estimation of these feats, it is my bad taste rather than my ignorance that sets me astray.

The evening on this occasion was warm, the room close, the dancers thirsty, and the arraki was poured forth like water. Its inspiration produced an amount of affection on the part of our dusky lady friends we could have dispensed with; they were curious about our pockets, smoked our pipes, and introduced new fleas to the old associates we carried ever with us. Finding my friend closely pressed by the assiduities of the younger lady in scarlet, and fearing that a similar fate awaited me on the part of the elder, I invited to sit beside me, and so oppose a barrier to the enemy, a remarkably good-looking Arab girl, who was standing in the doorway, smiling delightedly with white teeth at the dancers and the strangers. Nothing loath, the damsel took share of my shawl, my arraki, and my pipe, and slapped and scolded so bravely that the elderly invader was routed from my precincts. On this occasion my friend found out that many of the old prejudices rife in the days of Herodotus had disappeared; for he informs us that the Egyptian ladies had great horror of foreign gentlemen on account of their addiction to cow-beef, and adds, οὐτὲ γυνὴ ἀνδρ' Ἕλληνα φιλήσειε ἂν τῷ στόματι. I am bound to say of my young friend that she behaved extremely well, both as regarded my pocket and the fleas, for I am not aware of having suffered much on either score. She was a remarkable specimen of Nile beauty; and for those who do not dislike brunettes and mahogany coloring in the human species, was as pretty a girl as one could wish to see. Her figure was faultless, tattooed occasionally oddly enough, which adornment she exhibited with a little pardonable female vanity, and which is certainly quite as sensible as the patches of our great-grandmothers in the last century.

While on the subject of brunettes, I may mention that I have often heard persons who have lived a long time in India remark, that after a certain period the dark bronze color of the human skin becomes far more agreeable to the eye than the somewhat sickly pallor of European complexion; and they have particularly instanced the fine olive-brown of the high-caste Rajpoots. Not having seen Rajpoots except in pictures, I can say but little about them; but unquestionably one begins to take greatly to the dusky hues, that become duskier as we approach the tropics. We have particularly remarked the glossy rich coloring of the peasantry, as they worked almost naked at their shadoofs, or process of irrigation. As the sun plays over their dark muscular bodies without one ounce of superfluous flesh, bending and rising at their work, I can compare the tint to nothing but the shading of a good old mahogany table, lit up by a Christmas blaze, and over which the best of claret has been passed from hand to hand during half a century. The sun literally glances over their hard and polished figures. The ladies, as not being so much exposed to the sun and the same exercise, have not the same rich glossiness of coloring; but I am not surprised at the taste of many of my countrymen, who would have turned from the somewhat sickly and mottled complexions of many of our fair ones at home, to the duskier charms of the African girl, if the features at all corresponded, which they generally do not; for as a general rule the peasant women, who have slight pretty figures, become hideous from the hardships they undergo; while those of the higher order and of secluded and luxurious habits, from want of activity and wholesome exercise, very early in life become in shape close resemblances to well-stuffed pillow-cases.

We have hitherto had the river pretty much to ourselves, so far as European voyagers are concerned; but on the evening after leaving Osioot we heard a loud conference on deck, and two barrels blown off as a salute. On rushing out of our cabin to return the compliment, we found a French boat descending the river, the proud proprietors of which pointed out to us in triumph a prodigious crocodile at the bows. Whether it had fallen by their hands, or had been purchased, we could not decide; but we knew that such articles of curiosity are for sale, as we were offered a couple of days previously a remarkably inodorous specimen by a Bedoueen, who had shot him with an old gun nearly as long as his victim.

We were now advancing into the pet regions of crocodiles; and on the 22nd, when near the town of Hooa, we had good evidence of their abundance. The wind being light, and there being a remarkably nice-looking scrub at the foot of a mountain running into the river, a vision of roast mallard and lime-juice came across me, and as our boat was only just creeping onward, there was plenty of time to search for the savory bird in the recesses of the bank. While engaged in this occupation, and close to the water's edge, I was hailed by a native from above, who recommended me to be careful, for that the spot was haunted by crocodiles. "Kebir, kebir" (immense, immense), shouted he, extending his arms to give an idea of space. He had hardly said the word when, with a tumble and splash, one of these reptiles, alarmed no doubt by the conversation, rolled into the river, a few yards from where I had been standing. They are generally so like the mud on which they lie, that it is extremely difficult to perceive them; I have, however, seen some exactly the dark-green color of verdigris. Being admonished by the propinquity, I still advanced cautiously, and flushed almost immediately four more. Having only a light gun with shot, it was impossible to do them harm; so, signalling to my friend to come up with his rifle, I told him the state of affairs, and almost directly he got a shot, and severely wounded a huge lolloping brute, that was just getting into the Nile. He turned at once like a dying fish on his back, and kicked and lashed the calm water into waves, so much so that we entertained the most confident hopes of his capture; but I suppose he got over the inconvenience, for after all the excitement and turmoil, he subsided quietly, and we heard no more about him. We have been told, whether truly or not, our little experience does not enable us to pronounce, that the crocodile, when mortally wounded, always returns to the shore, and expresses his feelings by tremendous bellowing like a buffalo. At that interesting moment Dr. Darwin's pompous description would be highly applicable:—

> Erewhile emerging from the brooding sand,
> With tiger paw he prints the brineless strand;
> High on the flood with speckled bosom swims,
> Helm'd with broad tail, and oar'd with giant limbs;
> Rolls his fierce eyeballs, clasps his iron claws,
> And champs with gnashing teeth his massy jaws.

> Old Nilus sighs through all his cave-crown'd shores,
> And swarthy Memphis trembles, and adores.

Our sailors asserted that in some districts these animals are dangerous, carrying off women and children who go for water; so much so that they are forced to fence off a portion of the river with palm-branches for security against attack. They certainly are much more clever than they look; for they are wonderfully wary, and have a keen sense of hearing. It is remarkably curious, moreover, the perfect knowledge which these ungainly reptiles possess of the quarter from whence danger comes: they lie watching with the utmost unconcern the approach of a native, and still more strange to say, of a native boat; but on the slightest sign of a foreign dress, or as I must presume, of a foreign flag, they instantly roll into the water and disappear. We have constantly been pointed out by the natives crocodiles, which we have seen them approach within one hundred yards in their boats, without producing the slightest apprehension; and yet the moment our *dahabieh* hove in sight they became uneasy and restless, watching every movement warily. If we stopped, or attempted to approach, or put out the boat, as the French say, *ils s'eclipsaient*—they eclipsed themselves in a second.

Herodotus remarks that the crocodile is blind in water, but most keen-sighted on land. The first portion of his assertion we had no means of verifying, but to the latter part of it I can bear ample testimony. One day I had wistfully watched an enormous fellow, the largest I had yet seen, basking on a sandbank. In order not to disturb him we sailed to the opposite shore about a quarter of a mile distant; and after passing his resting-place a considerable way, and taking advantage of a turn, we landed without his being aware of our intention. It was, however, quite enough for him that the *dahabieh* stopped; he moved down into the water, without, however, leaving the spot altogether. Seeing this, and being in hopes that he might come up again, I crept behind a projecting bank on all fours, trailing the rifle after me, and got at last within eighty yards of him. Still, as yet, there was only his back and head visible. I remained, therefore, lying quietly in the sand for about a quarter of an hour, when his body emerged, and offered a fine chance just behind the fore leg. There was, however, a rise in the sandbank before me, which forced me to crawl about half a dozen yards further on to get a clear range and a fine rest for the rifle. Nothing but my cap, which was much the color of the sand, could possibly have been perceived; and yet, so quick was the crocodile's sight, that in one moment he disappeared. The island was a large one, with sheep and other animals occasionally upon it, and innumerable birds; but for all that he discovered in a moment the danger that lurked in the small suspicious object, and like a prudent reptile, took good care not throw a chance away.

As we neared Dendera, the river seemed really alive with these reptiles. They were rolling and tumbling one afternoon like salmon, and provokingly showing the mere tips of their ugly snouts. My friend went forth to stalk them, but returned long after nightfall wearied and unsuccessful. I remained in the boat and plumped a bullet into a great brute about two hundred yards off. He went through a series of most ungainly antics, and, having finished them, disappeared like his predecessor, and thus a second time our Nubians were disappointed of a crocodile feast, which they begged of us to procure for them.

A-propos to this feast, a curious circumstance has occurred on board. A few days ago a marked change all of a sudden seemed to come over the spirits of our usually merry, broadly grinning crew. The song was hushed, the joke checked, and the fireplace, on which their *pot-au-feu* cooked their favorite bread and lentil-soup, and round which they squatted so joyously of erst, was now deserted. In silence they munched dry bread, and softened it with Nile water. A general dreariness prevailed. At length we became aware of the prevailing gloom, and inquired into the causes. Our dragoman explained that—O horror of horrors!—Hubert had appropriated the pot in question, and boiled in it a portion of the unclean beast, namely, a Yorkshire ham, and that nothing henceforth would reconcile the men to cook food in a vessel so polluted. This was really a sad business, so we begged Mohammed to inform them that they might subject the pot to the roughest usage in the way of scrubbing, and so put all to rights. But the offer was of no avail. They protested that nothing would induce them to eat filth, and they retired to break their teeth and their fast on their parched brick-like bread. As a last resource I bethought me of a device, and knowing how greatly in these parts book learning is reverenced, I produced Lane's *Modern Egyptians*, and informing them that I had a great Muslim authority to quote to them, desired Mohammed to translate to them the following story:—" Some time since, a good believer having business with a baker of Cairo, found him in the act of withdrawing a dish of pork from his oven, which some filth-eating Frank, either by means of bribery or through the ignorance of the baker, had contrived to get cooked there, to satisfy at once his malignity towards true believers and his gluttony. The Mahommedan visitor instantly had the offending baker dragged off before the *zabit*, or magistrate. This worthy considered the matter too important to be decided by him, and referred the case to the Supreme Council, the Pacha's Divan; but the president of this also could not venture to give a sentence on a subject so portentous, and so the point was laid before the Muftee, or chief doctor of the law, whether the oven and the food therein had not been rendered impure by the association with pork, and whether citizens having eaten of food so cooked were not impure also. The Muftee, whose opinion on a case like this is as conclusive as would be the universal voice of the bench of bishops in England, on the question of altar candles and candlesticks, resolved and pronounced that all kinds of food not radically impure were purified by fire of any pollution they might have contracted, and, consequently, that whatever thing of this description was in the oven, even if it had been in contact with the pork, was clean as soon as it had been baked."

This precedent, added, no doubt, to great hunger, prevailed completely. One only difficulty remained:—Was the book really written by a good Muslim? As Mr. Lane was supposed by us, though erroneously, to have conformed to Islam, we had no hesitation in putting their minds at ease on this point also, and the effect was marvellous. In a moment every eye brightened up, the fire was lit again, and old Mohammed volunteered to clean the pot himself, and eat, moreover, the first pigeon cooked in it. Since then all has gone happy as a marriage bell. It is, however, somewhat comical to watch the grimaces of disgust whenever Hubert brings forth the ham for breakfast; and yet these very particular purists have entreated us to kill a crocodile, that they may eat and make merry withal. They have already devoured several cormorants, and are wanting more. The poor pig is certainly held in very low estimation, when even the smart Cairenes clean their teeth with a piece of soft wood, preferring this very inadequate mode of abstersion to the chance of touching the bristles of the impure beast. Even in the copious vocabulary of Arabic abuse so constantly exhausted in their wordy wars, there is one expression they carefully avoid even in the paroxysm of oriental fury (unless indeed to an inferior, who is unable to resent it), and that is, Hhanseer, or hog; for the law would take cognizance of such an unpardonable insult. This inimical feeling to the pig species seems from a very early period to have pervaded this portion of the East. Herodotus says, that the old Egyptians considered the hog to be an unclean animal, so much so that if any passer-by touched one accidentally, it was considered necessary that he should bathe himself, and thoroughly wash his garments. The swineherds were the pariahs of those days; they were not allowed to enter any temple, nor to marry out of their own peculiar caste; and only on certain occasions, and to Dionysus and Selene exclusively, were hogs sacrificed. They were, according to the same account, used for stamping in the seed in the moist muddy ground after the Nile inundation, and they were also employed in treading out the corn. It has been asserted that there were no representations of swine in any of the old Egyptian monumental drawings; but this is not the fact: they are drawn, although rarely; I have myself seen these animals delineated on more than one tomb at Thebes. It is curious enough to remark in this instance the strange revolution of custom. There is no doubt whatever but that Moses, who grounded much of his ordinances on the teaching and practice of Egypt, in whose learning he was profoundly versed, forbade to the Israelites the use of swine's flesh in consequence of the abhorrence in which the Egyptians held it. They were unquestionably impelled originally to this aversion from sanitary reasons—from the unwholesome nature of a gross uncleanly animal feeding on all sorts of garbage, whose extreme fatness would be a recommendation in a cold climate, but unnecessary, even injurious, in the sultry atmosphere of North Africa. Religion was invoked by the priests to the aid of the physician, and the pig was tabooed as an unholy animal, conveying pollution, only to be sacrificed to certain gods on certain occasions, and to be tended by the outcasts of the community. No tenet was held by the followers of Moses more rigidly than abstinence from the flesh of pigs; and Mahommed, who derived the greater portion of his theology from, and based many of his precepts on, the institutions of Moses, who indeed made every possible overture to the Jews, in order to be acknowledged by them the successor of their prophet, adopted, among many other ceremonial regulations, almost the entire table of meat forbidden in the Pentateuch. When the disciples of Mahommed entered Egypt, they found the feeling towards pigs among the Christian Copts very different to what it was in the days of the Pharaohs. They were encouraged, bred in large herds, and were the common food of the country. The sword of Amr soon put an end to this state of things; and thus in a curious circle, the Mahommedan came down as the destroyer of the swine of the Egyptians, he having derived his abhorrence of them from the Israelites, the Israelites from the forefathers of these modern Egyptians, whose ancient tradition has thus been restored to them by the instrumentality and succession of two foreign nations—Palestine and Arabia.

We have at last arrived (Jan. 25) at Kenneh, and the country is beginning to assume a different aspect from the lower regions. The river is covered with great floats, composed entirely of vessels of baked clay, of all dimensions, from the large and graceful amphora which the Fellah girls carry on their heads for water, morning and evening, to the goolleh, or small porous bottle, our refreshing companion in every excursion. These floats are precisely on the same principle as the Rhine wood-rafts, and proceed down the river manned by a crew who dispose of their earthen commodities either wholesale or retail, and work their way back again on foot. The complexions of the natives are getting duskier, and though as yet the thermometer tells no great tale, yet the dôm-palm that now has shown his presence among his lithe, slim brethren of the date, begins to tell of fiercer suns, and richer vegetation. Although both of the same species, these two trees differ essentially from one another. The date-palm grows up tall and stately, with a single trunk, and from the practice of the natives, who cut off the yearly growth of the branches, it terminates in a tuft of long, light, uniform branches waving gently downwards. The branch itself is leaved to the end from its commencement with narrow green leaves, gradually diminishing to a point. The dôm-palm is a much smaller tree, and, instead of growing tall and erect, invariably divides at a certain height into two branches, and these again, as they progress, become furcated, always in two sets. They differ altogether from the date-palm, having a much closer and more clothed appearance; and the branch is altogether dissimilar, having no leaves at the commencement, or at least so small as to be overlooked, while towards the end it bursts out into the semblance of a large green fan. We were at first much taken with their rich tropical appearance;

but, now that the novelty has worn off, we have returned to our old companion, the Nakhl el Bellah, the date-palm, which since we have set foot in Egypt, has cast such continual verdure and grace on the arid landscape, waving lithely in the morning breeze, and lit up by the last lingering ray of the departing sun. It is rather amusing, nevertheless, to hear English travellers telling tales of avoiding the midday glare beneath the cool foliage of the palm, "the cocoa's feathery shade," and French poets describing happy Arab maids and youths "sous l'ombre d'un cocotier." If one requires an exemplification of the grateful coolness thus afforded, one can have in a mild degree a practical imitation at home, by selecting a particularly hot and cloudless August day, fastening a fan on the top of a long pole, and enjoying oneself under it as best one can.[1]

It was a bright, brisk, and breezy morning, on the 25th of January, when we crossed from the Kenneh side of the Nile to mount our donkeys, which were waiting on the opposite shore to take us on to Dendera. After leaving the rich ground adjacent to the river, our course led us over the neutral territory, half desert, half reclaimed, occupied by some families of Bedoueens, who since

---

[1] Lieutenant Burton.

the days of Mohammed Ali have abandoned their wandering and predatory habits, and become more or less fixed in spots such as these, where they can get pasture for their camels and flocks, and a little precarious tillage for their simple fare. As we approached their low black tents, swarthy, naked, pot-bellied children issued out of them to look at the strangers; and ferocious dogs bounded forth to pull down the intruders; a formidable pack indeed would they have been for a solitary wanderer to meet, and differing altogether from the mangy, growling, but slinking pariah, the denizen of the dirt-heaps about Fellah villages. These were fine-looking brave fellows, and attacked us with such pluck and good will, that in spite of staves and stones, a speedy exit from their dominions was necessary to prevent the necessity of resorting to powder and shot in self-defence. After a ride of about two miles we reached the huge heaps of rubbish which cover the site of ancient Tentyra. The broken and crumbling walls of mud houses denote that a town formerly surrounded the great structures that now hardly emerge from the demolitions; but there was no one at present to disturb our explorations, except a few peasants digging up the earth in search of nitre at the outskirts of the old town. We halted at the *pylon*, or portal of the temple, from which there is an approach of 110 paces to the entrance of the building. Our stay in the immediate vicinity of this *pylon* was short enough, from the innumerable quantities of surly black and yellow banded hornets which had made it their habitation; indeed the whole outside of the temple was so infested by these insects, that we were obliged to keep at a respectful distance from many portions of it, which we should otherwise have liked to have examined more closely. The approach from the portal to the temple is flanked by a low, crude brick wall, evidently modern, probably erected by order of Mohammed Ali, who cleared out the main building of the accumulations of earth with which it had become more than half filled.

The first impression which comes across the visitor as he advances, is the disproportion between the size of the columns and the extreme lowness of the portico, which has rather the appearance of an entrance into some rock temple, than of a sanctuary of the extent and magnificence which one had figured to oneself from the description of former travellers. We see facing the view as we approach six columns above twenty-two feet in circumference, but apparently not more than about twenty in height, supporting the massive roof of an enormous structure. It is not until we arrive close to them that we find that hitherto we have seen only half their height, the other half being hid beneath the level of the earth, from which, as I remarked, they have been excavated. We find that behind this front row of six columns there are three other rows of six,

8*

making twenty-four in all, each covered with hieroglyphics and religious representations, and having the capital square in shape, with the features of the goddess Athor carved on it ("mooned Ashtaroth, heaven's queen and mother both") more or less defaced by the hand of man. The Greeks themselves, in their caryatides, seem to give a sanction to this principle; but the effect of the calm, benign human countenance surmounting these large columns was strange to an eye accustomed only to the classic capital; and yet the impression conveyed was most imposing. The multiplied features of the great goddess seemed ever proclaiming her immediate presence; and the gracious expression of repose that characterizes them is in harmony with the genius and spirit of the whole structure. On reaching the portico we descend abruptly to the floor and interior of the temple. It seems quite perfect. Chamber after chamber is explored, each covered with a profusion of ornaments and mystic devices; but in attempting to push these investigations still further, by ascending and descending a series of stone staircases, which lead somewhere upwards and downwards at the extremities of some very narrow passages, we were repulsed by the torrent of bats which came forth upon us, flew into our faces, extinguished our candles, and rendered the attempt hopeless. Probably these staircases lead in some cases to subterraneous chambers beneath the temple, in others to the roof, which is massive and flat, and gorgeously adorned on its ceiling. It was in this temple and on its ceiling that the celebrated Zodiac of Dendera raised much learned discussion before the discoveries of Champollion assigned a true date to so many edifices in Egypt. This zodiac is on the ceiling of the *pronaos*, or portico, and according to the astronomical calculations of the scientific, the antiquity of the temple was abridged or lengthened. De la Lande, from his observation of the double appearance of Cancer, was of opinion that the zodiac was composed when the summer solstice was in the middle of that sign, or about three thousand years ago; but Visconti made a far more happy conjecture from his computations, that the building was being erected about the time of the Nativity. The summer solstice was at that time in Cancer, there represented by a *scarabæus*. The temple was in fact commenced by the celebrated Cleopatra, whose representation, together with that of Cæsarion her son by Julius Cæsar, ornaments the external back wall. There is certainly but little in that figure that served, to me at least, to recall the wondrous beauty of her who subdued the subduers of the world. Much of that portion of the structure undertaken by her is still unfinished, and many cartouches on which would have been engraved her royal name are empty; for ere they could be completed, Actium had been fought, Agrippa in his light Liburnian galleys had routed the vast armada of Egypt, and the kingdom of the Ptolemies had become a Roman province. It is to Tiberius that the completion of the temple and its magnificent portico is due; but all the early Cæsars seem to have been among its benefactors. On the back of the portico are the names of Augustus and Caligula; and on the portico itself may be read in hieroglyphics those of Tiberius, Caligula, Claudius, and Nero. Surrounding the temple, and in the immediate neighbourhood of it, are various other buildings, one of them a species of sacred edifice peculiar to Egypt, and called by Champollion, as he read the name in hieroglyphics, a "mammeisi," or lying-in chapel for the goddess of the spot; an establishment not unseldom found attached to Egyptian temples of any great size, as at Erment, Edfou, &c. This building lies to the right of the great temple, as it faces the river, and was supposed, before its real object was discovered, to have been dedicated to Typhon, from the numerous grotesque and frightful representations of that monster, whom the Ptolemaic sculptors seem greatly to have affectioned; and which are as unfitting decorations as well can be imagined for the chosen retreat of either goddess or mortal in an interesting situation. Behind the temple is a small chapel of Isis, remarkable from the sensation which the engravings of the goddess in the form of a cow, upon its walls, produced on our Indian Sepoys, when marching from Cosseir to this place, for the invasion of the lower country. They prostrated themselves before these figures, declared them to be the handiwork of their ancestors, and having bedaubed themselves and the walls of the chapel with cow-dung, departed on their way rejoicing.

The difference of opinion that exists among eminent writers as to the merits of this structure, is curious.

Sir Gardner Wilkinson observes:—"Egyptian sculpture had long been on the decline before the erection of the Temple of Dendera; and the Egyptian antiquary looks with little satisfaction on the graceless style of the figures, and the crowded profusion of ill-adjusted hieroglyphics, that cover the walls of this and other Ptolemaic or Roman monuments. But architecture still retained the grandeur of an earlier period; and though the capitals of the columns were frequently overcharged with ornament, the general effect of the porticoes erected under the Ptolemies and Cæsars is grand and imposing, and frequently not destitute of elegance and taste. These remarks apply very particularly to the Temple of Dendera; and, from its superior preservation, it deserves a distinguished rank among the most interesting monuments of Egypt. For though its columns, considered singly, may be said to have a heavy, perhaps a barbarous, appearance, the portico is a noble specimen of architecture; nor is the succeeding hall devoid of beauty and symmetry of proportion."

Mr. Hamilton, in his *Ægyptiaca*, is far more warm in his commendations:—"After seeing innumerable monuments of the same kind throughout the Thebaid, it seemed as if we were now arrived at the highest pitch of architectural excellence that was ever attained on the borders of the Nile. Here we found concentrated the united labor of ages, and the best efforts of human art and industry, in that regular uniform line of construction, which has been adopted in the earliest times. After admiring the general effects of the whole mass, its elegance, solidity, correct proportions, and graceful outlines, it is difficult to decide what particular objects were to be first examined,—whether its sculptures and paintings, typical and ornamental; the distribution of the interior apartments; the details of the capitals and columns; the mystical meaning of particular representations here seen for the first time; the zodiacs or the other celestial phenomena, sculptured on the ceiling,—all seemed objects of high interest and importance, all invited a nearer and closer inspection."

Mr. Bayard Taylor's note of admiration is still more emphatic; and, though I cannot go with him in praising the lineaments of Cleopatra as we have them here, still his description is far too graceful to omit it. These are his words:—"The impression produced by the splendid portico, and twenty-four columns, each sixty feet high and eight feet in diameter, crowded on a surface of one hundred feet by seventy, is that of oppression from their grandeur. The dim light admitted through the half-closed front, which faces the north, spreads a mysterious gloom around these mighty shafts crowned with the fourfold visage of Athor still rebuking the impious hands that have marred her beauty. On the walls between columns of hieroglyphics and the cartouches of the Cæsars and Ptolemies, appear the principal Egyptian deities:—the rigid Osiris, the stately Isis, and the hawk-headed Orus. Around the bases of the columns spring the leaves of the sacred lotus, and the dark blue ceiling is spangled with stars between the wings of the divine emblem. The portico opens into a hall supported by six beautiful columns of smaller proportions, and lighted by a square aperture in the solid roof. On either side are chambers connected with dim and lofty passages; and beyond is the sanctuary, and other apartments, which receive no light from without. Part of the temple was built by Cleopatra, whose portrait with that of her son Cæsarion may still be seen on the exterior wall. The face of the colossal figure has been nearly destroyed; but there is a smaller one, whose soft voluptuous outline is still sufficient evidence of the justness of her renown. The profile is exquisitely beautiful. The forehead and nose approach the Grecian standard; but the mouth is more round and delicately curved, and the chin and cheek are fuller. Were such an outline made plastic,—were the blank face colored with a pale olive hue, through which should blush a faint rosy tinge, lighted with bold black eyes, and irradiated with the lightning of a passionate nature,—it would even now move the mighty hearts of captains and of kings."

At the risk of being thought disrespectful, both to Cleopatra and antiquity, I must decidedly demur to the latter part of the paragraph. Although the effigy in question is defaced, its outline can even now be recognised; and I am bound in sober truth to remark, that I failed to appreciate the grace, delicacy, and passion which Mr. Taylor so much admires. It is like the other figures in the temple—like, in fact, most Ptolemaic figures: round in face, not very graceful, with a decidedly "puffy" expression of countenance; and I am satisfied that, though it may have been the effigy, it never can have been the likeness of the "dark-browed Queen." It has not the stamp of individuality, as some of the older Egyptian representations have; so that you at the very first view have no doubt on your mind but that they are portraits and resemblances. To go no further than one example, can there be found a more striking contrast than the features of the wife of Rameses the Great in the Temple of Athor at Abou Simbel, bear to those of the other female figures there represented? or can there be a doubt, from the peculiarity of these features, but that they are drawn to resemble one orginal?

Sir Gardner Wilkinson is unquestionably right

in his remarks as to the inferior execution of the hieroglyphics and other devices on the walls and columns of this temple, in comparison with those on earlier monuments; but he should have been more liberal of commendation when describing its noble architecture and proportions. It is not to be wondered at, that the spirit of the old hieroglyphical devices and representations of gods had fallen off; for the spirit of the old worship had fallen off also. The reverence that should have animated the chisel of the graver, the pencil of the designer, and the mind of the overseeing priest, had passed away with the faith that had animated them; and profusion of ornament, rather than the excellence of thought, was the one thing aimed at. A graver in the days of Cleopatra executing the form of Osiris, and a Scotch Calvinistic painter representing the Assumption of our Lady, may be supposed to be imbued with very similar feelings. But as to architecture, the Ptolemies have but little reason to feel ashamed of being compared, as to the grandeur of their monuments, with the greatest of the ancient Pharaohs—Karnak always excepted, which nothing ever can approach. With this reservation, there is no structure in Egypt more grand or imposing than Ptolemaic Edfou, none more beautiful than this of Dendera.

Mr. Curtis, in his *Nile Notes*, stands forth a most energetic champion of Ptolemaic excellence, in which he discovers the rich addition of Grecian grace and lightness. I may well be excused quoting so long a passage, in consideration of its beauty, if not of its correctness. He says:—

"Our human interest enters Egypt with Alexander the Great and the Greeks, and becomes vividly and really warm with the Romans and Cleopatra, with Cæsar and Mark Antony, with Hadrian and Antinous; the rest are phantoms and spectres that haunt the shores. Therefore there are two interests and two kinds of remains in Egypt—the Pharaohnic and the Ptolemaic: the former represents the eldest, and the latter the youngest history of the land! The elder is the genuine old Egyptian; the younger, the Greco-Egyptian, after the conquest—after the glorious son had returned to engraft his own development upon the glorious sire. It was the tree in flower transplanted. The Greeks rarely spoilt anything they touched; and here in Egypt they inoculated massiveness with grace, and grandeur with beauty. Of course there was always something lost. An Egyptian temple built by Greek-taught natives, or by Greeks who wished to compromise a thousand jealousies and prejudices, must, like all other architecture, be emblematic of the time and of the people. Yet in gaining grace one is not disposed to think that Egyptian architecture lost much of its grandeur. The rock temples, or the eldest Egyptian remains, have all the imposing interest of the might and character of primitive races grandly developing in art. But as the art advances to separate structures, and slowly casts away a crust of crudities, although it may lose in solid weight, it gains in every other way...... When the Greeks came to Egypt, they brought Greece with them, and the last living traces of antique Egypt began to disappear. They even changed the names of cities, and meddled with the theology; and in art the Greek genius was soon evident—yet as blending and beautifying, not destroying; and the Ptolemaic temples, while they have not lost the massive grandeur of the Pharaohnic, have gained a greater grace; a finer feeling is apparent in them; a lighter and more genial touch—a lyrical sentiment, which does not appear in the dumb old epics of Abou Simbel and Gerf Hosayn. They have an air of flowers and freshness and human feeling: they are sculptured with the same angular heroes and gods and victims; but while these are not so well done as in the elder temples, and indicate that the Egyptians themselves were degenerate in the art, or that the Greks who attained the same result of mural commemoration in a loftier manner at home, did it clumsily in Egypt, the general effect and character of the temple is much more beautiful to the eye—the curious details begin to yield to the complete whole,—a gayer, more cultivated, further advanced race has entered and occupied. O poetic and antiquity-loving Howadgi, this jealousy of the Greeks is sadly unpoetic. Look at this little

Dekkeh temple, and confess it. Remember Philæ, and ask forgiveness. Why love the Ptolemies less because you love the Pharaohs more?"

Those who have seen Dendera and Esneh and Edfou and Kom Ombo and Philæ, will in a large majority answer this appeal, and abjure all jealousy of the Ptolemies and their noble structures; but although with the Ptolemies came the Greeks, and the Hellenistic spirit reigned at Alexandria and in her schools, yet, as far as the architecture of the interior of the country is concerned, I do not perceive it to be altered, modified, or even influenced in the slightest degree by the inroad of foreign taste. The same massiveness of structure; the same sense of immense weight; the same devices to increase the apparent distance of the god's shrine, by diminishing the doorways in height, as if by the effect of a lengthened perspective; the same forest of pillars supporting the flat roof: all these characteristics as much belong to the new as to the old Egyptian architecture. Where Mr. Curtis can discover this infusion of Grecian spirit, this "lyrical sentiment," I cannot form a conjecture. The infusion of Grecian spirit—that is of scepticism, and ridicule of the old gods and devices—may perhaps account for the decided falling-off in the religious decoration, a falling-off still greater in subsequent periods, witness the gravings on the interior of Kalabshe temple, a work of the Roman Cæsars. The old Egyptian religion had become a creed outworn; Osiris with his crook and scourge, hawk-headed Thoth, lion-headed Saté, Ammun with his lofty plume, become so many stereotyped ornaments, instead of carrying with them a deep significancy and feelings of awe, belief, and veneration. We may rest assured that even heraldic painters had a far higher sense of their art, when they imagined themselves to be painting most spirited and high-couraged lions, than after they had seen the real king of the beasts, and knew the unreality of the long-backed, weak-loined creature of conventionality it was their duty and fate to represent. And thus it was with Egypt: as scepticism waxed strong, art waxed weak; and thus it was in Greece, and thus it was in Italy, and thus it will be to the end of time—Art dies beneath the shade of unbelief.

Before quitting Dendera, as we are getting into the region of temples, it is as well to give some idea of the general construction of these buildings in Egypt. They are as dissimilar as possible from those of Greece. In Greek temples the æsthetic, in Egyptian the religious, feeling predominated; all the subordinate and accessory parts being calculated to bring the worshipper into the immediate presence of his God with an increasing impression of awe. The approach was frequently by a *dromos* (avenue), or double row of sphinxes, mysterious compounds of a human form with a lion or a ram, denoting the union of strength and intellect in gods and kings; colossal figures in attitudes of profound repose, or obelisks of granite placed in pairs, stood before the entrance. The sacred enclosure was approached through a lofty gateway or *pylon*, on each side of which was a wing (*pteron*) of pyramidal structure, the residence of the porters or the priests. Through this gateway, on which the emblems of the good genius Horhat, a sun with outspread wings supported by two asps, was inscribed, entrance was gained to a spacious court, open to the sky and surrounded by colonnades; and on the opposite side a second gateway led to a second open court, or to a hall lighted by small openings near the top of the walls, the roof of which was supported by thickly placed columns. In this court or hall the NAOS, probably the great body of the worshippers, assembled on occasions of great solemnity. Beyond it lay the proper temple, the cell or SEKOS, approached by a portico enclosed in walls without colonnades, and sometimes divided into several small apartments; in the remotest of these, behind a curtain, was the image of the god in his monolithal (made of a single stone) shrine, or the sacred animal representing him on earth.[1]

I may as well remark, that I should not recommend a visit to Dendera until returning from the upper country; the extreme preservation of this building somewhat spoils the traveller, unless he be imbued with a strong spirit of research, in investi-

[1] See Kenrick's *Egypt*.

gating other highly interesting but still not equally well preserved monuments. Moreover, all one's freshness and enthusiasm and desire to be astonished should be reserved for the marvels of the Theban plain.

From Kenneh to Thebes we occupied three helpless, stagnant days, with scarcely a breath of wind to aid our poor struggling Nubians to tow the bark, although the distance is but forty-eight miles. Once, and once only, came a few hours of respite to their toil; and this is a specimen of such interludes. It is mid-day; thermometer about 90; a gentle breeze has just ruffled the surface of the river, and tracking is over for the present. The Flea sable on gules ground, that has long curled round the flagstaff, has emerged, and is fluttering, somewhat feebly to be sure, but the flutter is a sign of life, and that is always something. At one end of the cabin table I am sitting, muttering strange gutturals, and drawing aspirates from the soles of my feet; old Mahommed is opposite gurgling harsh sounds; for a lesson in Arabic is going on, and my study this morning is the language of abuse; and the reis looks aghast as he croses the door, and hears me and my instructor call imaginary individuals robbers, and sons of dogs, and rascals and fools, and pandars and persons whose grandmothers have offended against propriety. My companion sits on deck, telescope in hand, looking out for crocodiles, and hubble-bubbling at a *shishé* with a long snake-like tube emerging from beneath his legs. Hubert is engaged in making up fine linen; he brandishes a laundry iron, and glares fiercely over his black beard at a shirt-front whose plaits refuse to be symmetrised by the hand of man. Our old cook has just given his usual greeting, "Good morning, sare; I good, you good, all good;" and bustles off to complete some cabalistic operation of stuffing cabbages with forced meat. Beyond on the bow, clustered together, are our blackies, exulting in their respite; they have got their broken *dharabuka* mended; one sings a song, another beats the instrument, the rest are clapping hands in time. A little Nubian boy, whom from his tricks and cleverness we have nicknamed "Nesnas," or monkey, is dancing in the middle of the party, and imitating, alas! far too accurately, the *ghawazi* he had seen the night before.

Such is the aspect of our interior. On the Nile shore everything is dead and silent, save the ever dreary, droning shadoof. Close to the right come down the Lybian mountains, fiery and shattered by the fierce heat, but greenly fringed by a belt of dôm and date palms. On the left the Arabian chain is far off in the distance, misty and dim from the mid-day glare. Dead, still, and sultry are the large river sandbanks. Grave storks are motionless upon them, meditating upon eel fixings. Groups of wild ducks are huddled together; but the ever-watchful pelicans are sidling off, like large white strutting females in the family way, and geese are uneasily watching the approach of the Howadgi.

This is a faint sketch of an ordinary day under the influence of a calm; but on a Monday, whether there come calm or storm, bustle and activity prevail; for that is the epoch when general ablutions take place, and accounts are settled. Every inch of the boat is then purified with soap and water, beds and sofas are beaten out, cockroaches astonished in their lairs, and fleas driven from their sanctuaries. Splashing, scrubbing, and soapsuds then prevail from the first early hours, and then enters Hubert staggering under the weight of the treasury, a huge box full of copper money, for change for larger specie is not obtainable, and Mohammed and myself balance long and mystic annals of expenditure in milk, in vegetables, in chickens and charcoal, and other usual Nile provender and necessaries.

Our only halt except at night during this period was for a few hours at Nagadeh, a Coptic town, celebrated for its manufacture of *melayas*, a kind of cotton plaid, in which article some of the crew, and especially the reis, were anxious to invest, in order to appear in suitable magnificence among their comrades at Thebes. While the bargaining was going on we occupied our time in shooting pigeons—massacreing would perhaps be the most suitable expression; for the pot and not amusement was the object. The quantity of these birds was prodigious; they flew in flocks to and fro by the river's edge, and sometimes as many as a dozen fell to one discharge of the gun. After picking up and sending on board above one hundred, some of the principal inhabitants begged of us very civilly not to shoot any more, for as many would die of their wounds as we had secured. They valued them chiefly, they said, for the guano they made in the pigeon-houses, which was most useful to rear vegetables, and did not seem to respect them much as articles of food. Not so our crew, for the benefit of whom we had been thus hard upon the good Copts of Nagadeh: their joy was unbounded, and for three successive days they had an allowance of three pigeons each—a luxury quite unusual.

On the night of the 28th we overcame the calms, and the crew seconding gallantly our wishes, we reached the first great goal of our destination—the hundred-gated Thebes. In Europe we hear so much of Thebes and Luxor and Karnak and Medinet Abou—all referring to the same locality, that it is well to make the distinction clear, for the sake of future description. In the first place, the word Thebes is the generic appellation of the whole great city on both sides of the river. It is a corruption by the Greeks (who invariably corrupted every proper name, to suit their own ideas of pronunciation) from the Coptic or Egyptian word Tapé, pronounced also Thaba, meaning the *head*, or capital of the country. As to its hundred gates, referred to by Homer, unless they be an expression to denote its magnificence, or unless he meant the gateways of its innumerable temples, they existed solely in his imagination; for Thebes never was surrounded by a wall.

On the right bank as you mount the river, is that portion of the city and its environs containing the small temple of Goornah, the Rameseum, or temple palace of Rameses II.; the great temple of Medinet Abou, and further on the Dayr-el-Medinet, a smaller temple of the Ptolemies, together with the whole of the Necropolis, including the tombs of the kings, queens, and priests of this metropolis of Upper Egypt. On the opposite side is the modern Luxor, where stands the magnificent temple of Amunoph III. and Rameses II., and about a mile and a half to the north is the greatest edifice ever built either in ancient or modern times, in which St. Peter's and St. Paul's would be lost but for their domes, and Westminster Abbey be but as a chapel—the Sanctuary of Karnak.

It is totally impossible for any one, without entering into antiquarian discussions, which would occupy at least a large volume, to give anything like a minute description of the remains of this magnificent city: a city of which the original grandeur and gorgeousness must seem to be a romance to every one except those who have actually visited it, and before which, as regards public buildings, the greatest cities that the world has ever seen sink into comparative insignificance. One's mind becomes prepared, after a visit to the Pyramids, to conceive the possibility of works of art of that enormous magnitude which Thebes reveals, yet it is most difficult to form a conception of the powerful will, and corresponding means, that transported from great distances and piled together the immense masses of stone of which these palaces and temples are constructed, not to mention the subsequent careful minuteness which literally covered them with the most highly finished and elaborate engravings; all telling the tale, both in sculptured stones and in writing, of the wars, the triumphs, the external and internal glory of their founders. While the Greeks and Romans, at the period when they were most lavish of their writing, only placed a short inscription of a few words on the front of their largest temples and most splendid buildings; for which reason the monumental style still denotes among us a short laconic style, as seems most suitable to the speaking stone—among the Egyptians the temples were almost covered with inscriptions. All buildings which were dedicated to the gods, to the kings, or to the dead, had generally representations or inscriptions upon all the walls, ceilings, pillars, architraves, friezes, and lintels, inside as well as outside. In place of only giving the most necessary information, the writing here forms in itself at the same time an essential ornament of the architecture. The variegated written columns on the white and grey surfaces, not only express a desire for ornamental drawing by the great variety in their lines, which run backward and forward with the utmost regularity, and satisfy the painter's eye by the brilliancy of the varied colors; but they also excite the observation of the unlearned by the figurative and direct meaning of the written object, taken from all the natural kingdom; and lastly the intelligent curiosity of the inquirer, especially of cultivated men, by the peculiar significance of their religious or historical purport. Thus, hieroglyphic becomes a monumental writing in a sense and to a degree of perfection beyond any other written character on earth. They had also so far overcome the technical difficulty of engraving these signs, both in the most fragile and the hardest kind of stone, that it seems scarcely to have been considered at all, though these signs were not composed of simple mathematical strokes, like the Roman or Greek monumental writing, or the cuneiform of the Assyrians, but were at the same time writing and artistic drawing. This practice has thrown much light on ancient Egyptian manners as well as history, for the written character was not alone the constant and indispensable accompaniment of architecture and of the large representations upon the walls of the temples, but was placed with an equal predilection upon all, even the smallest objects of art and of daily life. How precious among other nations of antiquity are those statues, vases, gems, or other articles, which bear upon them inscriptions with respect to their origin, their owner, or their intended use! But this was the universal, almost undeviating, practice in Egypt. There, no Colossus was so great, and no amulet so small, that it should not express for what it was designed by means of an inscription; no piece of furniture that did not bear the name of its owner. Not only the temple had its dedications, in which the builder was named, and the god to whom it was dedicated by him, but these dedications were considered of such importance that a particular class of independent monuments were especially devoted to them, *viz.*, the obelisks at the entrance of the gates, and, besides this, every fresh addition to the structure, every newly erected pillar, actually even the restoration of separate representations which had been accidentally injured upon the old walls, had a written information respecting which of the kings built it, and what he had done for the enlargement, embellishment, and restoration of the temple. They even went so far as to record the name of the king upon the separate building stones, as that of Shoofoo in the Great Pyramid; and it was usually stamped on the bricks of royal manufacture.

These preliminary observations, for the latter

portion of which I am much indebted to Dr. Lepsius, are meant to give a general idea of the astonishing profusion of sculptured ornament and writing which pervades all these buildings, and which modern science is daily proceeding to interpret; so that I am assured learned authorities profess, by translation of the older monuments, to give very shortly detailed annals of the reigns of some of the most remarkable monarchs of the golden era, as the more modern of these edifices have already enabled chronologists to fix with accuracy the dates and successions of the Ptolemies.

The sun was hardly risen on the morning of the 29th, when the cabin window at my bedside was thrown open, and I endeavored to get some idea of the right bank, which, in accordance with the suggestions of Sir G. Wilkinson, we first determined to visit. To the left the gay streamers of five English, two American, and one French *dahabieh* were fluttering around us, and the crews in groups cooking their morning meal on the strand of Luxor. Gorgeous dragomen were moving importantly to and fro, and female Howadgi, under white umbrellas and uglies, were sketching the majestic portal of Amunoph's temple, running parallel to the shore. Our destination was, however, not among them, but over the water, and provided with guide and water-carrier, we set forth early to visit the temples of the plain and the colossal figures, reserving the tombs for another day.

The first spot we stopped at was the somewhat comparatively small temple of Goornah, at the extreme north of the Theban plain. It was dedicated to Amun, the Jupiter of the Egyptians, and the tutelary deity of Thebes, and was founded by King Sethos, but completed by his son, Rameses II. This we are given to understand by the inscription of Rameses over the corridor on the architrave. The god Amunre is here delineated presenting to the great Pharaoh the emblem of life, and after the titles of the King it goes on to say—" Rameses, the beloved of Amun, has dedicated this work to the father Amunre, King of the Gods, having made additions to the temple of his father the king, the son of the Sun, Osiris." We were here beset by a host of Arabs, with curiosities and relics of various descriptions. I purchased a few ancient *scarabæi*, the larger of which were suspended round the necks of the dead, and the smaller used as signets; and I also became possessor of some recent imitations, for a regular manufacture of modern antiquities is now vigorously at work somewhere in the neighbourhood of this village. We also got some mummy cloth in wonderful preservation, of which nearly a thousand pieces had been found in one tomb, almost as fresh as if from the loom this year. Besides these, we invested in mummied cats, mortuary vases containing various seeds which were deposited in the tombs along with the body of the deceased; but the most interesting purchases were some vases, in which were placed various portions of the interior of the human body.

"As soon as the intestines were removed, they were properly cleansed, embalmed in spices and various substances, and deposited in four vases; these were afterwards placed in the tomb with the coffin, and were supposed to belong to the four genii of Amenti (the land of spirits), whose heads and names they bear. Each contained a separate portion. The vase with a cover representing the human head of Amset, held the stomach and large intestines; that with the cynocephalus head of Hapi, contained the smaller intestines; in that belonging to the jackal-headed Smautf, were the lungs and heart; and for the vase of the hawk-headed Hebhnsnof were reserved the gall-bladder and the liver. The most costly were of oriental alabaster, from ten to twenty inches high, and about one-third in diameter, each having its inscription with the name of the particular deity whose head it bore. Others were of limestone, and even of wood; but these last were often solid, and contained nothing, being merely emblematic, and intended only for those whose intestines were returned into the body. So careful, indeed, were the Egyptians of old to show proper respect to all that belonged to the human frame, that even the sawdust of the floor where they cleansed it was taken and tied up in small linen bags, which, often to the number of twenty and thirty, were deposited in vases, and buried in the tomb or near it."[1]

Having at a small outlay laid in a considerable stock of rubbish, my friend concluded by purchasing a human head in the most strange preservation, touched up, and colored to represent the flush of life, and with a set of teeth the strength and symmetry of which must have given but little employment to contemporary dentists.

We thence made our way to the next great edifice—the Memnonium, so called by the Greeks from another of their verbal assimilations. Having heard tell of Rameses II. by his distinguishing name of Miamun, they immediately connected him with Memnon, son of Aurora, and have given the Egyptian king a pedigree from their own mythology, making him the offspring of Tithonus and Aurora, and have connected him, moreover, with the Colossus of the plain, and endowed him with vocal qualities, of which more hereafter. The real name of this structure is the Rameseum, or temple palace of one of the greatest kings and warriors of the nineteenth Egyptian dynasty, who was considered until lately to be the Sesostris of general history.

This magnificent pile of building is in sad desolation, and but a portion of its former circuit re-

[1] Sir G. Wilkinson.

mains. Enough, however, is in existence to enable the visitor to complete in imagination that which in reality is wanting. Its main characteristic is a series of triumphs by King Rameses over foreign enemies, whom you see him in one place in the act of routing with his mighty bow and arrows:—

> ἔκλαγξαν δ' ἄρ' ὀϊστοὶ ἐπ' ὤμων χωομένοιο
> αὐτοῦ κινηθέντος· ὁ δ' ἤϊε νυκτὶ ἐοικώς·

in another, pursuing to their walled towns, and trampling down beneath his chariot wheels. After this series of highly animated war pictures, the King is seen returning homewards; he has now dismounted from his chariot, the horses of which are held by grooms; he then in full state receives the congratulations of the priests, and of the high officers, and presents his prisoners and his other offerings of captured spoil to his country's gods.

> Ipse sedens niveo candentis limine Phœbi
> Dona recognoscit populorum aptatque superbis
> Postibus; incedunt victæ longo ordine gentes
> Quam variæ linguis habitu tam vestis et armis.

But the most astounding of all objects in this grand and elegant temple was the stupendous granite statue of the King carved from a single stone. "He is seated on a throne in the usual attitude of Egyptian figures, the hands resting on the knees, indicative of that tranquillity he had returned to enjoy in Egypt after the fatigues of victory. But the fury of an invader has levelled this unrivalled monument. Its colossal fragments lie shattered around the pedestal, and its shivered throne evinces the force used for its destruction. It is difficult to realize the possibility of moving such a monstrous mass as this, and yet it has been transported more than 175 miles to the spot where it now lies, from the granite quarries of Syene. But if it be a matter of surprise how the Egyptians could transport and erect a wall of such dimensions, the means employed for its destruction are hardly less wonderful, nor should we hesitate to account for the shattered appearance of the lower part by attributing it to the explosive force of gunpowder, had that combustible been known at the period of its ruin. The throne and legs are completely destroyed, and reduced to comparatively small fragments, while the upper part, broken at the waist, is merely thrown back upon the ground, and lies in that position which was the consequence of its fall. There are no appearances, strange to say, of the wedge or other instrument which should have been employed for reducing these fragments to the state in which we find them. The fissures seen across the head and in the pedestal are the work of a later period, when some of the pieces were cut for millstones by the Arabs, but its previous overthrow is probably coeval with the Persian invasion. Merely to say this is the largest statue in Egypt will convey no idea of the gigantic mass which, from an approximate calculation, exceeded, when entire, nearly three times the solid contents of the great Obelisk at Karnak, and weighed about 887 tons."[1]

Travellers are very apt to fall into ecstasies and amazements at objects which their friends have not seen, and are not likely to see; but in real truth, and without the slightest exaggeration, I was perfectly bewildered by the sight of this stupendous statue. It is of the most beautiful rich red granite, polished like a looking-glass; the sacred characters, where uninjured by violence, are still as deep and clear and well defined as the most modern inscription—in fact, far more so; for, though I have seen modern inscriptions on granite, I have never seen any which at all can be compared with these in size, depth, and execution. But then the shattered block itself, even in its mutilated condition, is of a size that the marvels of machinery would seem to be an absolute necessity to stir it. It is difficult to conceive a statue the height of a tall tree, and proportionably great; but when you have in some measure reconciled your mind to that idea, then press in on you all the accessories: the first carving out of a mount of granite this mighty stone; then its exquisite finish without crack or flaw; then its removal (by land according to Herodotus) to its present site; and, lastly, its erection. It is positive bewilderment. But Thebes, with its palaces, its temples, its statues, its obelisks, and its tombs, is one bewilderment, from the day you furl, till the

[1] Sir G. Wilkinson.

day you lift your sail from beneath the columns of Amunoph. Your former admirations, as far as size is concerned, become almost insignificant—Rome and St. Peter's, London and St. Paul's, and the middle-age Gothic cathedrals of Rouen and Cologne, Strasbourg and York—insignificant in truth before the works of men who lived and built and died, without hearing a steam whistle, between 1500 and 2000 years ere Christ came on earth.

I ought not, however, to omit recording among the notices of the deeds of Rameses, justly called the Great, which the monuments acquaint us with, his patronage of learning and literature. His battles and campaigns did not divert him from the gentler arts of peace. In the temple we have just visited, he built a library for sacred books and historical records. Several hieratical papyri which we possess are dated from the Rameseum; and it is frequently spoken of in the so-called historical papyri. There is no doubt but that the example of the Theban monarchs influenced the Ptolemies in their establishment of the celebrated Alexandrian Library, and the 400,000 rolls with which it was in a few years enriched were, no doubt, derived from the institutions of the older Pharaoh. It is impossible it could be otherwise, as there is no private collection spoken of as existing at that period, except that of Aristotle. Diodorus refers to this library in his description of the temple of King Osymandyas, or Rameses, at Thebes; and just where the entrance to it should be according to his plan, Champollion read in hieroglyph a dedication to the gods Thoth and Safk, the male and female patron deities of arts, sciences, and letters, with the appropriate title of "Lady of Letters" and "President of the Library." Lepsius also mentions as having found in Thebes, to the south-west of the palace of Rameses, behind Dayr-el-Medinet, the tombs of two *Librarians* of the time of Rameses Miamun, and therefore probably belonging to this library. The occupants of the tomb were father and son, so that this, like most public offices, was probably hereditary. From thence we went southwards to the still larger pile of building of Medinet Abou. It is of earlier date, being commenced by Thothmes I., and added to by various kings. Of all the Theban monuments this is the best preserved, and every line of the gay coloring of the original decorations is uninjured, and affords perfect specimens of the effect of painting upon stone. As far as pleasure and interest is concerned, perhaps this is the most worthy of long study of all Egyptian temples; for besides the war scenes of the conqueror, and the religious processions and dedications of the King Priest, it has many delineations of the private life of the monarch, of his sports and combats with wild animals; and the eye turns gladly from the fierce energy of the combatants, and the turmoil and confusion of the battle, to the peaceful interior of the warrior's home, where his daughters, recognized by the royal side-plait, present him with flowers, and fan him with palm branches, and divert his leisure with games of chess and draughts, in which I may parenthetically observe, the King has the best of it by one piece.

But the sun is gradually sinking behind the Lybian hills, and we venture forth from the shade of columns and corridors to visit the colossi— the two that alone have survived, and have sadly watched for three thousand years over the Nile's green plain, the decline and fall of the glory of that race they were intended to perpetuate for all time. I have seen few things more solemn or more touching than the calm repose of these two sitting statues when evening begins to gild the opposite heights, and cast its shadows over the flat expanse below. When viewed from some distance the mutilations are unseen, and there in placid majesty, with hands upon their knees, they have brooded over the revolutions of ages, and seem yearningly to speak out the tale of their splendour and their doom. Their very isolation, apart from ruins and relics, amid the vegetation of richly waving fields, adds to the sense of hopeless melancholy loneliness with which they are invested. But they speak of days when they were not alone, but when the royal street of Amunoph the King ran between a row of stony companions great and towering as themselves, and how one by one they have perished by the mad fury of Cambyses, or the revenge of Lathyrus, until they alone are left to tell the tale of the vicissitudes of dynasties and kings, and the vicissitudes of creeds and faiths; of Pharaohs and of Ptolemies; of Cæsars and of Caliphs; of Osiris and of Jupiter; of Jesus and of Mahommed; and changes yet as strange as these may pass over their heads ere they sink beneath the clasp of the great river that annually, deeper and deeper within his embrace, vindicates them as his own peculiar children, the creation of a race by whom he was reverenced as a god.

These statues seem to have undergone a series of mutilations. They were each originally of one block, standing sixty feet high above the plain; the lower part of both, up to the face, is still perfect, but the countenances are so defaced, that on near approach we lose the charm, the calm, mild earnest expression, which was the type and characteristic of prime Egyptian art. It is, therefore, well at first to view them from a distance, and let fancy supply that of which closer inspection deprives them. The northern statue has been repaired, probably by Septimius Severus. This is the image of the poets; and the Greeks connected with it their charming legend of the Vocal Memnon, who every morning at sunrise greeted his mother Aurora, while she moistened him with tears of dew for his early heroic death. They are in reality both of them representations of Amunoph III., a predecessor of Rameses. The Arabs now call them Shamma and Tamma, or collectively Salamāt (the Salutations); probably referring to the legends of old time. The sides and legs of the northern statue are covered with inscriptions, chiefly Greek, engraved by persons who have heard this stony harmony; among the number the Emperor Hadrian, in honor of whom it sounded thrice. Whether these sounds were produced by priestly device, or by atmospheric influences, is now matter of controversy, and worthy of wiser and more scientific heads than mine. Humboldt has a passage on the subject of atmospheric influence in producing sounds from stones, and refers to this phenomenon; but still seems dubious whether the vocality of the statue was natural, or the deception of man. "The granitic rock on which we lay," he writes, "is one of those where travellers on the Orinoco have heard from time to time, towards sunrise, subterraneous sounds resembling those of the organ. The missionaries call these stones *laxas de musica.*" "It is witchcraft" (*cosa de bruxas*), said our young Indian pilot, who could speak Spanish. We never ourselves heard these mysterious sounds, either at Carichana Vieja, or in the upper Orinoco; but from information given us by witnesses worthy of belief, the existence of a phenomenon that seems to depend on a certain state of the atmosphere cannot be denied. The shelves of rock are full of very narrow and deep crevices. They are heated during the day to 48° or 50°. I several times found their temperature, at the surface during the night, at 39°—the surrounding atmosphere being at 28°. It may easily be conceived that the difference of temperature between the external and the subterranean air attains its maximum about sunrise, or at that moment which is at the same time farthest from the period of the maximum of the heat of the preceding day. May not these organ-like sounds, which are heard when a person lays his ear in contact with the stone, be the effect of a current of air that issues out through the crevices? Does not the impulse of the air against the elastic spangles of mica that intercept the crevices, contribute to modify the sounds? May we not admit that the ancient inhabitants of Egypt in passing incessantly up and down the hill had made the same observations on some rock of the Thebaid, and that the " music of the rocks " there led to the jugglery of the priests in the statue of Memnon? Perhaps, when " the rosy-fingered Aurora rendered her son, the glorious Memnon, vocal," the voice was that of a man hidden beneath the pedestal of the statue; but the observation of the natives of the Orinoco, which we relate, seems to explain in a natural manner what gave rise to the Egyptian belief of a stone that poured forth sounds at sunrise.

"Almost at the same period at which I communicated these conjectures to some of the learned of Europe, three French travellers, MM. Jomard, Jollois, and Devilliers, were led to analogous ideas. They heard at sunrise, in a monument of granite, at the centre of the spot on which stands the Palace of Karnak, a noise resembling that of a string breaking. Now, this comparison is precisely that which the ancients employed in speaking of the voice of Memnon. The French travellers thought like me, that the passage of rarefied air through the fissures of a sonorous stone might have suggested to the Egyptian priests the invention of the juggleries of the Memnonium."

Sir G. Wilkinson seems to consider that the sound originated by means of some imposture; the only point about which there is no question, is that most credible witnesses heard it, some describing it as if the effect of a blow, others like the breaking of the string of a musical instrument. While we were there an Arab climbed up, and with a hammer made a clear ringing metallic sound, not so loud certainly, but of the same tone as proceeds from a stone in my own place in Ireland, called the Bell Rock; but it was not the chord that Aurora struck on leaving the couch of Tithonus, for it was late in the day, and the goddess had long been occupied with her godlike household cares.

We reserved our visit to the Tombs of the Kings

until the morrow; for we had a busy day, and though early in the field, were by no means able to accomplish as leisurely as we could wish, all that I have described. Not so, however, an American acquaintance whom we met galloping on horseback from temple to temple, in hot haste, and who flouted us with our slow and humble donkeys. He had *done*, he said, by dint of taking a horse and hard riding, the Tombs of the Kings and Medinet Abou, and was now off to *do* the Rameseum; and when he was out of hearing we added, "and to write your name as your countrymen invariably do in the largest letters on the most interesting part of the most interesting monument."

But up! and let us be off to the Kings' Tombs, for the way is long, the heat powerful, and the research extensive. They are separated altogether from the other tombs; for the dust of the Pharaohs, sons of the Sun, must not mingle with that of ordinary mortals, and they are dissociated in death from those whom they so loved in life, for a mountain bar divides them from the last resting-place of their queens. Well, indeed, did the old inhabitants of Egypt select the spot, which Nature seems to have consecrated to endless repose. The old road over which wound the funeral train of these great monarchs, runs through a valley, solemn, sombre, and silent, and Death seems brooding over it even in the glare of sunshine: The escarpment of the rock rises rugged, austere, and barren on each side, rounding off above to bare summits, and their brows are covered with coal-black stones, torrefied by the summer furnace. Your eye wanders anxiously in search of one green palm, one trickling mountain stream, one bright flower, to divert the painful dreary gloom that weighs down your imagination, and oppresses your very senses. But when I say gloom, it is not the gloom of European rocks and crags with deep black shadows, nor is it the gloom of American funereal hemlock swamps: it is a gloom worse than all that—a gloom in bright mid-day, a gloom of a fierce, steady, unclouded sun, of a great eye looking down from heaven with fixed unspeaking stare. It is the death of Nature that is around you, apt concomitant to the death homes of mighty mysterious kings, whose very names have a strange portentous sound, and who loom in dim, undefined, and gigantic outline through the cloud-curtain which time has dropped between them and you. Our donkeys trod noiselessly over the sandy path; our guide and drivers refrained from conversations; there was not even the shrill whistle of the circling hawk in the sky above us, nor the chirp of the cicada beneath our feet: all was silence, deep and almost painful silence. The valley at last ended beneath the foot of a lofty peak which walled it off from all communications; and around, deep in the bosom of the mountain, are the sepulchres of the Theban dynasty.

The whole of the day was employed in inspecting these beautiful tombs, of which about forty-seven are known to have existed; some of these are completely closed up, and others hardly worth a visit, except to the antiquarian. The first that we entered, although not the largest, is the best preserved, and called Belzoni's Tomb, from the discoveries made in it by that energetic explorer. It is the tomb of Sethos I., father of Rameses the Great; and the decorations denote the prime Augustan era of Egyptian art. The total horizontal length of this tomb is 320 feet, and its perpendicular depth 90 feet. It consists of a series of galleries, halls, and antechambers, lofty, spacious, and cool, all painted and adorned with the gayest colors, and the most various sculptures. Belzoni, in his researches, had at a very early portion of the tomb arrived at a pit and wall, on which was painted a continuation of the subjects decorating its sides, and which was its apparent termination. "A hollow sound, however, and a small aperture, betrayed to Belzoni the secret of its hidden chambers, and a palm-tree supplying the place of the more classic ram, soon forced the intermediate barrier. The breach displayed the splendor of the succeeding hall, at once astonishing and delighting its discoverer, whose labors were so gratefully repaid.[1]" Over the entrance is the

[1] Sir G. Wilkinson.

mystic winged globe; and the carved doorposts were once provided with one or two massive folding doors to close it. The side walls, as you proceed, are covered with horizontal rows of colored hieroglyphics, with occasional figures of the King in the act of presenting offerings to the various deities. The minuteness and delicacy of these hieroglyphics is astonishing: it has been calculated there are 1200 on a space of between 40 and 50 ft. On the ceiling also, brilliantly painted, are represented symbolical signs representing heaven, as well as the hours of day and night, with their influences on mankind, and their astrological significations, all accompanied by explanatory inscriptions.

Then you enter the first hall, and on each column supporting it the King stands before different gods, and directs to them his justifications for the past life. All the subjects here are very beautiful; but there is one group from which I could hardly tear myself away. It represents the King standing in the presence of the goddess Athor, the Egyptian Venus. The soft and gentle Sethos, and the sweet face of the goddess, have a charm I cannot express; for the contrast lies between two gentlenesses—that of the man and of the woman; and the artist has caught them both. All the other conferences on the other pillars between the King and Anubis, and Osiris and Pthah and Horus, are interesting to some, no doubt, and to the scientific perhaps far more so than this; but

I confess it without shame, that we turned from jackal, hawk, and ibis-headed deities, with their symbols and their attributes, to the sweet face of woman, the rich ideal of sleepy, almond-eyed, full-lipped beauty, with which early imaginings had peopled the Nile valley, and late experience has sought for, alas! as yet, in vain.

But if that moon-crowned goddess is good to look on in all her comeliness of womanhood, yet turn not altogether away your eyes from him that pleads before her; for it is young Sethos, first of his name, priest and king, conqueror and architect—he who took Joseph out of prison, and made him lord of all his household, and brought Jacob out of Palestine.[1] The artist has not depicted him as the Assyrians did their fierce black-bearded kings—grim and stern, with the instruments and representations of bloody cruelty and revenge around; nor has he drawn him as he descended into this his rocky resting-place—full of years and honor; but there he stands, in the golden prime of youth, calm and mild, but of truly regal port, an Egyptian Paris worthy to present offerings to a Nile-born Aphrodite.

In all sepulchral delineations that I have seen, the decorator has portrayed the occupant of the tomb in his early days of manhood; indeed an old man is not to be found, that I am aware of, within the whole range of Egyptian art. This arose

[1] According to Lepsius.

partly, without doubt, from conventionality, but also from the fact of the Pharaohs having at once, on ascending the throne, commenced the construction of their tombs. These tombs at first consisted of the opening corridors running into the large vaulted hall intended for the sarcophagus; but often, if the king, after the completion of the tomb in its first and most necessary extent, felt his vigour still unimpaired, and promised himself a prolonged life, the central passage of this hall of pillars was cut in a still more deep descent for the commencement of a new hall. New corridors and lateral chambers were attached till the king for the second time fixed upon a goal, and terminated the sepulchre with a second hall of pillars, almost more spacious and splendid than the first. Smaller chambers on both sides were then added to this, if the time allowed, till at length the last hour struck, and the royal corpse, having undergone the process of embalming for seventy days, was entombed in the sarcophagus.[1]

Besides the particular groups on the columns in this hall of which I have made special mention, there are on the walls several extremely interesting drawings, one in particular, the procession of four different people of red, white, black, and again white complexions, who march four by four, followed by Ra, or the Sun. The four red figures are Egyptians; the next, a white race, with blue

[1] Lepsius.

eyes, long bushy beards, and clad in a short dress, are a northern nation with whom the Egyptians were long at war, and appear to signify the nations of the North, as the black procession those of the South. The remaining four, also a white people, with a pointed beard, blue eyes, feathers in their hair, and crosses or other devices about their persons, and dressed in long flowing robes, denote the East. These four groups are supposed to be a typification of the four divisions of the world, or of the whole human race, among which the King reckoned his subjects.[1]

The lower bordering of the walls is curious, representing a long serpent running round it, and supported by male figures as bearers; above this again are other delineations of gods and natural subjects; and still higher runs another serpent cordon, having legs as supporters, and human heads upon it to break the length. From thence you advance by another passage, highly decorated, to another chamber; and last of all to the grand hall, adorned with sculptures superbly painted, relating the life and actions of the deceased monarch, and the mysteries of Egyptian rite. In the side chambers are ceremonies connected with religion; and the transverse vaulted part of the great hall or saloon of the sarcophagus, ornamented with profuse sculpture, is a termination worthy of this grand sepulchral monument. "The chamber to

[1] Sir G. Wilkinson.

the left is remarkable for a broad stone bench cut out of the rock, and running round it, on which it is supposed the coffins of court officers were placed."[1] It is elaborately graved and painted, but sadly broken up, not by ancient but by modern barbarians, who have been anxious to bring home a specimen of its graceful decorations. After dwelling here as long as time allowed, we visited other tombs, that of Rameses III., called Bruce's, or the Harper's Tomb; that of Rameses V., Rameses VII., Rameses IX., Rameses IV., Sethos II., and Pthahmen. Some of these are larger and others smaller than the one I have described: all of them are interesting, but none of them finished with the same artistic skill and magnificence as that of the Pharaoh which we first inspected; but beyond obtaining a general idea, the shortness of time entirely forbade any minute examination.

As evening advanced we availed ourselves of a mountain pass, by which the long winding road of the valley is avoided, and at length, with a fine breeze fanning our parched cheeks, we stood on the top of the Lybian range, and looked down on the wide Theban plain. Above our heads was the high peak of the Gebel Assass, that so appropriately closes this Necropolis of Kings. To our left was the Goornah Temple, and the columns of the great Rameseum before us. The colossi were sitting, ever sad and solemn, among green spring crops;

[1] Sir G. Wilkinson.

to our right were the masses of Medinet Abou, while far away on the other bank rose up in the distance the gigantic portals of Karnak; but from the shore of Thebes the red granite obelisk seemed to pierce the clear air with its tapering spire, and the gay flags of *dahabiehs* were fluttering in front of the pillars of Amunoph. This, and the prospect from the hill behind Osioot, and from the citadel of Cairo, were the only really beautiful views I have seen in Egypt. There are many spots whose softness and grace have made themselves felt, and of which the general impression can never fade while memory remains; but yet these must have been seen and gazed on to be understood, and we might be altogether unable to describe the peculiar charm that has riveted itself so deeply into the imagination; but there was something tangible in these landscapes which the pencil of a painter could seize, and delight even those whose eyes had never rested on an African fringe of palms, or rejoiced in the sunny richness of an African rising day.

On looking over this extent of country and its grandly rolling majestic river, I recalled the famous letter of Amr to the Caliph Omar:—" O, Commander of the Faithful, Egypt is a compound of black earth and green plants, between a pulverised mountain and a red sand. The distance from Syene to the sea is a month's journey for a horseman. Along the valley descends a river, on which the blessing of the Most High reposes both in the morning and the evening, and which rises and falls with the revolutions of the sun and moon. When the annual dispensation of Providence unlocks the springs and fountains that nourish the earth, the Nile rolls his swelling and sounding waters through the realm of Egypt, the fields are overspread by the salutary flood, and the villages communicate with each other in their painted barks. The retreat of the inundation deposits a fertilizing mud for the reception of the various seeds; the crowds of husbandmen who blacken the land may be compared to a swarm of industrious ants, and their native indolence is quickened by the lash of the taskmasters, and the promise of the fruits and flowers of a plentiful increase. Their hope is seldom deceived; but the riches which they extract from the wheat, the barley, and the rice, the fruit-trees and the cattle, are unequally shared between those who labor and those who possess. According to the vicissitudes of the seasons, the face of the country is adorned with a silver wave, a verdant emerald, and the deep yellow of a golden harvest." Assuredly old Amr could wield his pen as deftly as Egypt found that he could wield his sword.

On the eastern side of the range of hills fronting Luxor are the tombs of Abd-el-Goornah, Goornet

Murraee, and the Assasseef, and in a valley to the south, those of the Queens. In the more elaborate of these excavations were deposited the remains of the priests and great private individuals, but the whole of the mountain side is literally one great sepulchre. Almost at every step you come upon mummy pits, either opened or closed; and mummy cloth, and the wretched remains of poor embalmed humanity, are remorselessly thrown about by the plundering Arabs, in their search for curiosities for the collector. In the words of the Psalmist, "The bones are scattered at the grave's mouth, as when one cutteth and cleaveth wood upon the earth," and skulls and hands and feet are soon kicked aside with indifference as one scrambles up the steep ascent. A French writer, whose name I have forgotten, amused me by some very serious animadversions against the mummying system, arguing that nothing could justify the inhabitants of this country in taking from the earth so much of the elements of decomposition, which are necessary for its generative powers.

By referring to the description of the rock tombs of private persons at Benihassan, one will arrive at a very fair idea of the general character of these. The sculptured and painted walls represent the occupations, the trades, the employments, the customs, the amusements, and festivities of the old Egyptians. To use the happy expression of Sir G. Wilkinson, all these delineations did not, except in special cases, refer peculiarly to the inhabitant of the tomb, but were intended to be an "epitome of human life." In fact these tombs were the property of, and constructed by, the priests, and "got up" according to their taste and fancy: and it was during his lifetime that the purchaser saw the tombs which were on hand for sale. There was always a sufficient number to suit his taste and means, and after he had become the happy possessor of his sepulchre, his name, titles, and employments, were inscribed; the name of the king or kings of his time was added, with perhaps a few incidental observations in hieroglyphics. The priests who, like the clergy in other countries —always excepting Great Britain and Ireland— had an eye to the main chance, kept up a kind of reversionary interest in the tomb, either by maintaining some quitrent, or renewal fine, or annual charge for ceremonies; for several of these tombs, owing to the laches of the family of the original proprietor, or perhaps its extinction, seem to have lapsed into the hands of the priests, and to have been sold to a second occupant. We find this out from the stucco that has peeled off the walls, and left exposed the original sculpture of an earlier period.[1] What a paradise for the hierarchy must have been these good old days of the Pharaohs, when only the lands of the priests were left untaxed; "for the priests had a portion assigned them

[1] See Sir G. Wilkinson, *Ancient Egyptians.*

of Pharaoh, and did eat their portion which Pharaoh gave them," and probably drank it too! In those rosy times there were no violent irreligious men to interfere with burial fees of parson, clerk, and sexton; and if they had chosen it, which fortunately they did not, they might have poisoned the air of their metropolis with the exhalations from the dead, without any extramural interment bills to raise up obnoxious opposition cemeteries, on the Assass, or at Goornet Murraee. As for a recalcitrant Dissenter refusing temple rates, or a Nubian insurrection against Egyptian tithes, there are narrow, dark, and massive chambers in every temple, above ground and below ground, where cogent arguments were employed on the slightest infraction of religion, by which expression was of course meant infraction of honest gains, whether in mint or cumin. Poor Mr. Horsman would have had a pleasant time of it then, had he scrutinised too narrowly the income of the dignitary of On, or called for an account of the revenues of the high priests of Thoth and Kneph and Amun, in their respective dioceses.

The scenes and drawings on these tombs throw considerable light on the amount of civilization of the period, and we are surprised by the proficiency of the Egyptians in some rather recondite arts at such an early era. You see actively employed at their various avocations glass-blowers, carpenters, curriers, boat-builders, chariot-makers; sculptors employed in carving a sphinx, and painters elaborately ornamenting mummy cases. Some of the designs of the chairs and vases are of the most graceful and ingenious patterns, worthy of Sevres and the Faubourg St. Antoine. One of the frescoes, representing an entertainment of about 3300 years ago, is worth description.[1] A party is being given at the house of the royal scribe, who, seated with his mother, caresses on his knee the youthful daughter of the sovereign, to whom he had probably been tutor. Women dance to the sound of the guitar in their presence, others place before them vases of flowers and precious ointments; and the guests, seated on handsome chairs, are attended by servants who offer them wine in golden goblets, each having previously been welcomed by the usual ceremony of putting sweet-scented ointment on the head. This was the polite custom of reception. In another of these tombs a servant is represented bringing the ointment in a vase, and putting it on the heads of the guests as well as of the master and mistress of the house. A lotus-flower is also handed to them on their entrance.[2] Elsewhere we have a picture of the arrival of a guest at the house of his entertainer. He comes in his chariot, attended by six running footmen, who carry his sandals, tablet, and stool. He is evidently by way of being fashionable, and has come late, for others are already seated and listening to a band of music composed

---

[1] Sir G. Wilkinson.   [2] Sir G. Wilkinson.

of the harp, guitar, double pipe, lyre, and tamburine, accompanied by female choristers. They too have their bouquets, which seem always to have been presented as a token of welcome on entering the house. Among the Egyptians of old time, the nosegay for the hand, and chaplets of flowers for the head and neck, seem to have answered to the coffee and pipe of modern days—" a far more praiseworthy and odorous custom," I fancy I can hear many English ladies exclaim. There have been found in the neighbourhood of the tombs, some of the wooden images of Osiris which were introduced into these repasts, and originated the poetical expression of the skeleton at the banquet. This image was from one to three feet high, in the form of a human mummy standing erect, or lying on a bier; and it was handed round to each of the guests, warning him of his mortality, and of the transitory state of human pleasures.[1] He was reminded that some day he would be like that figure; that men ought to love one another, and avoid those evils which tend to make them consider life too long, when in reality it is too short; and while enjoying the blessings of this world, to bear in mind that their existence is precarious, and that death, which all ought to be prepared to meet, must eventually close their earthly career. This sentiment, however it may have been perverted elsewhere, was not considered by the old Egyptian

[1] Sir G. Wilkinson.

as an incentive "to eat and drink, for to-morrow we die," but was perfectly consistent with their religious belief, to be reminded that their life was only a lodging, or "inn," on the path of every journeyer, and that their existence here was a preparation for a future state.

One of the tombs we this day visited, behind the Remeseum in the Assasseef, was of immense dimensions, far larger than any of those of the Kings; and, though greatly injured, gave a high idea of its original magnificence, and of the vast wealth that enabled a private individual, not only to accomplish such an excavation out of the solid rock, but to sculpture and adorn so large a superficies.[1] It consists of a series of galleries and chambers, extending to a length of 862 feet; and the area of the actual excavation is 22,217 square feet; and with the chambers of several large pits in it 238,09. From the nature of its plan, the ground it occupies is nearly one acre and a quarter. The owner of this roomy mortuary palace was named Petamunap, and was apparently possessed of unusual influence and consequence, since the granite gateway added by his orders to the temple of Medinet Abou, bears the name of Petamunap alone, amidst buildings in which kings were proud to inscribe their own. The style of the sculptures is, however, inferior to that of an earlier date, and

---

[2] Sir Gardner Wilkinson, *Modern Egypt and Thebes.*—Lepsius' *Letters.*

seems to denote that his era was in all probability about the twenty-sixth dynasty.

Several of these tombs are now occupied by Arabs as dwellings, which circumstance, as may be supposed, neither contributes to their preservation nor to their cleanliness. The tombs of the Kings are fortunately entirely free from all such inflictions. Indeed I may note down this day as the day of evil smells, for some of the tombs were infested by bats, which left behind them an indescribably sour odour; and he who has once been in the haunts of these foul mammalia will not readily forget it; others were thronged with young and old Arabs, not diffusing from their persons or their clothes the balmy gales of Araby the Blest; and, lastly, I bore ever in close contiguity a guide who was perfectly overpowering from his hatred of water, and his love of onions. Perhaps he eat these savory esculents on the principle of Callias (in the banquet of Xenophon), who affirmed that they inspired courage in the field of battle, or, as the only battle in these regions was about *buckshish*, more probably he was acting on the hint of Charonidas, that they were useful to deceive a jealous wife, who, finding her husband return with his mouth smelling of onions, would be induced to believe he had not tenderly saluted any one while from home. Be that as it may be, whether his reasons were military, domestic, or simply gastronomical, he was a perfect nuisance, and rendered the confined atmosphere of some of the tombs so intolerable, that I was obliged to leave them, after a very cursory examination. Perhaps some one asks, Why did you take him in at all with you? For this reason, my dear old lady, or young gentleman, because there are pits gaping most insidiously in some of these sepulchres, and as they are often forty feet deep, it is prudent to avoid the chance of subsiding into such abysses.

We wound up an active day by a visit to the last object on this the western bank of the river—the small Temple of Dayr-el-Medinet, the work of the Ptolemies Philopator and Physcon. It is very insignificant, both in size and interest, compared with the vast buildings we had seen, and the still greater Karnak, to be visited on the morrow; but still the detour to it was well repaid by the circumstance of its having on one of its chambers subjects totally different from any found in the other temples of Thebes, and which represent the trial of the soul after death:—" Osiris seated on his throne awaits the arrival of those souls which are ushered into Amenti (the land of spirits). The four genii stand before him on a lotus-blossom, and the female Cerberus is there, with Harpocrates seated on the crook of Osiris. Thoth, the god of letters, arrives in the presence of the King of Hades, bearing in his hand a tablet on which the actions of the deceased are noted down, while Horus and Aroeris are employed in weighing the good deeds of the judged, against the ostrich feather, the symbol of justice or truth. A cynocephalus ape, the emblem of truth, is seated on the top of the balance. At length comes the deceased, who advances between two figures of the goddess, and bears in his hand the symbol of truth, indicating his meritorious actions and his fitness for admission to the presence of Osiris. The forty-two assessors, seated above in lines, complete the sculptures of the west wall; and all these references to death were perhaps owing to the chamber being dedicated to Osiris, in his peculiar character of judge of the dead."[1]

And thus ended day the third on the Lybian boundaries of Thebes.

As the Arabian story-teller reserves until the last, despite the widely opened eyes and pleading countenances of his listeners, the main catastrophe of his wondrous tale,—on the same principle have I reserved great Karnak and its wonders for the last pages of my account of Thebes.

To give a general idea of the size of this enormous pile of building, together with its appertaining chapels, corridors, pylons, and propylæa, I should

[1] Sir G. Wilkinson.

say roughly, that the area it occupies is, perhaps, not quite as much as Hyde Park bounded by the Serpentine. It is, in a word, the largest building ever known, in which the Coliseum, large as it appears, would fill but a portion of the space.

Here stood the great royal temple of the hundred-gated Thebes, which was dedicated to Amunre, the King of the Gods, and to the peculiar local god of the city of Amun. The whole history of the Egyptian monarchy, after the city of Amun was raised to be one of the two royal residences in the land, is connected with this temple. All dynasties vied in the glory of having contributed their share to the enlargement, embellishment, and restoration of this national sanctuary. It was founded by the powerful King Sesortesen, under the first Theban royal dynasty, between 2600 and 2700 B.C., and still exhibits some ruins in the centre of the building of that period, and bearing the name of this king. During the dynasties immediately succeeding, which for several centuries groaned under the yoke of the victorious hereditary enemy, the Hyksos, or Shepherd Kings, this sanctuary was, no doubt, neglected, and nothing remains connected with that period. But after the first king of the seventeenth dynasty, Amosis, in the seventeenth century B.C., had succeeded in defeating the Hyksos, his two successors, Amunoph I. and Thothmes I., built round the ancient sanctuary a magnificent temple, containing chambers, and a spacious court with pylons or lofty portals, in front of which Thothmes I. erected two obelisks, one of which is still erect, the other prostrate and broken. Two other portals, with contiguous court walls, were built by the same king in the direction of Luxor. Thothmes III. and his sister enlarged this temple to the back, by a hall resting on fifty-six columns. The succeeding kings partly closed the temple more perfectly in front, partly built new independent temples near it, and also placed two more large portals to the south-west, in front of those erected by the first Thothmes; so that now four lofty pylons formed the magnificent entrance to the principal temple on that side. But a far more splendid enlargement of the temple was executed in the fourteenth and fifteenth centuries B.C., by the great Pharaohs of the nineteenth dynasty; for Sethos I. (our handsome monarch of the tombs, and father of Rameses Miamun) added the most gigantic hall of pillars that was ever seen in Egypt or elsewhere. The stone roof supported by 134 columns covered a space of 164 feet in depth, and 320 feet in breadth. Each of the twelve central columns is 36 feet in circumference, and 66 feet high beneath the architraves. The other columns are 40 feet high and 27 feet in circumference. It is impossible to describe the overwhelming impression which is experienced upon entering for the first time into this forest of columns, and wandering from one range into another, between the lofty figures of gods and kings represented on them, projecting sometimes entirely, sometimes only in part. Every surface is covered with various sculptures, now in relief, now sunk, which were, however, only completed by the successors of the builder, most of them, indeed, by his son Rameses Miamun. In front of this pillared hall was placed at a later period, a great open court, 270 feet by 320 feet in extent, decorated on the sides only with colonnades, and entered by a magnificent portal.

The later dynasties now found the principal temples completed on all sides, the entire length being about 2000 feet; and, being also desirous to contribute to the embellishment of this centre of Theban worship, began partly to erect separate small temples on the large level space surrounded by the enclosure wall, and partly to extend these temples externally. The head of the twentieth dynasty, Rameses III., whose campaigns in Asia in the fifteenth century B.C., were scarcely inferior to those of his renowned ancestors, Sethos I. and Rameses II., built a special temple with a court of columns, and a pillared hall above 200 feet long; and he founded at a little distance from it a still larger sanctuary for Chensu, son of Amun, one of the deities especially worshipped at Thebes. We next discern the signature and sculptures of Sheshonk, the warlike King Shishak of the Bible, who conquered Jerusalem about 970 B.C. His Asiatic campaigns are celebrated on the southern external wall of the great temple, where, in the symbolic form of prisoners, he leads 140 vanquished towns and countries before Amun. On his passage into Nubia, Champollion landed for an hour or two before sunset to snatch a hasty view of Karnak; and he at once, amid the various sculptures and heiroglyphics, pointed out among the triumphs of Sheshonk the inscription " Judah Melek Kah," or " King of the country of Judah."

After the termination of the family of the Ramessides, the kingly power was no longer in monarchs of the Theban line, but in those of Lower Egypt. Then came the invasion of the Ethiopians, among whom Shabak and Tarhaka, the So and Tirhaka of the Bible, reigned in Egypt at the commencement of the seventh century B.C. We find the monuments exactly confirming the history of the scriptures. These kings came indeed from Ethiopia, but governed completely in the Egyptian manner, and did not neglect to worship the Egyptian god-kings. Their names are found on several smaller temples of Karnak, and on a splendid colonnade in the great court in front, which seems to have been first placed there by Tirhaka.

According to historical accounts, this Nubian king returned of his own accord to his native country, and left the Egyptian kingdom to its legitimate rulers. The dispossessed Egyptian dynasty now returned to the throne, and once more, in the seventh and sixth centuries, developed all the splendour of which this country, as rich in internal resources as in external power, was capable of producing under a powerful and wise government. It opened for the first time a peaceful intercourse with foreign nations; Greek settlers came in, commerce flourished, and a new and enormous amount of wealth was accumulated, such as before had only been attained by the spoils of war and tribute.

But this flourishing period soon passed away. The storm of the Persians was advancing, and in the year 525, Egypt was conquered by Cambyses, and crushed to the earth with all the ferocity of a barbarian and a madman. During the whole of the Persian sway, we find hardly any addition to the architecture of this country; but when, one hundred years afterwards, Egypt recovered its independence, we again find the names of the native kings in the temples of Karnak; but after three dynasties had rapidly succeeded each other, in a space of sixty-four years, it fell a second time under the dominion of the Persians, who soon afterwards lost it to Alexander of Macedon, in the year 332.

Under the Grecian rule, Egypt still possessed sufficient vigor to retain its religion and institutions in the manner that had been carried down from ancient times. The Ptolemies in all respects took the place and followed in the steps of the ancient Pharaohs. Upper Egypt is richly endowed with Ptolemaic temples; and Karnak also bears testimony, if not to their good taste, at least to their good will. We here find the names of Alexander and Philip Aridæus, who preceded the Ptolemies in restoring that which had been destroyed by the Persians. Alexander rebuilt the sanctuary behind the great temple; Philip that to the front; the Ptolemies added sculptures to it, restored other parts, and even erected entirely new sanctuaries at considerable outlay, though no longer indeed on the grand scale of the Egyptian classic style of older days. Even the last epoch of declining Egypt, that of Roman dominion, is still represented in Karnak by a series of representations which were executed under Cæsar Augustus.

Thus this remarkable spot, which in the course of twenty-five hundred years had increased from the small sanctuary in the centre of the larger temple to a complete city of temples, presents, graved on stone, an almost uninterrupted thread of events, and the history of Egyptian monarchy as it rose and was temporarily obscured, and rose again, until its final decline under the dominion of the Cæsars. The appearance or non-appearance of the dynasties and individual kings in Egyptian history is almost uniform with the representation of them in and round the Temple of Karnak. This is a rough historical sketch of the rise and fall of

Karnak, derived from the resources of Dr. Lepsius, who passed two months in the occupation of one of the chapels of this temple, incessantly employed in copying its hieroglyphics and mapping out its remains.

But, as we are to visit this remarkable structure, let us do so in company with Mr. Bayard Taylor, and we cannot have a more correct or elegant guide:—"We mounted," he says, "and rode to the western or main entrance facing the Nile. The two towers of the propylon—pyramidal masses of solid stone—are 329 feet in length, and the one which is least ruined is nearly 100 feet in height. On each side of the sculptured portal connecting them is a tablet left by the French army, recording the geographical position of the principal Egyptian temples. We passed through and entered an open court, more than 300 feet square, with a corridor of immense pillars on each side connecting it with the towers of the second pylon, nearly as gigantic as the first. A colonnade of lofty shafts leading through the centre of the court, once united the two entrances, but they have all been hurled down, and lie as they fell in long lines of disjointed blocks, except one, which holds its solitary lotus-bell against the sky. Two mutilated colossi of red granite still guard the doorway, whose least stones are 40 feet in length. Climbing over the huge fragments which have fallen from above, and almost blocked up the passage, we looked down into the grand hall of the temple. I knew the dimensions of this hall beforehand; I knew the number and size of the pillars; but I was no more prepared for the reality than those will be who may read this account of it, and afterwards visit Karnak for themselves. Nothing could have compensated me for the loss of that overwhelming confusion of awe, astonishment, and delight, which came upon me like a flood. I looked down an avenue of twelve pillars, six on each side, each of which was 36 feet in circumference, and nearly 80 feet in height. Crushing as were these ponderous masses of sculptured stone, the spreading bell of the lotus-blossom which crowned them, clothed them with an atmosphere of lightness and grace. In front, over another file of colossal blocks, two obelisks rose sharp and clear, with every emblem legible on their polished sides. On each side of the main aisle are seven other rows of columns, 122 in all, each of which is about 50 feet high, and 27 feet in circumference. These have the Osiride form, without capitals, and do not range with the central shafts. In the efforts of the conqueror to overthrow them, two have been hurled from their places, and thrown against the neighbouring ones, where they still lean as if weary with holding up the roof of massive sandstone."

It is questionable whether the overthrow of these columns mentioned by Mr. Taylor be the work of a conqueror or of a native. I am inclined myself to believe that the great devastation of Karnak is to be ascribed to the terrible earthquake in the year 27 B.C., by which, Eusebius says, "Egyptian Thebes was levelled to the ground"—(Thebæ Egyptiacæ usque ad solum dirutæ sunt). The destruction has all the appearance of being the result of accident rather than of intention. In the spot where once rose the famous colonnade alluded to by Mr. Taylor, and where still remains the one beautiful solitary pillar, the remains of its comrades lie as they fell, the round even stones stretched out just like a column of draughtmen upset by children. It is unquestionably the result of a sudden fall, not of a protracted destruction, as it would be were it the work of man. The state of the obelisks of Thothmes II. is another confirmatory proof that the earthquake, and not Cambyses or Lathyrus, was the main cause of the havoc that surrounds you. One of them still stands perfectly uninjured; the other has fallen, and been broken in two apparently by the fall, but is in other respects uninjured. Had a hostile invader been wreaking his vengeance on the devoted sanctuary, he would hardly have spared one obelisk in one place, and another a little farther on, and satisfied himself with pulling down and then leaving unmutilated the other. This prostrate obelisk is 90 feet high, of rose-colored granite, and polished like marble. In consequence of its fall, one is enabled to inspect minutely its execution; and there is hardly any circumstance which so much struck me with the resources of the old Egyptians, as the apparent ease with which they worked this hardest of materials, so that every figure seems rather to have been impressed with a seal than engraven with a chisel. Some of the best judges who have looked closely into the execution of its devices, pronounce that those parts which represent animals in particular are treated with such accuracy and finish as not to be surpassed by the finest cameos of the Greeks.

There is no doubt, however, but that the hand of man has also fallen heavily upon Karnak. Whichever way you direct your footsteps, you meet the traces of the most wanton, energetic, and systematic devastation. A great deal of this is unquestionably owing to the fury of Cambyses, and to the exasperation of Lathyrus against the inhabitants of Thebes during the Ptolemaic period. After a siege of three years he took the town, and then reduced the grand metropolis of Egypt to so deplorable a state that it no longer deserved rank among the cities of that country. Recent excavators have just discovered and taken away some granite statues; arms, legs, and mutilated heads, strew the ground around their former site. An Englishman lately uncovered a beautiful white marble sphinx; and an American, we were informed, broke its nose off, and carried it away as a spoil for the delectation of the free and enlightened citizens of

Jacksonville or Lynchpolis. The learned Dr. Lepsius, the head of the Prussian Egyptian Fine-Art Commission of 1844, if he had not the way, had at all events the spirit of Cambyses, Lathyrus, and Mohammed Ali. On my inquiring as to many statues and ornaments, both in the temples and tombs of the kings, which had the appearance of recent fracture, how this sad fate had overtaken them, my guide invariably replied, that Dr. Lepsius was the enterprising man who had done the deed, and that he had been employed by Lepsius; he, moreover, took a pleasure and a pride in leading one hither and thither to show the handiwork of the energetic Prussian. One feat in particular seemed to create extreme delight and pride, and deserves particular attention. In the beautiful and perfectly preserved tomb called Belzoni's, which might have remained but for modern *virtuosi* an uninjured specimen of the finest and most costly decoration during the best days of Egyptian art, there is one chamber to which I have referred already, with a stone ledge cut out of the solid rock, and running round it. This ledge was most elaborately worked, the richest devices adorned it, and the most brilliant coloring was lavished on its sculptures. Dr. Lepsius required for the Berlin Museum a specimen of this design; and not being content with a plaster model, which would have fully answered the purpose, he has smashed in the most ruthless manner this stone bench, and the ground is strewn with fragments, the result of this wholesale and shameless destruction. A Prussian prince has also signalized himself in the same tomb, by knocking to the ground, either by gunpowder or the crowbar, a column richly painted and decorated with figures, and, as if to level it was his only object, he has not even attempted its removal.

I am quite aware of the justification resorted to by Lepsius and other scientific Attilas: if they did not take away these things, others would; if they did not mutilate whole figures, the Americans would carve their names on them, or break their noses; and, besides, that these objects are of value for scientific inquiry, and on being removed to Europe will be honored and preserved for the benefit of the curious and the learned. This is the exact argument, or words to that effect, employed by Lepsius, when observations were made upon his barbarous spoliations by one of his own countrymen. But such reasoning is perfectly illusory. The Egyptian government would immediately, if representations were made to it by the consuls of the chief powers, protect these monuments from desecration. Since the accession of Abbas Pacha, there has been every wish to do so; therefore it does not in the least follow, that if you do not mutilate, others will. I do not at all pretend to object to the removal of whole and distinct works, such as a sphinx, or obelisk, or statue, and any valuable inscription is perhaps equally fair game. But as for decorations and drawings which can be in no way available for historical or philosophical purposes, of which modern science enables any one to take the most exact copy by means of photography and casts, and of which the colors in general become effaced by the dampness of our northern climates, it is perfectly monstrous to attempt to justify the removal of them, and the wholesale macadamizing that follows. It is the example of men in so high a position as Dr. Lepsius which induces others to follow in their footsteps; and one can characterise such proceedings by no other name, than wanton, barbarous Vandalism.

"Nec meus hic sermo." Nor is this accusation mine only. Were I to be scolded by every friend who reads these pages for the digression, I could not omit to insert the indignant comment of Maxime du Camp, after visiting the Tomb of Sethos, the chief scene of Prussian demolition:—

"De tout ce tombeau magnifique, le plafond seul est resté intact. Ses murailles morcelées, ses legendes mutilées, ses cartouches effacés, ses piliers renversés, ses dieux et ses rois grattés n'en font plus a cette heure qu'une ruine lamentable. *Un homme a fait tout cela.* Un jour il est venu suivi par une bande de dessinateurs et il a copié les sculptures de ce sepulcre—a mesure qu'une inscription etait inscrite, qu'un dieu etait decalqué, qu'un Pharaon etait estampé, on refait l'inscription, on brisait le dieu, on abattait le Pharaon. Seul et mieux qu'une armée de barbares, il s'est rué sur ce monument. A travers ses galeries, ses chambres, ses couloirs et dans le stupide interêt de sa vanité imbecile, il a tout detruit. C'est un savant! Il n'a pas voulu que d'autres après lui pussent lire là ou il avait lu, pussent comprendre là ou il avait compris. Un jour viendra, sans doute, où il publiera sa decouverte, où il expliquera les hieroglyphes du tombeau de Meneptha Sethei I'. Ce jour la nous serons en droit de lui dire, 'Nous ne vous croyons pas! On sont vos points de contrôle? On sont vos textes, vos inscriptions, vos legendes, vos cartouches? ils ont disparu; ce que vous nous montrez aujourd'hui est au moins apocryphe; vous inventez car vous ne pouvez pas prouver; votre erudition est fausse; vous mentez.'

"Si jamais ce pauvre homme retourne en Egypt, et s'il va visiter les grottes de Biban-el-Molouk, il sentira un frisson agiter ses chairs, lorsqu'il entrera dans ces lieux ou il a poussé sa devastation puerilement interessée,—sur tous les murs il lira son nom maudit en toutes les langues; chaque voyageur a laissé contre lui un anathême qui portera ses fruits, car Dieu est juste.

"Tu sais, cher Theophile, qui je ne suis pas de ceux qui croient ingenument que la France est le plus beau pays du monde, et que le peuple Français est le seul peuple intelligent de l'univers, mais je te jure que j'ai été heureux de savoir que ce misérable porte un nom Allemand, et qu'il est né aù delà du Rhin. Au reste, partout ou il a passé, il a mutilé. Au temples d'el Assassif, de Denderah, de Karnac, d'Abydos, aux hypogécs de Syout et de Goornah; au tombeau de Sakara et des Pyramides, partout ses mains ont martelé avec une desastreuse intelligence; cela est bien raisonné au point de vue de sa mediocre ambition, car à cette heure que sagement pour lui il a aneanti les preuves d'une discussion sérieuse, il sait bien que nul ne pourra lui prouver son ignorance et l'inanité de ses travaux."

I am delighted with the just anger of the French writer, and think his congratulations to his friend Theophilus on their countrymen being free from the stain of this havoc, to be most natural and proper; but I fear he was not informed that Monsieur Champollion was the first of the moderns to set the example of pillage, by hewing off and carrying away the beautiful groups at the base of the second staircase, in the same tomb.

But to return to Karnak. For hours, literally for hours, you wander to and fro, endeavouring in some manner to grasp a conception of its former glory. You go from hall to hall, from portal to portal, from propylæa to propylæa, and you try to figure to yourself, what must have been its original majestic structure when these grand columns were intact, when the graceful obelisks pierced the clear air, when the massive roof closed over the brightly tinted stone pictures, when the approach to the temple was through the granite statues of multiform gods, and when a broad avenue of human and ram-headed sphinxes flanked the way for more than a mile and a half to the consort temple of Amunoph at Luxor. Were these great piles merely edifices of mute stone, they would be sufficient to excite our astonishment at the power, determination, and industry of the nation that had transported from afar, and reared such masses; but our astonishment gives way to admiration, when we inspect the details; when every pillar bears on it the effigies of kings and gods, with their symbols and attendants; when every roof is covered with carved and colored mystical devices; every wall presenting the aspect of fierce battles, triumphs, and processions; and, more than all, when every portion of the building in hieroglyphic pictures tells with stony loquacity the history of its founder, his wars and conquests, his pious care of the gods, and the gods' reciprocal benignity to him. I believe I may with safety say, that not a stone presented its surface to the view throughout the whole of Karnak, that was not more or less carved and decorated, except where it formed the necessary space between other decorations.

It is needless to enter into any scientific or learned descriptions of the various nations whom the Pharaohs are combating on the walls. The scenes are of the same kind as those represented on the Rameseum, and the Medinet Abou temple.

In one place the king fights and wounds with his arrows the chief of his enemies; elsewhere he has alighted from his chariot, and is engaged hand-in-hand; with one foot he stands upon a prostrate foe, and seizes him by the hair of the head. He is everywhere in the van, whether on foot or in his chariot, leading and cheering on his forces. Among the names of the nations conquered by Sethos, the most remarkable are those of Kanana, or Canaan; and in another place the sculptures represent a woody and mountainous country covered with trees like cedars, of which hieroglyphics tell us the name was Lemanon, in all probability Lebanon; but to us the most remarkable drawing is that of the victorious campaign of Sheshonk into Judea, referred to before.

After passing a whole day within the circuit of Karnak, we were getting ready for our return, when an amusing incident closed the proceedings. I had wandered by myself some way, and left my friend sketching an outline of the main buildings. A jackal passed within a few yards of me, taking a direction which enabled him to cut the beast off from his destination. The signal of a whistle and a wave of the hand, showed him that game was on foot, and away he went at racing pace; one bang and then another intimated that mischief was done, and the loud shout of Arabs and attendants convinced me the jackal had the worst of it. On rushing to the scene of action, I found my friend holding the struggling animal by the tail, while the bystanders heaved huge hieroglyphics at his head. When the noise subsided, Mr. K. informed me, that he had, after wounding his antagonist, seized him by the tail, and in so doing tumbled down; whereupon the jackal caught him in return by the leg, and as proof he exhibited the bleeding member, which, as well as his gunstock, bore marks of the encounter. There was not much harm done, but the leg has been slow in healing, and I watch diurnally the first symptoms of *rabies canina*, or, to translate it freely, jackal madness; for my friend, with the stern self-devotion of a Briton, has volunteered to be shot on its appearance. That last sad office is, however, reserved for the dragoman, as I have positively refused to imbue my hands with the blood of a fellow-countryman.

Greatly refreshed and cheered by this episode, we returned to Luxor, examined the Temple of Amunoph, the beautiful granite obelisk that stands before it, and the colossal granite statues of Rameses II., now almost buried beneath the earth. The fellow to this obelisk adorns the Carousel, in Paris; and, as its hieroglyphics have no doubt met every one's eye that reads these pages, this is their purport and interpretation:—" Rameses Amun Mai, Lord of Upper and Lower Egypt, son of the male and female deities, lord of the world, sure guardian of truth, approved by the sun, has made these works for his father Amun Re, and has erected these two great obelisks in hard stone before the Rameseum of the city of Amun." This obelisk was cut at the granite quarries of Syene, 138 miles distant, about the year B.C. 1570. His descendant Rameses III. added his name also, and some inscriptions, of which the purport is—"Thy name is firm as heaven, the duration of thy days is as the disk of the sun." The temple itself is a magnificent building, apparently in good preservation, but so built around by houses, by which its columns are utilised, and so choked up by sand and rubbish, that it is difficult to ascertain its extent.

It was constructed by Amunoph III., one of the most powerful Pharaohs of the eighteenth century, who had only built a side temple at Karnak, and had added but little to the principal temple there. In return, however, he erected here a splendid sanctuary to Amun, which Rameses the Great enlarged still more by an extensive court in front, in the direction of Karnak; and indeed, although distant a good half-hour from it, this temple must also be regarded as belonging to the space dedicated from ancient times to the great national sanctuary. This is proved by the circumstance, that the temple, though situated close to the Nile bank, has its entrance, contrary to custom, away from the river, and directed towards Karnak, with which, besides, it was immediately connected by colonnades, massive stone causeways, and the great avenue of ram and human-headed sphinxes to which I have before alluded. We paid our consul a visit, and had pipes and coffee in his house, which was cool, comfortable, and spacious, constituting as it does a portion of the temple. The Romans have utilised another portion, a little further on, having converted it into a hall of justice; and some very curious pictures and ornamental frescoes by them, still remain upon its walls, in copying which Sir Gardner Wilkinson, then at Thebes, received a sun-stroke, and was extremely weak and unwell in consequence.

I must here take the opportunity of paying Sir Gardner, not a just compliment, but a just tribute as to the excellence of his works on Egypt, and their scrupulous fidelity. His hand-book is just what it should be—a correct detail of what should be seen, witha s short, accurate, and, for a hand-book, as agreeable an account as possible of the principal objects worth visiting. His *Ancient Egyptians* is remarkable for its deep research, which leaves nothing connected with the manners and customs of this wonderful people unexplained. I believe subsequent investigation has altered his views as to Egyptian chronology, for the light which has now streamed in on the darkness of Egyptian early history was comparatively faint when he began to write. His Arabic vocabulary is the only one in English, that I have yet met with, which is in the least degree serviceable for Egypt, as, by attending to his rules, much of the difficulty of Arabic pronunciation may be overcome. His advice on all subjects respecting the equipment of the Nile traveller is excellent; and the whole book is as free from the jargon of would-be scientific and abstruse writers as the nature of the subjects treated can possibly allow.

Our consul we found to be a very excellent and obliging fellow, much better than he looked, being notable, although an Arab, for his swarthiness, and for the loss of his nose, which gave him rather the appearance of one of the colossi of the plain. He had letters and newspapers for us, and offered to obtain anything we required; but we were in the proud position of wanting nothing, except castor oil, of which useful medicine the consulate was minus. Instead of it he offered us our choice out of an accumulation of pills, to which it would appear that every passing invalid, no matter what his malady, had added his contribution out of his peculiar stock. Mustapha is the only consul here; and it is no small object to attain that dignity. With the union-jack flying from the columns of the temple of Amunoph, he bids defiance to beys and pachas, before whose desolating presence he would otherwise have to fall and lick the dust. His trading vessels go to and from Alexandria, without being deprived of half their crew, and left helpless on a sandbank, as it often occurs, if any wandering Turkish dignitary is in want of sailors. His men till his ground, and no conscription drags them to the wars. He is fearless of exactions and extraordinary infringements on his purse; and he has the proud satisfaction of superintending the administration of the bastinado, when any reis or boatman dare, in a moment of exuberance produced by arraki or hashish, to be saucy to the lordly wanderer from perfidious Albion.

But now home to bed. O, busy and most inquisitive Howadgi! Enough of mummied cats and vases and modern antiques hast thou purchased in these thy first soft days of virtuosohood. Too many ill-flavored bats hast thou roused from slumbers with thy intrusive torch. Sufficient skin has been abrased from thy shins as thou hast stumbled over blocks and columns; thou art, like Moses, wise in all the learning of the Egyptians, and knowest that a goose means the sun, and that a vulture denotes affection; long hast thou dallied with sweet Athor, moon-horned goddess, and formed acquaintance with her contemporary gods of evil favor and lineaments grotesque. Beware therefore, beware, if old Doubly Beautiful, anxious to reward thy antiquarian rummagings with savory meats, presents to thee a banquet difficult of digestion; for if so, assuredly this night the hawk-headed Thoth will sit above thy head, and expound to thee hieroglyphics, and the four-and-twenty genii of Amenti will assess peccant mummies on thy breast; and the ape symbol of truth will squat upon thy feet, and glare at thee if thou hast exaggerated or colored in this thy narrative; and Savak, crocodile-headed deity, will clamor and gibber at thee for *buckshish;* and Anubis, with foxy head and pricked-up prying foxy ears, will examine thy sides to take out thy interiors and embalm thee for seventy days. Off—off to bed, I say; for a north wind is rustling about the *Flea*, and a voice within thee whispers like a siren's song, "The south, the south! the golden-sanded, peaceful, gentle south! Away southwards—ever southwards. To the south! To the south!"

On the morning of the 2nd of February we weighed anchor; but the breeze of the night before falsified its promise, and after a long and weary walk in search of some small sphinxes, which we heard had been dug up in the neighborhood, but which Mustafa Pacha had carried off, we passed the night beneath an extensive sugar factory of the same grandee, in the vicinity of Erment, the ancient Hermonthis. The temple in existence is another of the buildings of Cleopatra, who is there represented, together with Cæsarion, as at Dendera. It is but a small building, which was originally attached to the large temple, which is no longer standing, and is another of those *mammeisi*, or lying-in houses, to which I have already alluded. Mustafa Pacha has, I understand, employed the best part of the large temple in the erection of his sugar fabric.

On the 3rd we got to Esné, and visited the

temple, which is interesting, being well preserved. We read on the portico and columns the names of some of the early Roman emperors in hieroglyphics; but we did not have an evening performance of the Ghawazi, or dancing-girls, for which this place is pre-eminently famous, for we saw the sirens occupied in a cleanly but still a repugnant operation—that of freeing each other's heads from certain encumbrances towards which we hold European prejudices, and our hearts became frozen against them. We consoled ourselves instead by dining on board a hospitable British boat, which had put into port at the same time, and where we had the company of a fair hostess—snowy fair to our eyes long accustomed to dusky charms growing duskier every day.

The next day we profited by the calm that still prevailed, and paid a visit to the really grand temple of Edfou, which, from its size and preservation, deserves a more than passing mention. It is of peculiar value, moreover, to one who has just left the shattered and somewhat confused masses of Theban structure; for it is so little injured by time and man, that it exactly fits itself to the various blanks that must be filled up, ere the mind completely grasps the idea of the Egyptian temple. This edifice is also of comparatively recent date, being founded by Ptolemy Philometer, and completed by

Physcon, or Energetes II., by Lathyrus the destroyer of Thebes, and by Alexander. The first impression on casting one's eye over the great size and solidity of the building, is that of its strength as a citadel, either to resist attack, or to repress revolt; for at a time when 13-inch shells and 64-pounders were unknown, a fortification such as this would have been a serious undertaking to reduce. It was dedicated to Horus, and to Athor, who is here in one place called the "Queen of Men and Women." Horus, as a child, is represented naked, as are all children on monuments, with his finger on the mouth. The Romans, not understanding the meaning of the title of this god, called him Harpocrates, but his real name is here written in full, Har-pe-Chroti, which means in the old Egyptian tongue, "Horus the child." They also misunderstood the gestures of the child that cannot speak, and converted him into the "god of silence," considering the finger on the mouth to intimate perpetual taciturnity. We certainly heartily wished that his influence in the Roman sense might still preside over this his peculiar sanctuary; for we were tormented incessantly by crowds of little naked vagabonds, until, to take refuge from them, we mounted by an excellent staircase, with various chambers leading from it, to the summit of its lordly propylæa. We here passed a considerable time looking down on the wide plain below, and the Arab town beneath our feet. The house of the

Turkish Governor rose high above the rest, and in its open verandahs we saw the gay dresses of attendants, and blue-shirted suitors waiting patiently for the presence of the great man. A prettily adorned mosque, with its white minarets, contrasted well with the mud square dwellings of the villagers; pigeon-houses were scattered here and there crenelated with earthern pots; too inquisitive spyglasses might have peered into the interior of peasants' hareems through the interstices of mat roofings; for slaters would be at a discount in this rainless district. Dogs were lazily basking in the sun wherever a friendly beam gave unusual solidity to these coverings, and muddy colored naked children were rolling on the heaps of broken pottery and rubbish which cover the site of ancient Apollinopolis. Behind us far extended the noble pillared court of the temple, and its covered chambers, which now constitute a portion of the village, providentially, perhaps, to save it from mutilation until Egypt falls into better hands, when it will emerge from its present superincumbent mud covering, and be the most perfect representation of Ptolemaic Egyptian architecture.

Among many names, most of them unknown to fame, scratched on the sandstone summit of the propylæa, we recognized those of some of the earlier explorers whose labors have directed attention to the historical remains on the Nile's bank: Belzoni, Irby and Mangles, and Caillaud, have all recorded their visit; but perhaps the most interesting signature was that of a young French officer of the 22nd Légère, dated 1799; for it recalled the expedition of the two *colonnes mobiles* commanded by Dessaix, in pursuit at that moment of the Memlook Mourad Bey. After thoroughly enjoying the view and the clear dustless breeze, we descended from our lofty post, and examined the temple carefully, as far as the encumbrance of potsherds, and the Arab village, would permit us; and, as the Egyptian Government have given some sign of life by clearing the temples of Dendera and Esné, one may indulge the hope of seeing at some time or another this noble building freed from all its disfigurements.

The fine propylæa which adorn the entrance to this temple, and the spacious open court with corridors, supported by twenty-two lotus-headed columns of great size, give it a superiority to Dendera, as far as first appearance is concerned; and it yet remains to be proved whether the interior be not equally elaborate. The exterior of the propylæa, instead of being adorned, as those at Thebes, with battles and profusion of sculpture, is more simple, but not the less impressive, being engraved in three tiers, the two uppermost consisting of gigantic figures of the king presenting offerings to the gods. On the lowest tier of all he is seen with outstretched mace holding prisoners by the hair, who raise up their hands for mercy. A bird of victory like an eagle hovers over him. The interior and the sides of the propylæa are similarly adorned, absurdly enough no doubt, as far as Ptolemies aping Pharaohs in dress and actions are concerned, but with an effect superior, in my opinion, to the minute details of the older architecture.

The afternoon of this day was marked in our Nile almanack with a white stone; for as a pelican was gravely looking at his reflection in the river, and perhaps pitying other birds for not having so large a beak as himself, a lucky ball from my rifle laid him low. It was a fine sight to see him fall on his portly back with outstretched feet, in the attitude of the horrified ducks in *Punch* when they behold the peapods first bursting open, and revealing to their view the deadly vision of green peas. A universal cry of "Tayib, Tayib!" "Wallah, Yallah!" and other exclamations of delight in Arabic and Nubian, proceeded from the crew. Out went the sandal, and the large bird was brought on board. The sailors begged the bag of his beak to form the drum of their *dharabuka*, and also requested permission to eat him, both of which demands were accorded; the latter, however, not without some allusions on our part to some persons straining at gnats and swallowing camels, referring to their abhorrence of ham, and affection for pelican. I secured the pad of the breast, which was as soft as grebe, in hopes of getting enough from other specimens to form a lady's muff; but we only shot one other of these birds, and he was too old for the purpose. Some of the flesh was sent up for breakfast; it was dark colored, and not bad; but it would have amused a third person to watch our mutual devices by commendations of its extreme excellence, to persuade each other to feed heartily upon it. The crew's repast was worthy of Vitellius; they picked pelican, body and bones, and on the strength of such perfect happiness, they broke forth into singing, and this is a translation of a portion of their melody:—

"Miss! I am thy slave. Thy hair is long and makes me sick with love. I have lost my sleep on account of thee. O my eye! When she dances, she dances well, and her hip movement is lithesome as a serpent!"

Chorus.—" On account of thee I have not slept. Go away, O thou of the evil eye, and leave us at peace! O, Cairene miss, place thy mosquito-net over us, that we may sleep! Cover thy face and eyes, that I may not see them: they make me sick with love!"

But now at last the north wind blew fair and free; and leaving Gebel Silsileh and its sandstone excavations unvisited, and flying quickly by Kom

Ombo temple, perched proudly on an eminence above the Nile, the only Egyptian temple thus reared aloft, we found ourselves one evening at the rocky entrance of Assouan, the old Syene, the limit between Egypt and Nubia. When morning dawned we were safely moored opposite craggy Elephantina, with five European boats in company, all but one with their prow homeward turned. The shore was busy with the various crews; and vendors of clubs from Sennaar, spears from Kordofan, ladies' trinkets and adornments from inner Africa, and baskets and daggers from the Nubian neighborhood, crowded about the boat. A caravan has arrived from the interior with bales of gum and elephants' teeth, and its swarthy guides were rejoicing around their merchandise in the first fruition of Egyptian fleshpots.

And now came the chief difficulty of our Nile journey—the mounting of the cataracts. To overcome this it is necessary to have the services of certain worthies called the Reises of the Cataract. They are at present four in number, and each in turn, attended by his merry men, takes charge of the boat committed to his care. Puffed up and elated by the unwonted prosperity of a continually increasing influx of travellers, these good folks have correspondingly increased their demands. A couple of pounds used to be the charge; now, however, it ranges from four or five to eight or ten. As our boat was small we expected to get off for the lowest price, and despatched our own reis to bargain and do battle with the formidable chief. He returned in the morning, and announced that for about £4. 10s. we should be taken up the next day. We therefore employed our time in visiting the granite quarries, which are interesting, as showing the birthplace of the red granite obelisks of Heliopolis and Thebes, and of many of the great colossal figures interspersed throughout Egypt, of red and dark-colored granite, for granite of every hue and grain abounds in this locality.

The conception I had entertained of these quarries was very different from their actual appearance. I figured to myself a fine granite mountain something like Killina, near Dublin, with deep precipitous cuttings in its sides. Nothing can be more dissimilar from the reality. The granite quarries are situated in a large plain, from which large masses of stone crop up every here and there, but only to an inconsiderable height—so inconsiderable indeed, that all the larger blocks are cut out longitudinally and not vertically. An immense unfinished obelisk is lying as it was originally worked; and some idea of the magnitude of the blocks may be conceived from its size, 117 feet long and 36 feet broad. The whole neighborhood bears traces of indefatigable industry; and the marks of the holes cut for the wedge seem as if only waiting for the return of the workmen from their dinner. The old method of cutting off the stone is curious.

They appear to have used wooden wedges as in India, which, being firmly driven into holes to receive them along the whole line of the stone, were then saturated with water and broke it off by their equal pressure.[1] This, then, was the inexhaustible deposit which for a space of eight hundred miles from Assouan to Alexandria, adorned the temples and palaces with obelisks and statues, lined the interior passages of some pyramids, and formed the external casing of others.

In the evening it blew a hurricane, and a few drops of rain, not dropping like the gentle dew from heaven, but spiteful and causing the sensation called pins and needles, beat into our faces as we crossed to the island of Elephantina. The storm now swept grandly over the Lybian girdle, and from the Santon's white monument on the western peak the sand-drifts clouded the sky with a deep lurid glare. Half stifled, we climbed up to the highest point of the island, and looked up the river. The sun was descending, not gently as is his wont, lingering and sad to leave the country that he loves, even for a period, but with the fierce angry glare of a baffled retreating foe. The usually calm surface of the Nile was broken up into short breakers, which were dashing over granite islands with which the channel is now encumbered. These islands are

[1] Sir G. Wilkinson.

composed of huge dark rocks, which look Plutonic, and as having been fused by the heat of ages; but above them, greenly waving, are mimosa bushes, and an occasional palm, not the less dear to the eye from its loneliness, shed its verdure over the arid rock. It was an angry, vengeful night, and we tossed and creaked against the shore.

Since my return to England I have seen a letter in the *Times*, under the head of "It never rains in Egypt," in which the writer contrasts an account of a heavy fall of rain at Alexandria with the assertion of Sir Archibald Alison, that "it never rains in Egypt," and that "it is said, no rain has fallen in that country for 1700 years." A more inexcusably careless statement I cannot well conceive than that of the historian. At Alexandria rain is by no means an uncommon occurrence; at Cairo it is much less frequent; in Upper Egypt and Nubia, it seldom falls. During my stay in Cairo, between the 20th and 30th of December, there was a heavy fall of rain during the whole of one night; and on alluding to the circumstance, I was informed that sometimes the streets are perfectly muddy from rain, and that it is a subject of much amusement to the more strongly shod Europeans to watch the Egyptians, especially the ladies, in gorgeous red and yellow papooshes, sliding about or even literally stuck in the mud. This casualty, however, but rarely occurs. Sir A. Alison may have been deceived by the statement of Herodotus, who says that a shower of rain at Thebes was one of the prodigies that portended the fall of Psammenitus, for he adds,[1] that the Thebans related that rain had never before fallen up to the era of that monarch, nor since then till the time of his own visit; or he may have heard the Arab saying, "that when Jacob lost Benjamin he cursed the land of Misraim, declaring it should never know rain; Joseph, on the other hand, blessed it, promising that it should never want water." It is strange enough that Herodotus, who generally had his eyes open, should have been so misled; for as he, no doubt, visited the tombs of the kings at Thebes, he would have seen, in the most remarkable of all these tombs, that of Sethos I., a precaution to avoid the inroad of rain-water, in the shape of a deep pit sunk before the second entrance, the filling up of which by Belzoni caused serious damage to this most beautiful monument, by the irruption of a torrent some years ago. He would also have remarked, as there is but little reason to believe that any change has since taken place in the Egyptian climate, the deep water-worn gullies on the side of the hills flanking the desolate valley leading to these tombs. The precautions taken in the Egyp-

---

[1] Herod. iii. 10:—ἐπὶ Ψαμμηνίτου δὲ τοῦ Ἀμάσιος βασιλεύοντος Αἰγύπτου, φάσμα Αἰγυπτίοισι μέγιστον δὴ ἐγένετο· ὕσθησαν γὰρ Θῆβαι αἱ Αἰγύπτιαι, οὔτε, πρότερον οὐδαμᾶ ὑσθεῖσαι, οὔτε ὕστερον τὸ μέχρι ἐμέν, ὡς λέγουσι αὐτοὶ Θηβαῖοι· οὐ γὰρ δὴ ὕεται τα ἄνω τῆς Αἰγύπτου τὸ παράπαν· ἀλλὰ καὶ τότε ὕσθησαν αἱ Θῆβαι ψακάδι.

tian temples to avoid the effects of rain on the colorings of the ceilings, show that it was an occurrence necessary to be guarded against, even in the upper country. Where the large blocks met there was often a groove cut, and a fresh block laid over the joining, to prevent the possibility of wet penetrating: a proceeding involving both time and trouble, although such considerations were but little regarded by the old inhabitants of the Nile valley. But, even more than this, the fine lion-headed gutters or spouts for carrying off the water from the roof of the Temple of Dendera, show that at a distance of not fifty miles from Thebes, and as far back as the time of Cleopatra, a downpour of rain was a casualty not to be overlooked. The same appendages I have also remarked in one of the Nubian temples. This little digression is *à-propos* to the shower we experienced at Assouan.

I inquired in the evening whether fever was at any time of the year prevalent in the vicinity of the cataracts; my reason for making the inquiry arose from the black appearance of the huge granite rocks which I had remarked in the cataracts during the day; for I remembered Humboldt's noticing the same fact in his description of the cataracts of the Orinoco, and his mentioning that the missionaries, as well as the natives, attributed the most noxious effects to these black rocks—*laxas negras*—

as they are called. I could not, however, ascertain that there was any prejudice against them. Humboldt observes that the phenomenon of the brownish black crust, which gives these rocks, when they have a globular form, the appearance of meteoric stones, does not belong to the cataracts of the Orinoco alone, but is found in both hemispheres; and he instances the Nile cataract of Assouan, and the rapids of the river Congo, as having the same appearance. The mud of the river is not the cause of this discoloration, but the action of oxides of iron and manganese. "Can it be," says the celebrated traveller, "that under the influence of excessive heat and constant humidity, the black crusts of the granitic rocks are capable of acting upon the ambient air, and producing miasmata with a triple basis of carbon, azote, and hydrogen? This I doubt," he adds, and proceeds to account for the malaria, only because these rocks retain a very elevated temperature during the night. After all, however, as I could not trace the slightest apprehension of insalubrity among the dwellers on the Shellal (or cataract) even in this burning climate, I am inclined to think that the black rocks have got a bad reputation most undeservedly.

Our crew had obtained leave to visit their Nubian relatives, who were scattered in the villages around, on the strict promise of returning with the dawn. At the dawn they came accordingly, and made obeisance, and then we got ready to go up the cataract. But if travellers propose, reises dispose; and our reis had two wives at hand: the first of whom he visited the night before, and the same compliment had to be paid to madam number two. The wind was blowing strong certainly, but still favorably, nevertheless our reis insisted that no sane human being would face the fearful dangers we had to encounter in such a storm. We protested, but in vain, and the reis cut short the argument by departing to the sweet company of the second Mrs. Ali. Having nothing better to do, we proposed a walk to Philæ, by the side of the cataract, the better to reconnoitre the horrors of the passage. Mr. Nisnas, the Nubian boy, volunteered his attendance; and having dressed himself in the great magnificence of a new blue shirt, and a clean turban, he proudly stalked before us gun in hand, displaying with much arrogance his finery to other little vulgar boys, among whom in his days of earlier youth and innocence he had rolled in the dirt, and cried for *buckshish*. The path winded along the side of the low broken rock-encumbered river, by the base of sterile granite crags; but at last we came to an oasis among all this aridity—a village embowered in palms and mimosas, with green rich crops of early corn, and green rich grass threading its little path through the hard soil, marking as it went the passage of the water-course, and slender trickling rill. It was a spot well calculated to charm and refresh the eye, parched with the glare of sand, and wearied with hot, burnished, refracting rock. In this village dwelt the friends of Nisnas. The naked children held aloof, awestruck at his blue shirt; but aged women and maidens rushed forth and embraced him fervently. We stood by serenely pleased with the sight of the dark Penelopes welcoming their restored Telemachus; but the face of Nisnas had upon it an expression of bore, and perhaps of annoyance, while with low plaintive chuckling, "con voce chioccia," as Dante calls it,[1] expressing their sympathy with the dangers he had encountered, they kissed him again and again, and welcomed him to his Nubian home after his toils and wanderings. When the chuckling and kissing was over, we proceeded onwards ever in search of the rush of waters, and the perilous fall, through which, by their own account, so many brave travellers had escaped destruction, by providential interference only. We also remembered what Cicero had narrated in his dream of Scipio, that the Nile at the cataracts precipitated itself from the loftiest mountains, and with such a roar that the inhabitants of its banks in that neighbourhood are deprived of the sense of hearing.

In Burckhardt's later days, however, this scene of terror was removed somewhat further, and he

---

[1] *Inferno*, canto vii. 2.

was informed that at Wady Halfa, the Second Cataract, the waters fell down as if from heaven; and Curtis, he whose sweet prose poem of *Nile Notes* had been ever urging us to the shores of Africa, wrote as follows, and his words were graven on our memory:—"The *Ibis* went up the cataract. We were on the seething struggle between two powers —narrow and swift, and dark and still, like a king flying from a terrible triumph, flowed our royal river. Huge hills of rugged rock impended; boulders lay in the water; white sand shored the stream, stretching sometimes among the rocks in short sweeps, whose dazzling white contrasted intensely with the dark barriers of death. High on a rocky peak glared a sheikh's white tomb, the death's head in that feast of terrible fascination and delight, and smoothly sheering precipices below gave Hope no ledge to grasp in falling, but let it slip and slide inevitably into the black gulf beneath. The wreck of a *dahabieh* lay high lifted upon the rocks in the water against the base of the cliff, its sycamore ribs white-rotting like skeletons hung for horror and warning around the entrance of Castle Despair. Every instant the combinations changed, so narrow was the channel, and every moment the scenery was more savage..... Black irregular mounds, and hills and regularly layered rocks, rise and slope, and threaten all around. Down the steep sides of the mountain, now here reaching the river, like a headlong plunge of disordered cavalry, roll fragments of stone of every size and shape. Like serried fronts immovable, breasting the burden, the black smooth precipices stand in the rushing stream; there, pile upon pile, fantastic, picturesque, strange, but never sublime, like foes lifted upon foes to behold the combat, the intricate forms of rock crowd along the shore. It is the desert's enthusiastic descent—its frenzied charge of death or victory—confusion confounded, desolated desolation, never sublime, yet always solemn, with a sense of fate in the sweet rushing waters, that creates a sombre interest, not all inhuman, but akin to dramatic interest." Prave 'ords these—Mr. Curtis! Would that I could add my testimony to their accuracy; for it is pleasant to narrate over a Christmas fire, to listening friends, the days of danger, nights of waking, through which one has in safety passed! But I am bound in sober truth to say that the inhabitants are not deaf from the roar of waters, according to Cicero; for they too well heard the fierce abuse they received, in return for their pestering for *buckshish*, and they fled incontinently; nor are there precipices, save when the strong current is over, and the river sleeps calmly as a millpond—in short, the whole cataract is nothing more than a succession of rapids, which a Shannon-boatman at Castle Connell would laugh to scorn. Its fall does not exceed five or six feet. "The general fall of the Nile through Egypt, below the cataracts, is about five inches to a mile, which gives about three hundred feet from Assouan to Rosetta."[1]

Carefully but with painful interest we inspected every reach, every nook and turn of the river, with the same feeling as we regard the fatal instruments on the dentist's shelf, which tell a tale of suffering of those who came before us, and of our own yet to come. At length, to our surprise and relief, Philæ, with its graceful columns and temples and arcades, stood right out of the river before our eyes; a European *dahabieh* was moored beneath it, and we knew the maximum of our danger, which was the minimum of our fears. On board this *dahabieh* was a hospitable host, and a drouthy assemblage of ladies and gentlemen, who had come by the short way from Assouan to make a morning call. A noble lunch was on the spacious board of the spacious cabin; champagne had been cooled in porous vessels of earthenware, and as they drank it, both they that were going up, and they that were going down, laughed in mockery at all the cataracts.

After lying there idly for two days, on the third we confidently expected a start; but again our reis, still fettered, I presume, by the ties of connubial affection, made excuses, and alleged the unwillingness, or inability, or extreme pressure of business on the part of the great man, the Reis of the Cata-

[1] Sir G. Wilkinson.

ract, and after that statement, departed to his home. Here were now three days uselessly wasted, but on the fourth we declared we would stand it no longer, and insisted on moving to the first gate of the cataract, and there sending for the mysterious being, the reis of the waterfall, whose name sounded in sombre tones like the Wizard of the Glen, or the Fiend of the Wolf's Cave, in some German tale of legendary romance.

We slipped from our moorings, and ran along with a fine breeze to the first pass, where we were assured he would be before us, but that he could not come and pay his respects to us at Assouan in consequence of some little difference of opinion between himself and the governor, who had been looking out for him for some time, to catch him, and bring the knotty point to an issue. To the gate then, as it is called, or first rapid, we came, closely followed by another boat, which, as having arrived before us at Assouan, had the right of priority. But no great man and his attendant satellites were there to haul us up, and a rumour reached the boat that the governor had descended with armed men and *posse comitatus* during the night, and was at that moment delivering to unwilling listeners a lecture on that somewhat confused subject, Egyptian finance. The dragoman of the other boat, a man of energy and suited to emergencies like these, proposed to its English proprietors to proceed to the reis's village, and there expound European notions as to the unpleasantness of such delays, and to lay, moreover, before the governor the Sultan's firman, compelling instant attention to its owner's will, like the magic ring of oriental tales. Away they went, master and dragoman, and after some hours returned bringing with them the great reis, whom we now saw face to face, and a necessary number of his followers.

We had fancied to ourselves this potentate of the rapids to be an aged, calm, and venerable man, such as the effigy of the God Tiber, or Father Thames, and in the eye of imagination we saw him descending the Arabian hill with flowing snowy beard, and a young uprooted palm-tree on his shoulder. Anticipations are, however, generally fallacious, and so were ours, when a great brawny, middle-aged, ill-favored Nubian jumped on board, and after jabbering and mumbling for a full hour in a most ungodlike, unpatriarchal manner, proceeded to haul us up the first obstruction. A good pull, a little pushing and poling, got us up comfortably enough, and then the cataract reis departed home again, although the sun was still high, leaving a request that we should have coffee and pipes ready for him in the morning, the coffee hot, and the tobacco the best Gebeli. These dainties, he said, would give him courage to complete the undertaking. We of course promised all he demanded, and would have promised anything else, eatable or drinkable, with the mental hope that it might choke him for his interminable delays. The spot, however, where we were moored for the night was very beautiful, and the more pleasing from its breaking, tumbling waters, after a month's residence on the calm bosom of a river ever serenely flowing.

While my friend amused himself with taking a sketch of our resting-place, I watched the Nubians crossing and recrossing the rapids on palm trunks, which they manage with much dexterity. They first place their trunk, about four or five feet long, in the water, and sitting astride on it, paddle away merrily with their hands; and the speed and security with which they manage to make their way, through rough and rapid waters, is curious enough. But they are all about here quite amphibious, and take the water like ducks, as I knew to my cost; for desirous of emulating their aquatic feats, I plunged into a rapid, and swam about very comfortably for some time, till being desirous of going ashore, I found myself unable to do so, being caught in some back water of which I was unaware. After much difficulty, and thoroughly exhausted, I reached a prominent rock in the river, and there ascertained my true position; but while lying panting and breathless, I recalled the old Egyptian oath, "By him who sleeps in Philæ," and thought how near I had the honor of sleeping too in Philæ, and reposing by the side of Osiris, slain like him by the fell Typhon of the waters.

The cataract reis being a late riser, did not appear the next morniug for many hours after dawn, and then commenced the operation, and a slow one it certainly was. First of all they sat down, and looked at the boat for a good half hour; then they squatted for another; then they took a pull, and bumped and thumped us over one rapid. At last they stuck fairly fast, and all the talk and shouting was ineffectual. The reis of the cataract stood commandingly on a lofty rock, and held his hands on high, during the conflict between the river and the *Flea*, like Moses when the Amalek fought with Israel at Rephidim. From this elevation he roared, and encouraged, and cursed; and then squatting down for breath, waited till his lungs enabled him again to roar, encourage, and curse. The men squatted also, and listened pleasantly to his execrations. After at least two hours had been thus consumed, they bethought them of doing what any one of common sense would have done at first. Four blacks one after the other took a header into the boiling current, and swimming as schoolboys call it wheel-wise, they reached the opposite rocks, which were certainly not far off, but so admirably did they swim that the stream seemed hardly to have any power over them. Fixing a rope to the bow, we got a pull on the boat at both sides, and away she went in no time. Half a dozen English sailors with running block and tackle would get the boats up, while half a hundred of these lazy, stupid fellows make it an affair of days. It is, however, a question whether a good deal of the pull and difficulty be not a matter of policy on their part, to preserve their monopoly and prestige; for if the operation were too simple and speedy, they would probably expect to get less money, being of opinion that noise, scolding, delay, and cursing, require corresponding *buckshish*.

At last, just as the sun was declining, we ran into the smooth calm water that encircles templed Philæ. The scenery during the day may be described as long reaches of water winding through innumerable low rocky islands; but here it assumes a different appearance. Huge boulders of immense granite lie tossed and tumbled, no doubt by the action of primeval deluges, in the wildest confusion over one another, and the hills thus formed come straight down to the river on each side. It is a curious view, and were it not for Philæ that rises midstream in such graceful, tranquil mien, it would be savage and austere. There is a story somewhere of a fair white girl ruling queenlike a wild Indian tribe, among whom chance had cast her shipwrecked; and Philæ seems like a spot that has drifted from some softer clime, and found herself queened and crowned among these rugged, stern associations.

But we had no time then to inspect Philæ closer; for the wind blew strongly and steadily, and in spite of the angry remonstrances of our own reis, who wished to return again to his wives, and thereby lose us the first real good breeze we were likely to benefit by, we gave the word "Forwards" in a manner that admitted of no reply, and stopped the reis's objurgations by language more forcible than polite, and by hints that his heels and the Governor of Assouan's sticks would probably form acquaintance on our return. So the reis sat sadly and sulkily on the quarter-deck, and thought of his dirty castor-oiled wives, and we slept soundly and comfortably below, while the *Flea* sped joyously and, for her nature, speedily by Nubian shores.

And now we were fairly in another country—in Nubia—the famous Ethiopia, where Neptune in olden times retired when disgusted with the frivolity and heartlessness of the other gods, and feasted and drank at the expense of and with the "blameless Ethiopians"; where in later days Candace ruled, a woman of masculine appearance and with one eye; and where at present the traveller thinks himself fallen into a community of portentous humble bees, from the incessant hum, buzz, and drone of Sakias[1] that line the water's edge, and sing their dreary chant incessantly during the twenty-four hours without respite or repose.

Nubia is altogether different from Egypt. We have now got rid of interminable mud banks, and rich extensive plains of cultivation, and chalky

---

[1] Water wheels for irrigation.

regular ranges of hills. Instead of all this, there is but a narrow strip of green running along the river's slope, planted with lupins, or chick-pea, or corn; and where there are no palms, it is fringed with castor-oil bushes, the resort of innumerable turtledoves, which seem to delight in this wholesome purgative. Occasionally the Sakias win by right of conquest a small territory inland from the desert, which is carefully and industriously tilled; but the poor Nubian is ever at war with his sandy foe, and this year his fond and faithful ally, the river, not having risen to near its usual height, has left him to combat at fearful disadvantage. But there are long sweeps of the most charming lake-like scenery; for as you look behind, the broad sea-like river seems closed in by hills, and you wonder where your boat has passed, and abrupt barriers straight before you seem to stand across your track and forbid further progress. And there are bold rocks in the water, and pretty landlocked bays such as are not to be found in all the land of Egypt; and volcanic-looking hills start up from the desert plain, and belts of palms and mimosas rising with the level of the line of sight, seem to clothe the feet of these strange heights with a verdure that does not really exist; and brilliant yellow sand trickles downward from the mountain tops, and streaking the black dross-like stones with streams as it were of golden Pactolus, collects into a larger flow, and fills the valleys and the plain with glowing tints, dear to the painter, and dear also to the poet. He who has furled sail beneath Korusko, will not readily accuse me of a traveller's over rosy-colored imaginings.

But it is the night and morning in which Nubia is particularly glorified. When the first bright streaks paint the mountain sides, ere the fierce heat of noon renders distance dizzy and indistinct; and when the moon floats high, and reveals the deep shades of crags and gorges, and throws her light, not rippling and dancing up to us as before, but deep, deep down to the depth of deep Nile fountains, forming golden ladders for water spirits to mount up to the enjoyment of nights so exquisite: then it is that the Howadgi feels himself within the tropics; the smoke of his chibouque curls softly around him, and the water rustles meekly by his *dahabieh's* side. Silent and satisfied with silence, he looks up from his deck at heaven's ebon vault, and sees Arcturus dipping into northern seas, and the great Southern Cross just rising over the verge of the horizon, pointing to the lands of "dusky idolaters dwelling under strange stars and worshipping strange gods." But Arcturus speaks of snow and mist and leaden, melancholy, tardy springs, such as Coleridge in his *Christabel* has described even unto shivering:—

> Is the night chilly and dark?
> The night is chilly, but not dark.
> The thin grey cloud that's spread on high,
> It covers but not hides the sky.

> The moon is behind, and at the full,
> But yet she looks both small and dull.
> 'Tis a month before the month of May,
> And the spring comes slowly up this way.

But old Homer has sung of nights that brood over Ionian shores, such as the Southern Cross well knows, although his eyes never rested on that noble constellation:—

> As when around the glittering moon, when the firmament is bare,
> The stars shine out right brilliantly, and breathless is the air;
> Then clear stand forth the mountain tops, and promontories steep,
> And hill-side dells are bathed in light, and the cloudless heavens sleep;
> And every single star is seen, and the shepherd's heart doth leap.

Still there is something chilly even here, and the shepherd beneath Olympus or many-fountained Ida, wraps his mantle tight around him, while we, stretched upon the deck, cast away handkerchief and waistcoat, and woo and solicit the night breeze.

When we emerged from our shelves the morning after mounting the cataract, we found we had made great way during the night, and had passed the Temple of Dabod, which lies on the western bank, as indeed do all the Nubian temples, with the exception of about three between Assouan and Wady Halfa. From this circumstance, I presume, that as at present, the eastern shore possessed advantages of fertility denied to the western, which was the reason of the temples being built on the latter, rather than on the former bank, owing to the great scarcity of land adapted to cultivation.

The spots chosen for the site of these monuments have generally been most happily selected. Sometimes the temples stood in bold relief on an eminence; in other cases, if not so picturesque, when seen from the river they command a noble view of it, or some great expanse of country. As we pursued our course, we hailed their graceful columns or portals from afar, as they broke the outline of the desert, for they are all without exception in the desert, and close to the water's edge. For this reason the remarks of the author of *Nile Notes* are more applicable to Nubian than Egyptian temples; for you can see from the deck of your boat, all that remains of the ancient splendour of the Nile banks through Nubia, which is not the case in Egypt, where at times you journey weary miles on assback over fields and deserts, ere you arrive at your destination. But hear what Mr. Curtis says, and his words will come more home to the recollection of those who have, and to the imagination of those who have not, visited these solitary relics of Africa's days of glory and civilization, than a thousand scientific descriptions, and a thousand learned disquisitions:—" There is something essentially cheerful in an Egyptian ruin. It stands so boldly bare in the sun and moon; its forms are so massive and precise; its sculptures so simply outlined, and of such serene objectivity of expression, and time deals so gently with the ruin's self, as if reluctant through love or fear to obliterate it, or even hang it with flowery weepers and green mosses, that your feeling shares the freshness of the ruin, and you reserve for the Coliseum or the Parthenon, the luxury of soft sentiment of which Childe Harold's apostrophe to Rome is the excellent expression. We must add to this, too, the entire separation from our sympathy of the people and principles that originated these structures. The Romans are our friends and neighbours in time, for they lived only yesterday. History sees clearly to the other side of Rome, and beholds the Campagna and the mountains before the wolf was whelped that mothered a world. But along these shores, history sees not much more than we can see."

With two or three exceptions, almost all the remains in Lower Nubia are of Ptolemaic and even of later times, and on many of the temples are found the cartouches of the Cæsars.

The theory that the Egyptians were of African descent, and spread themselves and their institutions from south to north, was formerly maintained by many learned personages, who supported their opinions with erudite treatises innumerable. The deciphering, however, of the hieroglyphics has completely upset all their arguments, and proves without a shadow of doubt, that the tide of Egyptian civilization flowed in a directly contrary direction, and that the further it advanced southwards, the more modern it became. The neighbourhood of Cairo contains, at Ghizeh and Sakara and Memphis, relics of the earliest dynasties of Egyptian kings, supposed to have flourished as far back as 3000 years B.C. As we advance to Benihassan, and the rock grottoes in the Arabian mountains, running to the famous Gebel Aboufoda, we find records of early but still later kings, from 2500 to 2000 years B.C. At Thebes we arrive at the Augustan era and culminating point of Egyptian greatness. Above Thebes, Ptolemaic temples and the cartouches of Roman emperors become more common; and although even beyond the second cataract the names and works of Thothmes II. and III., Amunoph II. and III., and Rameses the Great, appear, yet it is evident these powerful Theban monarchs held the upper country by right of conquest, and by right of descent. The remains still higher up at the island of Meroe, to the far south, are the latest of all, extending to centuries after the Christian era; but they have induced some writers to attach an earlier date to their erection, from the fact of the Ethiopean rulers having adopted the hieroglyphical devices of several of the earlier Egyptian kings.

It is curious enough that Mr. Hamilton, writing in 1801, at a time when hieroglyphics were a dead letter, expressed his astonishment that a dynasty so powerful and enlightened as were the Ptolemies, should have left no temples nor architecture of their period. He imagined that, had such monuments existed, their appearance or dedications would have revealed them; but he shrewdly adds, "that perhaps inability to decipher the hieroglyphic characters may be the cause of the ignorance of the existence of these buildings." Although at the period when Mr. Hamilton wrote, the celebrated Rosetta Stone, which gave the first true direction to Egyptian philology, was in English possession, yet neither Dr. Young nor Champollion had arrived at the investigations which have since directed so much attention to the monuments of the Nile valley; but even then an inscription, both in Greek and hieroglyphics, connecting the Ptolemies so closely with Egyptian worship, and which is given by Mr. Hamilton *in extenso*, both in Greek and English, might have convinced him that his remark as to the existence of Ptolemaic remains was more than conjecture.

The first temple we visited, that of Dakkeh, on the western bank, is covered with the cartouches of the Ptolemies. We had previously taken advantage of the favorable breeze, and passed without a visit, reserving them for our return, the temples of Dabod, Gertassee, Kalabshee, Dendoor, and Gerf Hoossayn. The temple last but one named, that of Dendoor, is just upon the tropic of Cancer; and we determined that our entrance for the first time on the tropics should be considered a great occasion, and celebrated by a bottle of champagne, one dozen of which only was brought for solemn festivities, and which gave me, in consequence of my water-drinking habits, exactly one dozen of headaches.

This Temple of Dakkeh is worth a visit. Its portals stand out boldly from the desert, and it looked so gay and well preserved, and so dissociated from the long Nubian *boulevard* which seems ever to line the river's bank, that even Mohammed the dragoman, who had not been before in Nubia, and held the Nubians, or barbarians as he called them, and all appertaining to them, in an estimation half of fear and half of contempt, begged leave to be allowed to visit it.

This temple, though far from extensive, is tolerably well preserved, the propylon especially, which is of plain stone, and covered with Greek votive inscriptions, inscribed chiefly by Roman authorities from Syene. They mention the governors of the Ombos district, and of parts about Elephantina, coming themselves to worship the great Hermes. In fact, expeditions to the different temples of Ethiopian gods seem to have been quite the fashion among the Roman officials of Syene; for we find records of these visits inscribed on the greater number of buildings, as far as the Roman sway extended. They seem to have been a kind of religious pic-nic; and as at the period alluded to, strange rites, and worships of strange gods from Syria, Asia Minor, and Egypt, were as much the rage in Rome as spirit-rappings at present in America, no doubt the god Mandouli of Kalabshee, and Hermes Patnouphis of this temple, were greatly patronized, now that the old gods of Olympus were becoming commonplace and out of use.

The chief interest, however, of this temple is the fact of its having been constructed mainly by an Ethiopian king, whose shield and name we find among the cartouches of Ptolemies and Cæsars. King Ergamun or Ergamenes, its founder, contemporary of Ptolemy Philadelphus, about 285 B.C., was a remarkable man in the annals of Ethiopia. He appears to have been a kind of Victor Emanuel in his resistance to ecclesiastical tyranny and encroachment. Diodorus mentions, that before his period, the priests enjoyed such unlimited power, that whenever they chose, they sent a message to their king, ordering him to die, for that such was the will of the gods, whom to resist was impiety. Up to the time of Ergamenes, the kings had been submissive to this command. Ergamenes was, however, a man of different character. He was instructed in the science and philosophy of the Greeks, and having with his troops proceeded to the chief temple, he there and then slew the priests, and abolished the ancient customs, substituting others according to his own will. Although resisting the intolerable yoke of the priesthood, Ergamenes seems to have been a pious and enlightened prince, and by no means to have failed in observance of the deities of his country. He is here seen presenting offerings to the gods, and over one of the side doors he is styled "Son of Kneph, born of Sate, nursed by Anouke;" and on the other side, "Son of Osiris, born of Isis, nursed by Nephthys." His royal titles and ovals are read by Sir G. Wilkinson as "King of men, the hand of Amun, the living, chosen of Re, sun of the Sun—Ergamun ever living, the beloved of Isis."

That any man in possession of regal authority should submit to the dictates of a priesthood, and give up his life at their bidding, seems incredible enough; but the veracity of the historian is vindicated by the observance until lately of similar customs in Fazogl, the most southern province that has lately come under Egyptian rule. It was the custom there to hang a king after he had ceased to be popular, which occurred not more than about sixteen years ago, to the father of the king who was reigning in 1844. On these occasions the relatives, ministers, and head men, assemble round the royal throne or stool, and announce to the potentate, as he no longer pleases the men and women of his country, the oxen, asses, fowls, &c. &c., but is extremely unpopular with them all, that it is good he should sacrifice himself for the publc satisfaction and benefit. He appears generally to have acquiesced very readily; for the people of the country state that once on a time, when a king was recalcitrant, his wife and mother made the most pressing remonstrances to him, not to disgrace his family and lineage by resistance, upon which he yielded to his fate; and Werner, in his narrative of the expedition to the White Nile, mentions a tribe on its banks whose kings, when they feel the approach of death, give notice to their ministers, and are strangled to prevent their dying in the ordinary vulgar way, like their slaves and subjects.

Besides the interest attached to the history of gallant old Ergamenes, Dakkeh once was famous for its professors in the necromantic art, and from Dakkeh and Echmin came, at the bidding of Pharaoh, those potent enchanters who did battle for Egypt and Egypt's gods, against the signs and wonders of the prophet of the Lord of hosts. And yet never spot seemed more unsuited to the practice of the black art, than this bright, cheerful, level expanse of sun-gilt desert, without the aid of dim mysterious caves, and solemn ancient groves; nor did the potency of their ancient spells avail the present inhabitants, who crowded unpleasantly upon us for *buckshish*, to avert sundry hard pokes in the ribs with the muzzles of our guns.

It is from Egypt, in consequence of its reputation for the skill of its adepts in magic, that the word Alchemy is derived, although the *al* or *el* is the

Arabic article *the;* and from the same derivation comes our word Chemistry. This word signifies "Egyptian art"—"The art of the black land." Egypt was written in heiroglyphic characters, *Chmi;* and Plutarch (*de Isid. et Osir.* cap. 33) knew that the Egyptians called their land Χημία, on account of the black, colored earth, the deposit of the inundation,—"Et viridem Ægyptum nigrâ fecundat arenâ." The word Chemistry is first found in the decree of Dioclesian "against the old writings of the Egyptians which treat of the chemistry of gold and silver." περὶ χημίας ἀργύρου καὶ χρυσοῦ.

Had our Nubians been aware of the ancient celebrity of this locality, they would, no doubt, have attributed the misfortune of the afternoon to the malice of the powers of evil; for as we slowly pursued our onward way, and were quietly rejoicing in our cabin's shade, a strange sound of rushing waters fell upon our ears, and presently a stream was perceived meandering across the cabin floor. Alarm rose high on board the *Flea;* it was clear that it had sprung a leak; but where, it was difficult to ascertain; for the approach to the shore was full of rocks, and it was next to impossible to make the land. On this trying occasion we became fully aware of the incompetency of our reis. He cried and moaned, and hid his face in his hands. The vessel was lost, he said—nothing could save it. He advised us to hail the first boat going down stream, and make our best way back again, and in piteous accents declared he should never be able to show his face among other reises, should he ever regain the port of Boulak. But the pilot we had taken at Assouan to guide us to Wady Halfa was a man of different stamp; in a moment off went his whole suit of clothes, a blue shirt, and animated by his example, the crew followed him into the water. After some examination, during which time we were busily engaged in raising our perishable effects on the main deck, the leak was discovered. It originated from some of the caulking having been torn out by the frequent collisions we had engaged in that morning with the rocks. Meanwhile the decks were torn up, every basin and porringer set to work; but a few hours' hard baling put all to rights. The accident had the effect of giving us a lesson, that we did not understand Nile navigation as well as the natives; for we had insisted on the crew tracking during the day, attributing to mere laziness their assertions that the shallow rocky bottom in this locality rendered tracking extremely hazardous,; not as in Egypt, where a run aground on a sandbank was of little consequence. In spite of their better judgment they obeyed, and a narrow escape from shipwreck was the result.

Taking warning by this mishap, we remained opposite Goorti the 15th and 16th, and had excellent quail-shooting in the narrow strips of chickpea along the bank. These dainty birds were deftly drest by Hubert, with coverings of ham fat and vine-leaves; nor were they the less appreciated for the ugly faces our crew made at their cuirasses of the unclean beast.

The next day we only advanced about three miles, and stopped to see the somewhat uninteresting Temple of Maharraka, the Hierosykaminon, or sacred fig-tree of the ancient geographers; and a rude representation of the goddess Isis sitting under a fig-tree still remains on one of the walls. We now bid farewell to Ptolemaic and Roman temples; all the remains of architecture higher up the river are the works of great Egyptian monarchs, who have left these monuments of their conquests. When I say up the river, I only mean to about fifty miles beyond Wady Halfa.

On the 18th we made some better progress, and got to Korusko, having passed by Wady Sabooa, or the Valley of Lions, so called, not from the presence of the king of the beasts in the neighbourhood, but from an avenue of sphinxes erected by Rameses the Great, in front of a temple built by him. The temple has it shrine in the rock, and the exterior is built of sandstone; some of the sphinxes, and the statues which terminated the approach, still remain; but from the attrition of the desert sand swept along by fierce desert gusts, they are much worn away. They appear never to have been at all worthy of the epoch when they were constructed, being apparently the rudest specimens of art. The western portion of the temple, hewn in the rock, is so completely filled with sand, that we found it impossible to penetrate it, nor, indeed, did our inability to do so cause us any regret.

This day we had to bewail the irreparable loss of our thermometer, which was broken by some accident. We had hitherto made it our custom to mark the temperature at sunrise, noon, and about ten o'clock at night. As we were desirous of forming some idea of the amount of the heat we had to encounter in our daily rambles in search of the ornithology of Nubia, we noted the rise of the mercury, not as the thermometer stood in the shade, but as it hung in front of our cabin. For the last few days the temperature was like a furnace; it gradually rose as we advanced from 105 to 112, to 123, to 130, to 140; and after the thermometer was *hors de combat*, we had to experience still greater heat. Although this was only February, yet we found the harvest almost finished; and if such were the heat at this early period of the year, it is difficult to conceive what it must be in the month of June, when it reaches its height. As it was, it scorched our hands to touch at midday the iron plates in which the thowl-pins were fastened on the boat's side; and when out shooting, I have been obliged to keep my gun under the skirt of my coat, or I should have been unable to hold the barrels while loading. It seemed so strange and incredible on reaching Cairo, to find letters describing the horrors of an English winter, rivers bound with icy chains, earth hard, and metallic with frost, water congealed in the jug, roaring fires, and fur integuments, just at the very period when we were being melted, grilled, stewed, and cooked in every possible manner by the fierce sun of Nubia.

Although we are not yet very far from the boundaries of Egypt, it is easy to explain this difference of temperature. In Egypt you sail generally through a wide alluvial plain, and the wind has room to sweep over broad expanses of cultivated soil; but in Nubia the desert runs to the river's edge, and every here and there high ranges of hills flank the waters on both sides, and impede the current of air; and when the breeze does blow at night, it blows from hot burning sands, which have not time between sunset and morning to cool themselves from the conflagration of the day.

This evening we were moored at Korusko, a small village on the eastern bank, inhabited by Arabs, but important as being the best starting-point for Khartoom, by caravan across the Nubian desert. The Nile from this point takes a westerly direction, and the navigation from Wady Halfa is impeded by a series of cataracts; the chief traffic, therefore, to Khartoom leaves the hill at this point, and to avoid the bends proceeds directly to the south, strikes the river again at Abou Hammed, and coasting its banks, descends as far as Berber, from whence the Nile is clear of obstructions to Khartoom. The journey is about twelve days to Berber, and thence by water from six to ten days to Khartoom, according as the wind favors.

This city of Khartoom is about the only exception to the desolating and blasting influence exercised wherever Turkish supremacy exists. As a general rule, wherever the crescent flies, insecurity, neglect, and bad government destroy whatever prosperity might have prevailed in more auspicious times. But in the present case, Khartoom not only has not been subjected to this general depression, but has actually risen within the last thirty-three years from a mere collection of wretched huts, into a large and highly flourishing town, rapidly increasing in size and importance, and containing, it is supposed, at present between 30,000 and 40,000 inhabitants. Our old cook, Hassaneen, who had been there twice in his culinary avocations, spoke of it with rapture, of its size and bazaars and gardens and vegetables and esculents of all sorts; but longer and more fondly did he dwell on the beauty of the

Abyssinian slave girls, and the low rate of purchase at which they might be procured.

Ismail Pacha, son of Mohammed Ali, has the credit of being its founder, after his conquests of Sennaar and Shendy, in the years 1821 and 1822. He had the sagacity to perceive the admirable position which the confluences of the two great rivers, the Blue and White Nile, afforded for concentrating to this spot the trade proceeding from Sennaar and Abyssinia by the Blue Nile, and by the White, the ivory, gum, gold dust, and other products of the great Negro kingdoms to the south and west. It there stands a kind of central point among the conquered provinces of Sennaar, Kordofan, Berber, and Shendy, and has become the seat of government of the Soudan, as the Negro territory of Egypt is called.

When Ismail Pacha, in the midst of his conquests, was burnt to death by the Sultan of Shendy, he was succeeded by the Defterdar Bey, son-in-law of Mohammed Ali, who was sent from Egypt to the newly conquered countries, as a kind of exile, in consequence of his execrable cruelties, which had roused the indignation of every European representative. In spite of the general tendency of all oriental officials, especially in Egypt, to find fault with and undo whatever has been commenced by a predecessor, the Defterdar was sensible of the great military and commercial advantages possessed by Khartoom, and made it the residence of the pashalik. Converging into this apex of a triangle flow the Blue and the White Nile. The Blue Nile, or to give it its exact Arab signification, the Blue-Black Nile, was once supposed to be the true Nile; but its sources were undeniably discovered by Bruce, and arrived at in N. lat. 11°, among the mountains on the south-west frontier of Abyssinia. The White River, however, has been traced as far as N. lat. 4°, and was even then a noble river, flowing through primitive Negro kingdoms, thickly populated, and through a highly fertile country. Some idea of this fertility may be conceived from the estimate of the number of one Negro tribe, that of the Shillooks, N. lat. 12°, whose territory of about two hundred miles in length is supposed to contain between two and three millions of inhabitants—an amount equal to the whole population of Egypt.

On visiting the village of Korusko, we found that almost all its male inhabitants had started with their camels, to convey the new governor of the Soudan to Berber. Haleem Pacha, brother of the Viceroy, having got heavily into debt, has applied for and obtained this government, where there is little fear of his being pestered by duns, at all events. He is said to be a charming young man, and from having been educated in France, to speak French like a native. Most orientals, however, are very charming young men till placed in authority, when their charming qualities rapidly disappear, and there cannot be a better example than Said Pacha, who

13*

before his accession was supposed to be *bonhommie* and kindness personified; but whose follies and cruelties since his elevation have made even the iron but more regular tyranny of Abbas to be regretted. However, Haleem Pacha is an ardent sportsman, and an undeniably good shot; in fact, a love of hunting and shooting is the ostensible reason for his voluntary departure into a climate at all times treacherous, but positively pestilential during the summer months. This young Pasha has, I understand, taken up very warmly a French scheme for penetrating to the sources of the White Nile, and there is no reason to despair of the success of the next exploring party. Already have adventurers advanced further than where the Mountains of the Moon were supposed by old geographers to hide these mysterious fountains; and it is expected that about the equator, the springs of this great river will be at length discovered, and reluctant Isis be compelled to lift that veil, that no European has yet raised.[1]

Any account of the Nile is so connected with Egypt, that I cannot help quoting an admirable passage from Mr. Bayard Taylor, who a few years ago sailed up the White River as far as the country of the Shillooks, when the fears of his crew compelled

---

[1] Haleem Pacha returned to Cairo after a short residence at Khartoom; the climate he found unbearable. The expedition to the source of the Nile failed from the bad management of the French commander.

him to return. Writing of the Nile's appearance at Khartoom, he observes:—" The Nile was to me a source of greater interest than all the Negro kingdoms between Khartoom and Timbuctoo. There, 2000 miles from its mouth, I found its current as broad, as deep, and as strong as at Cairo, and was no nearer the mystery of its origin. If I could ascend the western of his two branches, I might follow his windings further, and still find a broad and powerful stream, of whose sources even the tribes that dwell in those far regions are ignorant. I am confident when the hidden fountains shall be reached at last, and the problem of twenty centuries solved, the entire length of the Nile will be found to be not less than 4000 miles; and he will then take his rank with the Mississippi and Amazon, —a sublime trinity of streams. There is, in some respects, a striking likeness between the Nile and the former river. The 'Missouri' is the true Mississippi, rolling the largest flood, and giving his color to the mingled streams. So of the White Nile, which is broad and turbid, and pollutes the clear blue flood that has usurped his name and dignity. In spite of what geographers can say, and they are far from being united on the subject, the Blue Nile is not the true Nile. There, at the point of junction, his volume of water is greater; but he is fresh from the mountains, and constantly fed by large unfailing affluents; while the White Nile has rolled far more than one thousand miles on nearly a dead level, through a porous alluvial soil, in which he loses more water than he brings with him."

My friend employed the afternoon in taking a colored sketch of Korusko, which is one of the prettiest spots in all Nubia; I say colored sketch, for without color who could venture to give an idea of the characteristics of an African landscape! And here the pencil must be deeply steeped in carmine and violet, to represent the evening hue on the amphitheatre of cone-shaped hills which shut and guard this little gem of green from the remorseless craving desert; and it must be dipped, too, in ruddy gold, to trace the yellow sands that trickle down these mountain sides like mountain streams, and relieve and soften the dark black shadows of the huge rounded rocks, that are heaped upon their flanks, and look as if they had been polished and rubbed over with plumbago; and the emerald must also lend its tint to the diminutive rich fields of rice, which look like the goffres sold on the French *boulevards*, barred and cross-barred as they are with little rivulets of civilization. The river is broken with rocky islets; but there is verdure on them, and the lupin is in full flower under the steep banks; beneath the thick foliage of palms the sakia is singing its endless song; and as we gladly plunged into the shade of trees, and rested our wearied eyes on palm shoots and waving rice, the freshness was to us as the freshness of falling waters. The hateful sound of *buckshish*, which ever resounds through the length and breadth of Nubia, had ceased for this day its persecution, and long and fondly shall memory dwell upon Korusko.

We had purchased a lamb at Goorti, for the purpose of endeavouring to allure hyenas to destruction; but as yet in vain. We had sallied forth at deep hours of the night into wild and savage mountain gorges, and there, armed to the teeth and ensconced behind rocks, had waited for and fallen asleep too in waiting for beasts of prey, which the lamb tied to a stone invoked with repeated bleatings. In vain had the deep stillness of these mountain passes been broken by the shrill complainings of our little black orphan; neither hyena nor wolf appeared, and the lamb used to follow us of his own accord back to the boat as faithfully as a dog. This evening, however, he received a warning not to trust to previous immunities. He was put out as usual to feed on the bank, and was cropping his supper, when a wolf rushed down at him through the lupins. The poor animal instinctively perceived its danger, ran up the plank that connected the boat with the shore, quite an unusual feat, and jumping into the hold plunged its head among the cook's clothes, and refused to be comforted or reassured. The whole affair was so rapid, that we had no time to resort to our guns; but in the hopes of again alluring the wolf, we tied the lamb to a stake, and my friend volunteered to shoot the aggressor from his cabin window, which looked landwards. A few hours afterwards I was tempted to peep in, and found my companion fast asleep, with his rifle protruded from the window. I went on deck and found the crew asleep also, and on going ashore to release the lamb found him also enjoying a pleasant slumber. I may add, though on many subsequent occasions his assistance was required in midnight excursions, yet that no tooth of wild beast ever assailed him, and that when he did die, he gave up the ghost like a good and orthodox Mahommedan lamb, after having the *bismillah* duly muttered over him.

The river from Malkeh has now begun to take a considerable bend, and from Korusko to Derr the direction is N.N.W. The light wind enabled me to put ashore and examine the temple of Amada, which lies not far from, but on the opposite shore to, Derr, the capital of Nubia. The early names of Thothmes II., of his son Amunoph II., and Thothmes IV., occur there; and Mr. Harris found also the name of Sesortesen III., by whom it appears to have been founded. The sculptures in this temple are remarkable for the excellent preservation of their coloring, which they owe to the unintentional aid of the early Christians, who, desirous of hiding the emblems of ancient idolatry from the eyes of their flocks, covered them with mud and plaster, and then redecorated them, as I before mentioned, with Christian devices. Norden describes this temple as "fort remarquable par les peintures de la Trinité, et des saints qu'on y voit exprimées"; and, as the plaster in various parts has peeled off, it is strange enough to see Amun and Kneph and Athor standing alongside of highly orthodox but extremely ill-executed Coptic saints.

The same day we passed Derr, the capital of the country. A long wide beach of sand extends before a range of low mud cabins ensconced in palms; and one square edifice, muddier and loftier than the rest, proclaims itself to be the abode of the resident dignitary and Governor-General of Nubia. The whole of this district on the east bank abounds in palms; it is reckoned that 20,000 are taxed between this place and Korusko. The date-trees are counted by the official tax-collector every five years, and each tree is assessed at a tax of a piastre and a half, or about 4*d.* annually. No matter how many of them die in the mean time, the tax remains the same, until the expiration of the five years. They say the trees are seven years coming to maturity, after which they produce dates for seven years, and then gradually decay. The crew here intimated their intention of spending their next *buckshish* in dates, and doing a little speculation by reselling them at Cairo.

In the rear of this town is a temple cut in the rock of the time of Rameses the Great; its dimensions are small, and the sculptures unworthy of the period when they were executed.

As we sailed leisurely by the town of Derr, and on our return wandered about shooting without let or hindrance in its palm woods, we recalled the times when this point was almost the *ultima thule* of North African expeditions,—when Memlook beys and greedy native Kacheffs interposed insurmountable obstacles to further advance, and plundered and insulted, and encouraged their defendants to plunder and insult, every traveller and merchant, whether native or foreign. It was from here that in 1738, Norden, whose accurate accounts of the state of the country are most interesting, and the strict fidelity of whose drawings renders them highly valuable to compare with the existing remains, was obliged to retrace his footsteps. Belzoni, Bankes, Irby and Mangles, in the years 1817, 1818, and 1819, when endeavouring to open the great temple of Abou Simbel, testify to the interruptions, annoyances, and danger arising from this nest of extortioners. But the iron hand of Mohammed Ali swept away Memlooks and Kacheffs, and the Howadgi can now sail from Philæ to Wady Halfa, with as little interference as he would experience from Twickenham to Richmond, always excepting the perpetual assault of *buckshish* on his ears, which, however, but little affects his pocket or security.

This habit of shouting after strangers for *buckshish* becomes really a puzzle, for most unquestionably the cry is generally raised when there cannot be the slightest hope of obtaining anything. When riding by a village, or sailing swiftly along and far from the shore, one hears this wretched word screamed after one in the distance, and at times when I have called to the most vigorous vociferators, and even held out a copper piece, they never ventured to approach to receive it, evidently expecting the proffered gift to be merely a bait to bring them into contact with the stick. They are even at times so unconcerned about the matter as not to trouble themselves with repeating the whole word, but merely raise their heads from their work, and after a faint exclamation of "Sheesh Howaga," continue their avocations.

In Egypt one is but seldom subjected to this annoyance, and then only from children; but in Nubia it never ceases from old and young, men, women, and children. I remember asking, through one of our sailors, of a sturdy Nubian who sat by the door of his house, shouting for *buckshish*, what service he had performed for us that we should give him anything. He apparently thought there must have been something abstruse and remarkable in the question, for he gave no reply, but seemed to ponder over the matter, muttering, however, to himself the whole time *buckshish, buckshish*, until we went away. If this word were roared at one merely for purposes of annoyance, as some persons suppose it is, they would surely choose expressions more forcible and irritating; and as I never heard of any traveller giving money to these noisy applicants, I can only conclude that it proceeds from a kind of instinct, inherited from their parents, congenial with their birth, suckled in their mother's milk, inveterate, unalterable, resisting remonstrance, argument, reproof, or fear, coming from their lips with their first lispings, and exhaled with their last breath, part and parcel of their nature, as swimming to a duck, or chattering to a magpie.

A fine breeze from the north bore us on the 21st past the commanding heights of Ibreem, which tower over the water like the robber castles on the Rhine. We looked at its fine bold position with our glasses, and it seemed a strong but altogether deserted and abandoned town; and I heard from another traveller, who had scrambled to its summit, that it was, as we imagined, altogether devoid of inhabitants, except owls and beasts of prey in abundance. It appears to have been a station occupied by the old Egyptians, for stones, with their sculptures on them, are incorporated in the walls; the greater portion of which are of Roman origin. Sir G. Wilkinson mentions that the name of Tirhaka the Ethiopian appears on some of the blocks.

At the foot of the hill, cut out of the solid rock,

we perceived excavations; and the same writer states that they contain paintings and the names of the great kings, Thothmes I., III.; Amunoph II., Rameses II., with statues in high relief at their upper end. I landed with my faithful Nubian attendant, Himmed, and he scrambled like a wild goat up to and through them, and called out in ecstasy, " Ya Howaga, tassoweer khateer, khateer"—(O foreigners, quantities of drawings, quantities). He had so thoroughly identified himself with our antiquarian explorings, and had seen us pay so much respect to ancient monuments whenever we came across them, that he had imbibed a great taste for rummaging, and was always ready either to climb a rock or descend a pit, and his reports from above or below were accurate enough. My refusing, however, to risk my neck in climbing with boots on, to the grottoes in question, greatly lowered our researches in his estimation. He had evidently imagined we had some fine money-making objects in view, which were to be accomplished in some mysterious, inscrutable manner; and finding that I disregarded all his entreaties to ascend, he came to the conclusion (very apparently henceforth), that antiquity was a humbug—that, in short, there was nothing in it.

Ibreem was the ancient Primis Parva of the Romans, where an outpost garrison was kept to resist the incursions of the Ethiopians; and this may be said to be the furthest point where Rome planted her legionaries in garrison. Petronius, the Roman general, took this place by assault from Candace, the Ethiopian queen; and though he pursued her as far as Napata, now El Berkal, yet this spot is evidently the advanced post of Roman power on the Nile's banks. In after times it was employed for similar purposes by Sultan Selim, to keep the Nubians in subjection; and the descendants of the European soldiers quartered there were expelled by the Memlook beys, when they were driven out of Egypt by the victorious troops of Ibrahim. Burckhardt mentions the comparative fairness of the complexions of the inhabitants, and says that they boasted of being the descendants of the Bosnian troops of Sultan Selim.

It gives one a high opinion of early Egyptian power and civilization to reflect that, although Rome, with its organization, wealth, discipline, and insatiate love of dominion, stopped at this spot, and has left but a few mouldering walls as a record of its sway, yet that the Nubian monarchs of the eighteenth and nineteenth dynasties—the Thothmes' and Ramessides and Amunoph—had advanced far away southwards, following the Nile's course, erecting everywhere monuments of their piety and prudence. Although they fought and built and flourished from 1900 to 1500 years before Rome's inroad, still to this day, grand and elegant structures, magnificent in conception, and skilfully, even elaborately finished in execution, attest the civilization, wealth, and instruction that once prevailed in districts now almost unknown except to a few intrepid travellers.

The European rivers Rhine and Danube, with their castled crags and fortresses perched like eagles' nests amid rock and forest, confer a legendary and poetic interest to the great streams rolling at their feet; but that interest differs altogether from the sensations of awe and amazement, as the temple fortresses (for these temples were fortresses as well as sanctuaries) rise into view, and recede into the broken outline of the desert, while the broad wing of your *dahabieh* swells with the steady north wind, and carries you by shores and over waters of Ethiopia, the name of which, "the land of sun-burnt faces," brings back to you all the wonderings of your early days of travel-reading. But the robber chiefs, Rhine-graves, barons, and petty feudatories of the German rivers, are beings of yesterday; their names are no secret, nay, we have eaten, drunk, talked politics, and played whist with their lineal descendants; their very castles owe their interest to the stout burgher assaults of Rhenish confederations, and to French republican artillery. Their ruin is their picturesqueness. Here, however, there is a mystery thrown over these massive edifices, built as if to last for all time, by men undoubtedly mighty in their generation, wise and enlightened in all the arts of peace, but also vigorous, energetic, and ambitious, extending by force of arms their sway and manners among tribes and lands which remained after their disappearance, for thousands of years, unsubdued by the greatest masters in the practice of war. But here we stop, for there is a wide gulf between us and them. There is neither kindred nor connection, not even sympathies between us. They speak to us in strange characters, in an unknown tongue; but we fancy they proclaim victories in unknown lands—that they pompously announce their lineage with unknown gods. They appear to us as visitants from another and totally distinct period of the world. It does not require one to go all the way to Nubia to form a parallel between the two specialities—that of the Nile and of the Rhine; between the thoughts that crowd over one, as one sits alone on a sculptured stone in the sanctuary of an Ethiopian temple, the work of great Thothmes or greater Rameses, and the pleasant enjoyment of looking forth on a warm autumn day, from a feudal ivy-clad ruin on the gay scene below. The sensations are different indeed: the one is pure unmixed delight in the natural beauty of slopes "that promise corn and wine," of white city walls that gleam joyously as they nestle on Rhine banks, and cast their broad shadows along with that of the square Teutonic church towers, on Rhine's bosom; the other is almost painful—it is a kind of nightmare, as you plunge deeper and deeper into the speculations which these enormous blocks and chiselled walls and cartouches of kings produce—and down you sink into an abyss of ages, giddy and confused, until a Nubian like a good water-dog drags you ashore and to common life again, by a stentorean shout into your ears, of "Buckshish, Howaga—buskshish."

But to return to Ibreem; its position and appearance are so notable that I must not leave it yet, but transcribe the faithful description of it from a modern writer who pushed his investigations to its summit, and looked over its abrupt cliffs sheering down five hundred feet, into the Nile.

"Ibreem stands on a prolongation of the Arabian mountains, and is entirely isolated, except towards the east; loftier by far than every thing around it, you enjoy from its summit an almost boundless panorama. The desert in front stretches away, waving and sinking to the verge of the horizon; while northward and southward, the Nile is beheld flowing and winding between green banks, till in the extreme distance it looks like a blue riband, laid gently upon a golden ground.

"The houses of Ibreem, built and roofed with stone, are in many, if not in most cases, so perfect, that a new comer would only have to sweep out a little dust, to render them habitable. The chambers are spacious, the windows large, and the air breathing through them as pure as ether. What a delicious life might not one lead in the aërial dwellings, with one happy companion, far from the influence of our poisoned civilization, over-canopied and hemmed round by an atmosphere filled with sunshine by day, and at night glowing with innumerable stars."

I am bound to declare that to the last paragraph I cannot subscribe; nor do I think the companion who is to settle at Ibreem with Mr. St. John would long be a happy one, however estimable and agreeable may be the qualities of that gentleman.

On the 22nd of February, we reached the great object of our wishes—the last and culminating point of the remains of old Egyptian glory, between the first and second cataract—the famous Rock Temples of Abou Simbel. Slowly approaching from afar, we had been collecting with our glasses impressions of the distant appearance of the colossal likenesses of Rameses the Great, cut from and adhering to the mountain, and just emerging from the sand that is ever poured from the desert round their flanks. Gladly, when the light breeze brought us to land, we scrambled up the steep ascent, and visited first the small temple dedicated to Athor, which lies northward to the immense temple of Re, or the Sun. Both these temples are hollowed into the interior of the mountain, and the entrances of both guarded by four figures. On each side of the door of the smaller temple are two standing colossal figures of the king, with smaller figures beneath them representing the royal children.

When you step over the threshold, you enter into a chamber supported by six square pillars, bearing the head of Athor. On one side of the door, Rameses is portrayed with mace uplifted, holding by the hair, in act to strike, a captive, and presenting him to the hawk-headed deity Thoth. The lineaments of the prisoner, and type of countenance, totally different from the representations of Asiatic conquered nations on the walls of the Theban temples, at once declare his African origin. On the other side of the door is similarly presented a captive to Osiris. Upon the walls of the interior of the chapel the king is represented making offerings to Osiris and Athor, receiving the blessings of Thoth, and presenting lotus and incense to Amun. He is accompanied by his queen, Nofriare, who offers the sistrum and lotus to Athor. This drawing of the queen, to which I have before alluded, is remarkable, as it bears strong evidence of being a portrait; unquestionably the great statues in front of the other temple were intended to be representations of the king himself. In the drawings of the queen there is an identity throughout which shows them not to have been ideal. She is tall and slight, with rather piquant expression of countenance, and *nez retroussé*; and the contrast between her irregularity of features, and the noble and accurate beauty of the goddess to whom she presents her offerings, will be immediately remarked by any one who is provided with a good strong torch. These portraits of the queen were far more interesting to us, than the representations of Athor in the form of a cow in the sacred ship, or other curious devices dear to the antiquary; for the likeness of a lady of an extinct race who ruled in queenly state some three thousand years ago, gives rise to pleasant lucubrations. Her name, as read in the hieroglyphics, Nofri-ari, signifies "Beautiful eyes" (La reine aux beaux yeux), from Nofer, *good* or *handsome*, and Ari, *eye;* and we made various conjectures whether her attractions, or noble race, or consanguinity, made her consort of the great conqueror. And then we drew conclusions from her features as to her character; and, though holding conflictory opinions as to her temper, were both of us unanimous, that had she lived under happier and Parisian auspices, she would have been an arrant coquette, and have dressed herself more becomingly, and less *skimpily*. The *nez retroussé* forced this uncharitable judgment from us. The best group, in which the queen is represented, is on the corridor wall, on the right-hand side as you enter from the first chamber. At the end of this corridor, are two small chambers, and facing the entrance to the temple is the shrine where the statue of the presiding goddess was installed. Although small, this temple is so extremely well preserved, and there is such a diversity of groups, in many of which the queen prominently figures, that we took an inventory, as it were, of the representations, and occupied a good two hours ere we emerged to visit the greater Temple of the Sun.

After skirting along a kind of glacier of golden sand, which had completely filled up the slope of the *façade*, we stood in full view of this marvellous undertaking. Cut out of the solid rock were originally four colossal statues, likenesses of Rameses II. One of them is unfortunately shattered, by what catastrophe I am ignorant. They are sitting beneath a *façade* from ninety to one hundred feet in height, facing the Nile obliquely, with a northeasterly aspect. They are about sixty feet in height, on pedestals of at least seven feet more; and, with the exception of the coloring with which they were decorated having faded from lapse of ages, they are as fresh and as perfect as when first completed. Over these figures, where the cut-away stone meets the unhewn mountain, runs a band of gigantic hieroglyphics, giving the name and titles of the king; and this again is surmounted by an ornamental work of sacred apes, symbols of truth, which are also carved out of the rock, and form a finish to the summit of the *façade*. Over the door is a hawk-headed figure of the god Ré, or the Sun, surmounted by the Sun's globe; and tablets carved on various smooth portions of the rock adjoining the *façade*, with the greatest care and finish, narrate incidents of the king's achievements in different years of his reign, one of them commemorating events as late as the 38th year of his monarchy.

Among the many inscriptions in various languages (some Phœnician) which cover the legs and pedestals of the colossal figures, there is one so very remarkable and curious, as confirming a somewhat naughty story in Herodotus, that I think it worthy of mention. He tells us, "that in the reign of Psammitichus the Greek mercenaries employed by that king, Ionians and Carians, had been stationed at Elephantina to protect the country from the Ethiopians; and having been kept three whole years in garrison without being relieved, they resolved with one accord to desert the king and go over to the Ethiopians. As soon as the news reached Psammitichus, he pursued them, and having overtaken them, in vain endeavoured by entreaties and every argument to persuade them not to abandon their country, their gods, their children, and their wives." [Here follows some very improper narrative of the retort made by the soldiers, which I omit.] "But, deaf to his arguments, they continued their route, and on arriving in Ethiopia they gave themselves up to the king of the country, who rewarded them with the possession of lands belonging to certain refractory Ethiopians. They, therefore, settled there, and the natives became more civilised by adopting their customs." Such is the narrative of Herodotus: and, strange to say, Mr. Bankes and Mr. Salt discovered an inscription on the leg of the second colossus to the south, written by the troops of the same King Psammitichus, who were sent in pursuit of the deserters. It is in a curious style of Greek, with a rude indication of the long vowels, and clearly of the highest antiquity; in fact there is no doubt thrown by Lepsius or Sir G. Wilkinson, who have subsequently uncovered it from the sand, upon its authenticity. It commences:—"King Psammatichus having come to Elephantina, those who were with Psammatichus, the son of Theocles, wrote this." It then mentions their voyage, and the name and lineage of the writer, who is undoubtedly Greek. Here, therefore, is a rude inscription written about 680 B.C., and again brought to light after submersion in sand for probably more than two thousand years, confirming very notably a gossiping story in Herodotus.

At the entrance to the temple, on the pedestal of the colossus to the left, are the records of those who, after this lapse of ages, first reopened the temple. One says—"This temple opened in 1817 by his Britannic Majesty's Consul in Egypt." This was the enterprising Mr. Salt. Another tells us—"The Southern Colossus was laid open to the base by W. Bankes, Esq. A.D. 1819;" and over the entrance is carved, "June, 1831, Robert Hay, Esq., laid this door open, uncovered the two colossal statues to the base of their pedestals, and two tablets of hieroglyphics." The credit, however, of discovering this grand sanctuary is due to Burckhardt, and the discovering of it to Messrs. Irby and Mangles, who, unable to overcome the laziness, cupidity, and tricks of the natives and their chiefs, set to work themselves with the gallantry of British sailors to clear the sand-drifts from the entrance. After working eight hours a day for a fortnight, they succeeded in gaining admission; and any one who knows not what a Nubian sun is, even in February, as I have well known, can form but little idea of the indomitable pluck and perseverance that carried them through their labors, embedded as they were in sands that scorch the feet, under a June sun, and with the thermometer at 110 in the shade.

But now, as we stand on the edge of the slope of the sand, down which we are to slide ere entering the small orifice or door that remains uncovered, and that leads into this Hall of Eblis, let me shut up all my own notes, and transcribe the vivid sketch of Canon Stanley, a fellow collegian, who visited Abou Simbel in 1852. My only object being to bring home to the reader's mind a true picture of all that has impressed itself upon me, I am glad ever to borrow from others those sketches the brilliancy and fidelity of which I cannot hope to equal. Besides, if I have appeared somewhat enthusiastic in description, and exalting things I have seen, as if in triumph over those who have not seen them, it is pleasant to call into court a witness of undoubted veracity, and sober judgment: and this is the evidence of Mr. Stanley:—

"Why the great temple of Ipsambul" (another

term for Abou Simbel) "should have been fixed at this spot, it is hard to say. Perhaps because after this point begins the more strictly desert part of Nubia, known by the name of the Belly of Stone, and thus for a long way further south on the western bank (to which all the Nubian temples but two are confined) there are no masses of rock out of which such a monument could be hewn. The great temple is in the bowels of a hill obliquely facing eastwards, and separated from the smaller temple which immediately overhangs the river, by the avalanche of sand which for centuries had entirely buried the entrance, and now chokes up its greatest part.

"There are two points which give it an essential and special interest. First, you get here the most distinct conception of the great Rameses; sculptures of his life you can get elsewhere; but here alone, as you sit on the deep pure sand, you can look at his features inch by inch, see them not only magnified to tenfold their original size, so that ear and mouth and nose, and every link of his collar, and every line of his skin, sinks into you with the weight of a mountain; but these features are repeated exactly the same, three times over; four times they once were, but the upper part of the fourth statue is gone. Kehama is the image which most nearly answers to these colossal kings; and this multiplication of himself—not one Rameses but four—is exactly Kehama entering the eight gates of Padalon by eight roads at once. Look at them as they emerge—the two northern figures from the sand, which reaches up to their throats; the southernmost, as he sits unbroken and revealed from the top of his royal helmet to the toe of his enormous foot. Look at them, and remember that the face which looks over from the top of that gigantic statue is the face of the greatest man of the old world, that preceded the birth of Greece and Rome—the first conqueror recorded in history—the glory of Egypt—the terror of Africa and Asia—whose monuments still remain in Syria and Asia Minor—the second founder of Thebes, which must have been to the world then, as Rome was in the days of the Empire. It is certainly an individual likeness. Three peculiarities I carry away with me, besides that of profound repose and tranquillity, united perhaps with something of scorn: first, the length of the face compared with that of most others that are seen in the sculptures; secondly, the curl of the tip of the nose; thirdly, the overlapping and fall of the under lip.

"One of the two southern colossal figures, I said, was shattered from the legs upwards; but the legs are happily preserved, and on them, as on the Amenophis of Thebes, are the scrawls, not of modern travellers—nor even, as at Thebes, of Roman pilgrims, but of the very earliest Greek adventurers who penetrated into Africa. Some of them are still visible; the most curious, however, has been again buried under the accumulation of sand. It is the oldest Greek inscription in the world, by a Greek soldier who came here to pursue some deserters in the last days of the Egyptian monarchy.

"And now let us pass to the second great interest of Ipsambul, which is this: every other great Egyptian temple is more or less in ruins; this, from being hewn out of the rock, is in all its arrangements as perfect as it was when left by Rameses himself.

"You can explore every chamber from end to end, and you know that you have seen them all. The fact of its being a cave, and not a building, may of course have modified the forms; but the general plan must have been the same; and the massive shapes, the low roofs, the vast surface of dead wall, must have been suggested in the temples of Lower Egypt, where these features were not necessary, by those in Ethiopia, which were.

"The temple is dedicated to Ra, or the Sun. This is represented in a large bas-relief over the great entrance between the colossal figures. There is Rameses presenting offerings to the Sun, which you recognize at once, here and elsewhere, by the hawk's head. This in itself gives the place a double interest: not only was the sun the special deity of the Pharaohs, which mean 'Children of the Sun,' but he was the god of Heliopolis, and such as we see him here; and such, in great measure, as was his worship here, such was he and his worship in the great temple of Heliopolis, now destroyed; from which came the obelisks of Europe; of which Joseph's father-in-law was high priest, and where Moses must most frequently have seen the Egyptian ceremonies.

"Now climb up that ridge of sand, stoop under the lintel of the once gigantic doorway, between which and the sand there is now left only an aperture of a few feet, and dive into the dark abyss of the temple itself: dark it must always have been, though not as dark as now. All the light that it had came through that one door. First, there is the large hall with four pillars ranged on each side, colossal figures of Osiris; each figure with the feet swathed, the hands crossed on the breast; the crook and knotted scourge, his universal emblems, clasped in them; the face absolutely passionless, broad, placid, and serene as the full Nile; the highest ideal of repose, both as the likeness of death in the mummy, and as the representative of the final judgment. From this hall, richly sculptured round with the Homeric glories of Rameses, we pass into another filled with sculptures of gods. We have left the haunts of man, and are advancing into the presence of the divinities: another corridor, and the temple narrows yet again, and we are in the innermost sanctuary. In that square rocky chamber to which we are thus brought by the arms of the mountain closing us in with a closer and ever closer embrace, stood, and still stands, though broken, the original altar. Behind the altar, seated against the rocky wall, their hands upon their knees, looking straight out through the door of the sanctuary, through the corridor, through the second hall, and through the first, to the small aperture of daylight and blue sky, as it is now—to the majestic portal as it was in ancient times—sat and still sit the four great gods of the temple. There they sat, and looked out, and as you stand far back in the temple, and light up the adytum by kindling fires once more on that forgotten altar, you can see them still.

"There is the Hawk-head of the Sun—next to him Rameses himself—next Amun, the Jupiter of Egypt, the great god of Thebes; you see his tall cap or tiara towering high above the heads of all the others in high relief against the wall—and in the remaining corner, Kneph with the ram's head, the spirit of the universe. As the whole temple has contracted in proportion as it has receded inwards, so also have the statues in size. The sculptures of the adytum on each side represent the processions of the sacred boat, floating to its extremity. There is no trace of habitation for the sacred hawk, who, if he were in the temple, must have been here, sitting at the feet of Ra. So at least it follows from Strabo's clear account, that in the adytum of every Egyptian temple the sacred animal was kept, whatever it might be, corresponding to the statue of the Greek or Roman sanctuary—to the No-statue of the Holy of Holies in the Jewish temple.

"The chief thought that strikes one at Ipsambul, and elsewhere, is the rapidity of transition in the Egyptian worship from the sublime to the ridiculous. The gods alternate between the majesty of Ante-diluvian angels, and the grotesqueness of pre-Adamite monsters. By what strange contradiction could the same sculptors and worshippers have conceived the grave and awful forms of Amun and Osiris, and the ludicrous images of gods of all shapes 'in the heavens, and in the earth, and in the waters under the earth,' with heads of hawk and crocodile and jackal and ape? And, again, how extraordinary the contrast of the serenity and the savageness of the kings! Rameses, with the placid smile, grasping the shrinking captives by the hair, as the frontispiece of every temple; and Amun, with the smile no less placid, giving him the falchion to smite them. The whole impression is that gods and men alike belong to an age and world entirely passed away, when men were slow to move, slow to think, but when they did move or think, their work was done with the force and violence of giants.

"One emblem there is of true monotheism—everywhere a thousand times repeated—always impressive, and always beautiful—chiefly on the roof and cornice, like the cherubim in the Holy of Holies: the globe, with its widespread wings of azure blue, of the all-embracing sky, 'under the shadow of thy wings shall be my refuge.'"

Such is Abou Simbel; and I will not weaken this admirable sketch by any touches of my own, or by any descriptions of the fierce fights, the clash of chariots, and all the pomp and circumstance of war, which are carved upon the walls of the interior: they are of the same style as those on the great buildings of the Theban plain—the Rameseum, Medinet Abou, and Karnak; the difference is the difference of light and darkness. The Theban sculptures are of the sun, sunny and human; the Nubian, in their gloomy vaulted hall, seem unearthly, shadowy, and mysterious. The victim, decked with bright flowers and gilded horns, might well have been "led lowing to the sacrifice" in the gay shrines of Karnak; but the black lamb, meet offering to the infernal powers, should here have had its blood poured forth into the trench, and round it the pale shades from the world of Nox and Erebus would have flocked to drink.

On the opposite side of the river, cut out of the rock, is a small chapel containing the cartouche of Amunoph III., and dedicated to Amunre and Kneph; but it has also been, like many of the ancient idolatrous temples, employed by the early Christians, and crosses and inscriptions denote its change of destination.

Further on, about five miles to the south, I remarked some tablets cut on the side of the lofty and precipitate cliff that runs down into the water; they represent a king presenting offerings to six sitting deities. There are two lines of figures about three feet high, and a very small and indistinct shield of the king which I was unable to decipher. This tablet is curious, as, from being inscribed on the precipitous face of the rock, there would have been no support for the carver, while so employed; —but in the stone, which projects on each side, where the clearance was made for the tablet, there is a hole through which a rope was evidently passed, and which thus acted either as a guard to his back, or to support a seat from which he worked. Beyond this is a grotto originally painted, and with a statue, which is now all but demolished; the figures and hieroglyphics in it are faint from exposure to weather; but by its side, to the south, an inscription in large letters still remains in good preservation.

And now by this time night has come on, and our southward journey is near over; but to catch the first feeble puff of wind we are anchored in midstream of the broad glassy river. The last mountains that have girded our Nile path have left us, and are being scattered one by one behind like footmen flagging in a race, rising conically from the plain, detached and separate, lofty and abrupt at first, then smaller and smaller, dwindling into hillocks. Far away into measureless distance is stretched the red, sandy, stony desert, "that great and terrible wilderness where there is no water." Over the mountain tops at our back, rises the full moon, and the stars rain light on the drooping pennons of the *Flea*. As we lay on deck we gazed right up into the unfathomable vault of heaven, which rose like a dome of polished steel above us, grand beyond conception from its immensity and depth—beyond conception I well may say to those who have ever looked up into a northern sky, obscured with vapour, and depressed and limited from the atmosphere of fogs and humidity that closes it in. Such a night I never before saw (for the Nile valley too has its mists), and perhaps never shall see again. It seemed heaven's gala, and the firmament was alive with its million lamps of light. "There Argo steered its eternal voyage towards Colchis; there the mighty hunter Orion drew his glittering bow; there the virgin Cassiopeia sat on her starry throne; and there the hair of Berenice waved in golden brightness among the gods. Above all there extended lovingly across the heavens the white track made by the milk of Hera's breast, which as it fell from the summit of Olympus was converted into countless stars."[1] Nor were Arabian legends wanting too to tell us that on this night the rebel genii were active and stirring, and listening to the secrets of the angels, as they discussed in the lower heavens the ineffable secrets of super-

[1] Isis.

natural power and futurity and fate; but the falling stars hurled swiftly through the air in lines of fire showed us that these arch enemies of mankind had been discovered, and were being pelted back again by the messengers of Allah to the regions of their master Eblees.[1]

Hours such as these convince us how greatly climate, and climate alone, influences our peace of mind, even our well-doing. If under that fierce sun glaring down on us with his burning eye, thoughts of Europe have of late come over us, and of green fields and of old oaks and dashing rivulets, or even of cool panelled libraries, and periodicals and *Times* newspapers, let but the first star peep out like a little beacon over the summit of the Arabian chain, and Europe and the *Times* newspaper are foiled for ever. And yet our best qualities, our life, activity, and greatness, and independent spirit, is owing to that uncertain, rigid climate, which makes exertion a necessity, and commands us to be up and work. But here repose is the essential charm, and a dream-life the fulfilment of living. Business there is none, nor thought for to-morrow; for the least food suffices to satisfy hunger, and the Nile water is ever there to drink, and for raiment a blue cotton shirt is ample covering. I could make a suggestion to any family encumbered with nervous, irritable individuals:—take them off to Nubia.

---

[1] The Arabs account in this manner for the phenomenon of falling stars.

The sun will tame them by day, and the moon and stars will soothe them by night; but as the patients would die in the summer, they might be removed to the Ionian Islands during that interval, until the cure should be perfected. I must justify my enthusiasm for Nubian nights by quoting Humboldt's description of the first impression produced on him by the aspect of the heavens within the tropics:—

"From the time we entered the torrid zone, we were never weary of admiring, at night, the beauty of the southern sky, which, as we advanced to the south, opened new constellations to our view. We feel an indescribable sensation when on approaching the equator, and particularly on passing from one hemisphere to the other, we see those stars which we have contemplated from our infancy progressively sink, and finally disappear. Nothing awakens in the traveller a livelier recollection of the immense distance by which he is separated from his country, than the aspect of an unknown firmament. The grouping of the stars of the first magnitude, some scattered nebulæ rivalling in splendour the milky way, and tracts of space remarkable for their extreme blackness, give a peculiar physiognomy to the southern sky. This sight fills with admiration even those who, uninstructed in the several branches of physical science, feel the same emotion of delight in the contemplation of the heavenly vault, as in the view of a beautiful landscape, or a majestic site. A traveller needs not to be a botanist, to recognize the torrid zone by the mere aspect of its vegetation. Without having acquired any notions of astronomy, without any acquaintance with the celestial charts of Flamsteed and De la Calle, he feels he is not in Europe, when he sees the immense constellation of the Ship, or the phosphorescent clouds of Magellan, arise on the horizon. The heavens and the earth—every thing in the equinoctial regions, presents an exotic character.

"The lower regions of the air were loaded with vapours for some days. We saw distinctly for the first time the Southern Cross only on the night of the 4th of July, in the sixteenth degree of latitude. It was strongly inclined, and appeared from time to time between the clouds, the centre of which, furrowed by uncondensed lightnings, reflected a silvery light. If a traveller may be permitted to speak of his personal emotions, I shall add, that on that night I experienced the realization of one of the dreams of my early youth.

"When we begin to fix our eyes on geographical maps, and to read the narratives of navigators, we feel for certain countries and climates a sort of predilection, which we know not how to account for at a more advanced period of life. These impressions, however, exercise a considerable influence over our determinations; and from a sort of instinct we endeavour to connect ourselves with objects on which the mind has long been fixed as by a secret charm. At a period when I studied the heavens, not with the intention of devoting myself to astronomy, but only to acquire a knowledge of the stars, I was disturbed by a feeling unknown to those who are devoted to sedentary life. It was painful to me to renounce the hope of beholding the beautiful constellation near the south pole. Impatient to rove in the equinoctial regions, I could not raise my eyes to the starry firmament without thinking of the Southern Cross, and recalling the sublime passage of Dante, which the most celebrated commentators have applied to that constellation :—

> Io mi volsi a man' destra e posi mente
> All' altro polo, e vidi quattro stelle
> Non viste mai fuorch alla prima gente.
> Goder parea lo ciel di lor fiamelle;
> O settentrional vedovo sito
> Poichè privato sei di mirar quelle!

"The pleasure we felt on discovering the Southern Cross was warmly shared by those of the crew who had visited the colonies. In the solitude of the seas we hail a star as a friend from whom we have long been separated. The Portuguese and the Spaniards are peculiarly susceptible of this feeling: a religious sentiment attaches them to a constellation, the form of which recalls the sign of the faith planted by their ancestors in the deserts of the New World.

"The two great stars which mark the summit and

the foot of the cross having nearly the same right ascension, it follows that the constellation is almost perpendicular at the moment when it passes the meridian. This circumstance is known to the people of every nation situated beyond the tropics, or in the southern hemisphere. It has been observed at what hour of the night, in different seasons, the cross is erect or inclined. It is a timepiece which advances very regularly nearly four minutes a day; and no other group of stars affords to the naked eye an observation of time so easily made. How often have we heard our guides exclaim in the savannahs of Venezuela, or in the desert extending from Lima to Truxillo—'Midnight is past, the cross begins to bend.' How often these words reminded us of that affecting scene, where Paul and Virginia, seated near the source of the river of Latanier, conversed together for the last time, and where the old man, at the sight of the Southern Cross, warns them that it is time to separate."

The night was far spent when we turned in, and on the morrow when we came on deck, the long low-lying palm-groved reach of Wady Halfa was on our left. The word "Wady" is so constantly used by travellers in Arabia, that as it conveys a distinct idea of the country to which it is applied, and as

I have myself alluded to places on one or two occasions to which this word is attached, it may be useful to explain its signification. The general meaning is that of a *valley*, but its constant application is to the hollows in a country, with or without water, although in Arabia these hollows have been the effect of great torrents. Mr. Stanley remarks:—" For a few weeks or days in winter, these valleys present, it is said, the appearance of rushing streams. But their usual aspect is absolutely bare and waste, only presenting the image of thirsty desolation the more strikingly, from the constant indications of water which is no longer here. But so essentially are they in other respects the rivers of the desert, and so entirely are they the only likeness to rivers which an Arab could conceive, that in Spain we find the same name reproduced by the Arab conquerors of Andalusia; sometimes indeed fitly enough, as applied to the countless waters of southern Spain, only filled, like the valleys of Arabia, by a sudden descent of showers, or melting of snow; but sometimes to mighty rivers to which the torrents of the desert would furnish only the most general parallel. Few who pass to and fro along the majestic river between Cadiz and Seville remember that its name is a recollection of the desert far away; the Arab could find no other appellation for the Bœtis than that of the great valley, Ouad-el-kebeer—Guadalquiver." In the present instance it is not so easy to ascertain whence the term Wady was applied to this long tract of cultivated land, which extends for some miles along the eastern bank of the Nile. It is true that it lies between ground rising on each side; but such is the formation of the whole of the valley through which the river runs; nor is there here any of those peculiar appearances which confer the name of Wady.

On running our boat alongside the shore, we found no Europeans; but the place was busy enough from the arrival of some caravans from Dongola. All the merchandise was unloaded from the camels, and was formed into separate little camps upon the strand. Guarding the depôt near our boat were two Negro slaves, or, as they termed them, servants, of Kordofan origin. With the exception of a scanty covering round the loins, they were perfectly naked, and the finest men I ever laid my eyes on. Considerably above six feet in height, erect as young pine-trees, and with that marvellous development of sinew so seldom seen except in pictures, they looked like sons of Anak, as they stalked among their masters, and the sailors and idlers along the beach. Although jet black, and of Negro features with woolly hair, they had none of the repulsiveness which characterizes some of the Negro tribes of the west coast of Africa. It would have done a painter good to have seen the muscular neck, and head set so firmly but gracefully upon it; the drooping shoulders, and long, powerful, sinewy arms. We were so attracted by their appearance, that we made one of them come on board, wishing to have a talk with him about home; but he could scarcely understand any questions we desired to ask him, not being yet up in his Arabic. When he was departing we gave him a small trifle in money. The poor fellow seemed quite taken aback with such notice, and was most grateful for the present. He had not much reason to rejoice in it long, for his master, with eye of a lynx, watched the interview, and immediately on his leaving the boat, snatched away from him the piastres, which shows that, whether he was called slave or servant, the absolute authority was much the same. In consequence of this interference, we gave him and his companion, every afternoon during our three days' stay, a good feed of captain's biscuit, and to prevent that from being taken away also, we made them eat by the boat's side. They seemed merry, submissive creatures enough, and their great occupation was to watch all our movements. Wherever we turned, we found them looking after us, and always squatted with their faces towards our anchorage. Very likely their masters, from pique at not being made much more of than their slaves, and driven to jealousy by the captain's biscuit, had told them that we only wished to lull them into security to devour them at our leisure; for it is notorious, according to Negro tradition, the avidity with which white men prey on the flesh of their darker brethren. I believe, however, these to have been strong-minded slaves, for they evidently did not think the devil to be half as white as he was painted; so they came and eat their biscuit very gratefully every day. It was a shame to see such fine fellows so cringing and submissive, for they looked when they stalked and strode about like kings' sons; and when they lay in the moonlight, stretched out and asleep by their packs, they were the realization of Longfellow's grand lines:—

> Wide through the landscape of his dreams
>   The lordly Niger flow'd,
> Beneath the palm-trees on the plain
>   Once more a king he strode,
> And heard the tinkling caravans
>   Descend the mountain road.
>
> Before him like a blood-red flag
>   The bright flamingoes flew;
> From morn till night he followed their flight,
>   O'er plains where the tamarind grew.
> Till he saw the roofs of Caffre huts,
>   And the ocean rose to view.
>
> At night he heard the lion roar
>   And the hyena scream,
> And the river-horse, as he crushed the reeds
>   Beside some hidden stream;
> And it passed like a glorious roll of drums
>   Through the triumph of his dream.

We did some business with their masters, in leopard skins, of which they had a large stock, for housings for the horses and dromedaries of folks great in authority and wealth; and many a gaping spear-wound showed that they were dearly earned, and that their original owners had died hard and desperately before surrendering their spotted hides. We were informed by the merchants, that they had been purchased from the tribes far, far away on the banks of the White River.

In the afternoon we were visited by a sportsman of great renown in this locality—one Mohammed Faraj by name, and were assured that if we submitted ourselves to his guidance, he would put us in the way of slaying gazelles, wolves, and probably hyenas. We closed with his proposal, and, armed to the very teeth, sallied forth about ten o'clock at night under his auspices, in order to be at the proper spot about half an hour before the rising of the moon. At that time the gazelles, which are literally the harts of scripture " panting for cooling streams," rush down to the river to quench the intolerable thirst of twenty-four hours' abstinence in the parched desert. As they return back to their arid fastnesses, they amuse themselves *en route* by an inroad into any green crops that may be at hand. Hence, by killing a few of these invaders and frightening their comrades, you do the poor cultivator an inestimable service, and wherever he has tillage you will always find him as anxious to induce you to kill the gazelles, as an Irish peasant is to get you to have a shot at the crows which are rooting up the newly sown wheat—" bad luck to them.!"

After tumbling over water-courses, and scraping our shins on sharp doura-stalks, for it was dark as pitch, we came to the spot selected. This was a wide piece of uncultivated ground, about half a mile in width, running straight from the desert to the Nile, and flanked on either side with green crops of chick-pea and rice. A hole about four feet deep, and wide enough to hold two persons, had been dug to conceal the hunters at each corner of the cultivated land, and there, with rifle and smooth bore extended, we waited very impatiently, my friend in one, and I in the other excavation, until the rising of the moon should throw some light on the proceedings of the gazelles, or other more formidable antagonists.

The night was singularly unpropitious, a thin cloudy veil was spread over the sky, and when the moon did rise, I could hardly distinguish objects five yards before me. Mohammed Faraj, who up to this time had sat in the corner eructing[1] incessantly, for which I as constantly kicked him, now became very keen and silent, and gazed anxiously over the brink of the pit. His quick ear had caught a sound, and soon I could distinguish the

[1] He had supped on board, and this is the mode of expressing delicately a sense of repletion, and of hospitality received.

rustling of some large animal apparently not far distant. It was coming nearer and nearer, though still invisible from the dense background of palms in the direction whence it proceeded. Mohammed Faraj clutched my arm to be ready; and the whole battery was quickly brought to bear on the point of approach. At length, quite close to where we were squatted, we saw, but very indistinctly, the form of some strange but very large beast. I did not yet dare to fire, being utterly unable to catch the sight of the rifle, and waited till it came nearer. Closer and closer it now came, and seemed to be sniffing us out. In a few more seconds, and it would have been on the brink of our hiding-place. It was necessary, hit or miss, to fire. The rifle was raised, and as the trigger was on the point of being pulled, the monster, standing almost over us, burst into a terrific—bray, which was echoed and re-echoed by about twenty of his long-eared comrades in the village. Some men came up presently in search of the straggler, and the noise they made spoilt all chance of sport for that night; so home we went, and abused the donkeys and the devil who had incited them to kick up such a disturbance.

And here it must be explained why we abused the devil, and his influence upon asses; for it is not generally known that there is an important Arabian tradition on this matter.[1] The last animal that entered with Nooh, or Noah, into the ark, was

[1] See Mr. Lane's *Notes to Arabian Nights*.

the ass. Now, Iblees, or the devil, whom may Allah curse! clung to his tail. The ass was just entering at that moment the ark, when he stopped short and refused to advance further. Thereupon Nooh said to him, "Enter! woe to thee!" But the ass was still agitated and unable to proceed, so Nooh said in his wrath, "Enter, though the devil be with thee!" So the ass entered, and Iblees the accursed entered with him. Then Nooh, when he saw him, said, "O enemy of God, who introduced thee into the ark?" Iblees answered, "Thou! Thou said'st unto the ass, Enter, though the devil be with thee." Hence the well instructed in tradition say, that this is the reason why the ass, when he seeth the devil, brayeth. If the story be true, the devil was very busy under my window during my stay at Cairo, for there was a donkey tied there that never ceased to give warnings of his approach.

The next day we crossed the river, and met our donkeys behind a square mud-walled building, constructed as a resting-place for the Dongola caravans. Our object was to visit the Second Cataract from the lofty hill of Abouseer, which commands a view of the whole adjacent country. The distance was about five miles along the edge of the river,[1] over

---

[1] I have subsequently heard that very fine white sapphires can be picked up here; they are round, of a light color, about the size of marbles.

sand-drifts, and broad flat patches of smooth rock bestrewed with gaudy pebbles. There was not a tree of any sort, or a particle of green in view; the day was intensely hot, but a strong north wind, which sent the sand skurrying along with a dry hard sound, made it bearable enough. After a three hours' ride, gradually ascending all the way, we found ourselves at the foot of the summit of the rock, which from the lofty ground is perhaps not more than thirty feet high, and looks from below like a kind of cap. The whole cliff is calcareous, and the part at which we arrived is covered with the names of visitors of every country. A few steps took us to the summit of the cliff, which on the eastern side drops in a sheer precipice to the river's edge. It is at least three hundred feet in perpendicular height. "The view on three sides is uninterrupted for many leagues, and the panorama is truly grand, and unlike probably any other in the world. To the south, the mountains of the Batn-el-Hajar (belly of stone) rise like a black wall, out of which the Nile forces its way, not in a broad sheet, but in a hundred vexed streams, gurgling up amid chaotic heaps of rocks as if from subterranean sources, foaming and fretting their difficult way round endless islands and reefs, meeting and separating, seeking everywhere an outlet, and finding none, till at last, as if weary of the long contest, the rocks recede and the united waters spread themselves out sluggish and exhausted on the lands below. It is a wonderful picture of strife between two material forces, but so intricate and labyrinthine in its features, that the eye can scarcely succeed in separating them, or in viewing it otherwise than as a whole. The streams in their thousand windings appear to flow to all points of the compass, and from their continual noise and motion on all sides, the whole fantastic wilderness of rock seems to heave and tug, as it is throttled by the furious waters." Down among the little islands fringed with acacias we saw some of the natives jumping from stone to stone, and swimming the torrents in search, as we were told, of the eggs of aquatic birds which build in this solitary spot. The desert spread uninterruptedly around, and the air trembled over it from the radiated heat. To the south, dimly appeared the outline of a remarkably high hill, no doubt the same which was seen by Lord Lindsay, and which he took for the mountains of Dongola. But the range in the Dongola district is at least two hundred miles further to the south, and the fine sand that floats throughout the atmosphere is unfavorable for a distant view. The Nile is here about two miles in breadth, and for the space of ten miles its tortured waters hurry on, craftily winding in innumerable streamlets, or boldly dashing in innumerable falls and rapids.

We remained for some couple of hours here, carving our own names on the rock side, and looking over the names of those who had come before us; but the crosses placed before several signatures by the pious hands of friends or relatives, showed that even of the travellers of the last few years many had ceased to be. There was among these the name of my own cousin, T. K., and some loving recollection had graved this sad prefix and the words "Alas! poor," before the signature of Eliot Warburton. Like Old Mortality I cleared out these letters, which were somewhat indistinct, and some who shall come after me will, like myself, recline beneath that lonely African rock, recall his bright clever eye, his kindly voice, and gentle courtesy, and, rising to return, say with the same unfeigned sorrow for his early end, " Alas! poor Eliot Warburton!"

This place is legitimate for name-writing, that unhappy passion which seems to be the end and object of many English, but mostly of American travellers. Some names literally haunt you; they are inscribed on every monument in the most conspicuous spot, from the beginning to the end of your Nile journey. Quite oblivious of the schoolboy line

> Nomina stultorum semper parietibus insunt—
> The names of fools are ever graved on walls—

these vulgar and vain people seem to think that there is some imperative necessity for them to record their visit; and that posterity will take more interest in their insignificant and worthless signatures than in the monuments which are being thus perpetually desecrated and defaced. One person who had travelled in the steamer with me from Marseilles, and rejoiced in the name of John Gadsby, of Manchester, was a perfect fanatic in this occupation, and seemed to have carried an ink-bottle or a portable paint-pot about with him, for the express purpose of daubing every temple and interesting object with his name. This Mr. Gadsby is the author of a most peculiarly dull, ill-written, and uninstructive book, entitled *My Travels*, so that perhaps all these inscriptions may have been in the way of business, to convince the public that nothing had escaped his inspection—a sort of *visa*, in short, to the locality. The poor man, however, had some one not far behind him, or perhaps in company, who did not wish him well, for every signature was coupled with some remarkably uncomplimentary observation underneath. At Abouseer a memorial of one's journey is fair enough; the expanse of rock is like the traveller's book at foreign inns, and it is pleasant to look over it, and recall the names of those one has known either as friends, or as famous by reputation. It is the furthest spot in Africa on which the ordinary traveller sets foot, and from whence the eye is strained to the south, and thoughts of Dongola and Shendy and Kordofan and Sennaar and Abyssinia come across the mind. How many of those who have there recorded their names have felt that unspeakable fascination in African travelling, that has led such gallant hearts to untimely and unknown graves! How many, like ourselves, have left that rock wishing that the camels were lying packed and growling at its base, that the water-skins were charged, and the dromedaries ready to carry us off to the lands of ivory and gold dust, the jungle of the lion, and the deep water-reaches of the river-horse. But, Inshallah, Inshallah.

But our donkeys were our only caravan anxiously waiting, poor hungry beasts, to carry us back to the *dahabieh* and to their dinner. Mine, probably being the most hungry of the three, bore me gallantly home, and I arrived on an eminence strewn with ruins, and opposite to the boat, at least half an hour before the rest of the party approached. Finding all signals unseen or unheeded by the servants on board, I amused myself by poking with a stick in the sand around the ruins; a sculptured hieroglyphic sign, a goose surmounted by the sun's disk, caught my eye upon a block of stone, and on clearing the sand away I found the cartouche of one of the Thothmes' gaily painted and in perfect preservation, which shows that there once stood on the spot a structure built in the days of those monarchs. There are hardly any vestiges of the original building left except some scattered stones, and the foundations of pillars, now almost buried in the sand.

My friend this evening, nothing daunted by our ill luck of the night before, went forth again to the chase with Mohammed Faraj, but returned about one in the morning empty handed. He had, however, got a shot and wounded one of a party of gazelles that were jumping up and down, and romping in the green crops about him; and in coming home he fell in with a society of wolves which were lounging about in the open ground. He tried in vain to get a shot; the wolves, he said, knew exactly his gun's range, and just kept beyond it; if he walked towards them, they walked off, if he ran after them they trotted on very unconcernedly, and in short, though treating him with the utmost nonchalance, never gave him a chance of spreading their *spolia opima* on the quarter-deck of the *Flea*.

At midday on the 25th the crew broke forth into singing, and for the first time dashing their oars into the water, commenced the downward journey. A temporary lull in the north wind that had been blowing hard for the last two days, enabled us to make some little way, but it came on again as fierce as ever, nor was it till the 27th in the afternoon, that we arrived at Abou Simbel. Here we resolved on remaining, my friend occupied in sketching the *façade* of the great temple, while I organised a symposium in honor of Athor in the smaller one. In the centre of the first chamber our table was spread, and the columns were decked with torches and candles for a grand illumination; but we took care that the goddess should not have cause to complain that her bright eyes had been smudged with smoke, or her features desecrated by wax-droppings. Everything was done with seemliness and care. When nightfall came, the feast, in other words our dinner, was brought up from the boat; champagne in honor of the Egyptian Venus bathed itself in a pail hard by. Our Nubian boys climbed up the pillars and acted as torchbearers on the occasion. It was strange to see the old cavern in a blaze of light, and the gods waving and flickering on wall and column, Saté and Anouké, and statuesque Osiris, and Amun with his upright plume; and the crew peered in at the door, "dark faces pale against that rosy flame," marvelling much at the spells we were preparing for extracting the hidden treasures. So we feasted right merrily in company royal and divine, and poured out the first libation at the feet of Athor, nor did we omit to honor with similar observances slim Queen Nofriare. The saucy *nez retroussé* before commemorated, had perhaps more to do with this gallantry and expenditure of champagne, than even her alliance with imperial Rameses. We did not, however, conclude the night by sleeping in the temple, and enjoying visions of the good ancient times of Nubia, or revelations from queen or goddess, but retired to the boat in the hopes of a lull in the wind during the night, and some better progress than we had hitherto been making.

The crew for the last few days have been incessantly gambling at a kind of odd-and-even game, which they play with four small square pieces of dried date. These pieces of date are white inside and red outside; they are thrown up into the air with a peculiar crack of the finger-joints, and according as the colors turn up, odd or even, the players win and lose. The sailors first commenced with dates for stakes, but finding them to be not sufficiently exciting, they have latterly been gambling away all their little earnings and *buckshishes*. In fact they never ceased while they had a moment's idleness, and Mohammed the dragoman stated to me his conviction, that the repeated adverse winds were all to be attributed to these wicked propensities; for that no vessel could have luck or grace with a gambling ne'er-do-well crew on board. In spite of his remonstrances, and the cook's execrations at them for making a gambling-house of his quarters, this perpetual pitching and tossing and finger-cracking went on for nearly a week, until the whole capital of the players was concentrated into one or two hands, who very prudently did not risk their solid winnings, against promises to pay, which were the only stakes the victimised majority had to offer.

During the three succeeding days we were floating down the river, seldom rowing, and with no respite from adverse winds. We employed the time in walking along the shore endeavouring to procure along the mimosa and tamarind fringe, specimens of the birds of Nubia. We only found one kind we had not seen in Egypt, a species of fulvous-colored thrush, which by its peculiar cry gave us notice of its whereabouts in the thick mimosa brakes. We were very much disappointed with the results of our chase, the varieties of birds being very few indeed; to make up any deficiency, however, in number, the quantities of the common house-sparrow were quite astonishing. In the evening they flew along the banks in swarms, with a noise like a rush of shrapnel, as a Crimean friend of mine describes it; and the crew, in imitation of the people of the country, used to hide in recesses and beat them down as they passed with branches of trees for vengeance, and for grills. I say for vengeance, for the boatmen here and in Upper Egypt complained bitterly of their mischief, of which we were constant witnesses. With as much impudence as distinguishes their European relations, they took toll of every boat that passed their habitations, for it was building time, and they were busy in getting materials for their nests. To effect these domestic purposes they attacked the rigging of the boats, and from their pertinacious peckings soon unravelled a portion of the ropes. A weak point once established, was instantly taken advantage of by winged cohorts, and the result was a serious damage to the vessels' rigging; so much so that I have seen the tops of the masts of the vessels going down stream all covered over and bound tight with palm matting to resist these marauders.

Lower Nubia is certainly the worst country for sporting and ornithological amusements that can be well conceived, and one can form a correct opinion of its capabilities in these respects, while walking along the border of the river, as birds must resort to that narrow tract for their food, and if they were there, one could not fail to meet them. A pair of loose leathern trousers would be invaluable for forcing a way in search of one's victims, for the brakes are so thick and the thorns so formidable that it is very difficult indeed to secure small birds that fall among the bushes. Our Nubian boys dreaded acting as retrievers; their poor naked legs were not able to resist spikes, some of them at least two inches long, and as sharp as needles. Practical experience of their effects made me sympathise with our attendants' dread of these thorns, for the bank giving way under my feet, I subsided one morning into a wilderness of mimosa, and came forth from it like a second St. Sebastian, all bristling with these pestilent spines; and the points of more than one of them even to this hour remind me vividly of the misery that unlucky slip of the foot caused me.

We have been accompanied for the last few days

by innumerable armies of the common as well as of the Lybian crane. It was amusing to see them draw up in immense masses on the sandbanks every evening about sunset. They looked so sleepy standing on one leg with their long beaks under their wing, that we thought nothing would be more easy than to comply with the supplications of the crew to get a few, to give them courage, as they said, to row strenuously, for cranes' flesh they affirmed to be very good meat indeed, nearly as good as that of crocodiles. We found ourselves, however, quite mistaken in reckoning on an easy approach, for though a rifle might have done execution in their serried ranks, yet, like wise birds as they are, they had sentinels in advance in a very different attitude from their drowsy selves, standing on both legs and with beak in air, to give notice of the slightest danger. These sentinels did their duty well; for though I repeatedly tried stalking and every device to approach within gunshot, I never succeeded in deceiving their vigilance, and was only enabled to get a specimen of the Lybian crane for myself, and a dinner for the crew, by a haphazard shot among them with the rifle.

We liked the poor birds too, for they amused us, and kept us company all the way home to Cairo. Every evening we watched them forming their long and regular array, and at midday we heard their garrulous calls and conversations in the clear sky where they floated and gyrated in wide sweeps and circles so high, that they appeared like little burnished beetles as the sun's rays were reflected from their glossy backs.

It was not till the 2nd of March that we reached the gloomy mysterious temple of Gerf Hossayn, the ancient Tutzis. It stands back from the river, and is excavated in the rock to the depth of 130 feet, commanding a noble view over the level ground and the Nile below it, and the bold scenery on the opposite shore, where the town of Sabagoora, ruined by Ibrahim Pasha after a desperate defence by the Nubian chief who held it, is spread over the summit and slope of a lofty hill.

" But for the name of Rameses graven on every wall and every pillar throughout the temple, one would be inclined to assign it to the earliest period of Egyptian, or, more strictly speaking, of Ethiopian architecture. It is almost impossible not to believe it more ancient than any other monument in Egypt except the Pyramids. There is not a trace of the taste and beauty of the era of Rameses. A ruined portico (square columns faced with colossal statues) leads to the first and largest of the excavated chambers. This is a spacious hall, supported by six enormous square pillars, faced like those of the portico with statues of Osiris, above eighteen feet high, cut in full relief, mild, chubby, undignified countenances, the arms crossed, holding the scourge of power, and the crook of peace; the legs naked and shapeless, more like pillars than human stumps. The attitude of the lower part of the body reminded me of the Esquimaux, their pendent sashes of the Highland sporran, the head of some animal projecting in the usual place, with seven tassels below it. Statues of Pthah, or Vulcan, to whom this temple is dedicated, of Athor the lion-headed, and of Anuke, or Vesta, are sculptured in recesses behind the columns on each side of the hall. Beyond it are the cella supported by two large columns, and the adytum, or innermost shrine, at the further end of which, on a high platform, sit four most mysterious-looking colossal figures—a large hewn stone on the floor in front of them, perhaps an altar. In the small lateral apartments are benched recesses, probably for embalming. All the chambers are sculptured, but they are so black with smoke and dirt, and the rock has in many places proved so unfaithful to its trust, that we could make nothing of them. Negro and Nubian boys ciceronied us with burning ropes through this extraordinary excavation. Mithra's cave itself could scarcely have been gloomier than the Rock Temple of Gerf Hossayn." This is a description from Lord Lindsay, and remarkably faithful, as all his lordship's descriptions are. I cannot, however, forbear from adding another from Eliot Warburton, as it lays more stress on the impression produced upon the visitor, than on exact detail; and it, moreover, so entirely coincides with my own ideas of the place, that, as my object is to represent impressions produced during my Nile explorings rather than mere measurements and facts, I have never, as I before said, scrupled to substitute the accounts of others for my own, where they have struck me as being particularly apposite. "But," says he, "we are now approaching Gerf Hossayn, which appears to me the most striking and characteristic spot in Nubia, even while having Ipsambul vividly in recollection. It is the strangest, most unearthly place I ever beheld. It was dark when we arrived in its neighbourhood, but that mattered little, as its mysterious recesses were only visible to torchlight in the brightest noon. We passed through some cornfields, then came a strip of desert, then a tall cliff, and in it the enormous propylon of the temple. This, though built by human hands, stands out from the face of the mountain as if it had formed part of it from creation; four giant statues leaning against square pillars support its massive entablature. The vista of this colossal portico leads to a portal in the living rock, some twenty feet in height, and this is the entrance to the temple. The *coup d'œil* as we entered was very imposing; a group of our swarthy Arabs were waving blazing torches, and looked like officiating demon priests, to the calm, awful, gigantic idols that towered above us; the temple seemed full of these grim statues, though there are only two rows containing four in each. The massive pedestals on which they stand are but ten feet apart, which adds considerably to the effect of their enormous size. Hence we passed into a lesser hall, and then into the adytum; numerous torches here gleamed upon walls, shadowily giving out pictured battles and kneeling priests and stern deities; and in the centre of the shrine was a ruined altar, beyond which sat four gigantic idols with strange-looking crowns upon their heads, and mysterious emblems in their hands. It must be either a very strong or a very indifferent mind that can remain without some sense of awe in such a scene, or deny that it was well calculated to inspire such religious feeling as the eye alone can communicate to the soul."

There were few things that struck me more than the extraordinary and unaccountable differences in the execution of the Nubian rock-temples of the same era. They are all of the time of the great Rameses. Nubia was, under his reign, an Egyptian province. The art and science of Egyptian statuary and architecture were at their highest point. The erection and adornment of the gods' sanctuaries were essentially part of the regal functions. There is no doubt that a prescriptive code existed, laying down canons and regulations for the fixed proportions of the figures of gods and men, from which the artist was prohibited to travel. There are even strong grounds for supposing that the higher order of artists formed a branch of the priesthood. There, therefore, seems to have been no cause why any discrepancy should have arisen; on the contrary, there was every reason for uniformity in the style of public works of the same age, under the strictest system of prescription and centralization that can well be imagined; and yet nothing can be more dissimilar than, on the one side, the rock-sanctuaries of Abou Simbel and Beit Wellee (of which I shall have to write hereafter) and on the other side, those of Gerf Hossayn and Derr. The two first are executed in the very best style; the others, Gerf Hossayn especially, would seem to be the work of a barbarous race intent on producing something striking and enormous, but incapable of grace, and ignorant of design. The statues are, as Lord Lindsay calls them, rude and shapeless, and reminded me much of Gibbon's famous description of the appearance of the Huns. "These savages of Scythia were compared (and the picture had some resemblance) to the animals who walk very awkwardly on two legs, and to the misshapen figures, the Termini, which were often placed on the bridges of antiquity. They were distinguished from the rest of the human species by their broad shoulders, flat noses, and small black eyes deeply buried in the head; and, as they were almost destitute of beard, they never enjoyed either the manly graces of youth, or the venerable aspect of age."

It would be easy to understand that effect was alone aimed at, if all the Nubian excavated temples were equally unartistic; but as in some of them just as much minuteness, finish, and taste is observable as in the finest buildings of the Theban plain, so the want of these qualities in the others, and the striking difference of Gerf Hossayn, is worthy of consideration. In a country of free and enlightened citizens, where each congregation enjoys the right of building its own place of worship, in all extremes of false architecture and bad taste, discrepancies as strong as those I have referred to would be but natural; but the strict uniformity of design and execution pervading the same era, in the days of the Pharaohs, forbids the idea of Gerf Hossayn being the free kirk of an Ethiopian dissenting brotherhood.

The same afternoon we visited the temple of Dendoor, and no contrast could be stronger than that of the gloomy funereal vault of Gerf Hossayn, and this gay, pretty, objective little temple. It stands just within the tropic of Cancer, and conveys the idea of its tropical site as it basks in the full glare of sunshine. It is of comparatively modern date, probably of the time of Augustus Cæsar, whose name appears on it in hieroglyphics, and is of small dimensions, consisting of a portico with two columns in front, two inner chambers, and the adytum. In front of the portico is a pylon opening on an area enclosed by a massive wall, and facing towards the river. This raised area adds greatly to the embellishment of the structure, forming as it does what was a smooth terrace of stone work overlooking the river. The drawing made by Norden from his boat of this temple is particularly faithful as to its form, but it wants the rich warm tone of Roberts' sketches, without which no drawing of external scenery or building in Nubia can give adequate impressions. Photographs are cold abominations.

We made some little way during the night, and early in the morning arrived at the village of Kalabshee, a place of extremely bad reputation among dragomen and Arabs, from the lawless character of its inhabitants. It is a perpetual thorn in the side of the Egyptian governors of the country by reason of the "ignorant impatience of taxation" and conscription, evinced by its owners, who resist if the forces sent against them be small, and fly into the desert if they see themselves likely to be overmatched. We had, however, nothing to complain of, for in no part of Nubia did we find the natives more civil, obliging, and unobtrusive than here. A large concourse of the villagers, men and women, assembled on the shore, and squatting opposite our boat, did some smart business with the cook in the way of eggs and chickens, while we purchased Nubian daggers from the men, and that remarkable article of female attire called "rahat" from the women. This rahat consists of a leathern thong, which is fastened round the loins, and from which depend a number of leathern strips, decorated with cowrie shells, and in cases where the fair or, rather, dusky wearer, wishes to be extremely fashionable, with an extra adornment of blue beads, and small circles of mother-of-pearl. The garment is decidedly summery, but is the only article of attire worn by young girls; and though a blue cotton chemise is sometimes added, still the rahat always forms a portion of the dress until after marriage. We were often solicited by elderly ladies to purchase this whole wardrobe from off the persons of their daughters, but we preferred buying some that had not been worn, the absorption of castor-oil, with which the ladies' hair as well as bodies is smeared, rendering those that had been already worn by no means acceptable or odoriferous.

The Nubian dagger is a short, broadish weapon about eight inches long, and in general requisition. It is worn fastened over the elbow by a leathern thong, through which the hand passes. Our sailors said their countrymen were ready to use it on the slightest occasion; but though we witnessed occasionally an altercation, we never saw any very bloody spirit manifested, nor did the poor people who came to be cured of every kind of accident and disease, display among their other mishaps, any wounds inflicted by these weapons.

After the bargaining and marketing were concluded, we addressed through our Nubian interpreter the assemblage on the shore in a very neat and appropriate speech. We informed them that we had heard of their evil ways, how they mobbed, annoyed, and shouted after travellers, who came to their country, poor innocent lambs! only to do good, administer strong doses of jalap to the sick, and give generous *buckshish* in return for services, but not for shouting and importunity; that we, above all travellers, laid much stress on peace and quiet, and would not go to the temple at all, unless they promised good behaviour, and that we would take a guide and pay him well if we were not obstructed. Our observations were highly approved of, and I am bound to add that the understanding we came to was preserved inviolate. It was absolutely necessary to make some such arrangement, for the temple is the largest building in Nubia, and there is so much to see in it, with its pylons and halls and staircases, and ornaments, and inscriptions, that it would have been intolerable to have been pursued by a crowd of *buckshish*-hunters, swarming from the huts which are built everywhere in and about its precincts.

In front of the temple is a wide stone terrace extending towards the river, which must have added greatly to the splendour of this fine building. From it you enter through a noble portico into a wide open court; or, rather, I should say, scramble, so encumbered is it with rubbish at present. The walls are covered with inscriptions, and on the right-hand side of the doorway as you pass into the inner chambers, is the celebrated one of Silcho, a chief of the Nubadæ and of all the Ethiopians, as he calls himself. He was one, without doubt, of the petty kings of the Nubadæ who, by a treaty made with Diocletian, protected the Roman frontier from the incursions of the Blemmyes, and according to his own account he seems to have treated them summarily enough. After stating very modestly, "that he is a lion to the lower districts, and to the upper a citadel," he adds, "that he had divers battles with the Blemmyes, and that, as they will contend with him, he will not suffer them to sit down in the shade, but only in the sun, nor will he allow water to be brought into their houses, for his servants carry off their women and children." It is certainly to be hoped that he fought better than he wrote, for the Greek in which he delivers an account of his achievements, would have excited some disapprobation at Athens, in the times of Lysias and Isocrates. Passing from this court you enter into several chambers, in one of which the colours are perfectly well preserved, owing to its having been employed as a place for Christian worship, and besmeared in consequence with plaster, which has subsequently peeled off, leaving the original figures exposed to view. There is a drawing of Thoth in striped pantaloons, and another deity in a pair of tesselated inexpressibles, the gorgeous patterns of which, a few years ago when loud dressing was the fashion, would have made the fortune of a West-end tailor. Although there is a great variety in these figures, there is nothing particularly interesting about them, beyond the brilliancy of the colours in which they are painted, and as being a specimen of the restoration of the old Egyptian worship by the Cæsars. The present temple stands undoubtedly on the site, and probably employs in its construction the stones of an older edifice the work of the powerful Theban kings, for the name of Thothmes I. has been found on a statue lying near the quay. It was built in the reign of Augustus, and never completed, like many, indeed most Egyptian buildings; but it was subsequently added to and adorned by other Cæsars, particularly Caligula, Trajan, and Severus.

Although art, national spirit, and even religious faith, were to all purposes dead at the period when it was being constructed, the temple itself is a noble building, and it is well worth while to mount by an excellent staircase to the summit of the inner portal, and look over its extent. The artistic spirit had died out, but the physical energy and powerful will of the Roman conquerors were still sufficient to rear a vast and massive structure. It is surrounded by two walls of circuit of square stone, both of which are joined to the propylon, and constitute the whole *enceinte* into a formidable fortress quite adequate to afford refuge against, and to resist the attacks of wandering marauders.

About half a mile from this temple you ascend the hill, and come to the Beit-el-Wellee, or the House of the Saint, a small temple excavated in the rock, and dedicated to Amunre, with Kneph and Anouke; and Sir G. Wilkinson justly remarks that it is not without considerable satisfaction that the Egyptian antiquary turns from the coarse unmeaning sculpture of the Roman era, to the chaste and elegant designs of a Pharaonic age. The casts in the British Museum are from these sculptures, and I borrow from Lord Lindsay an animated description of them:—"The most spirited sculptures we have seen in the valley of the Nile are those in the small rock temple of Beit Wellee, half an hour's walk from Kalabshee, founded by Sesostris to commemorate his victories over the Cushites or Ethiopians, and the Shorii, an eastern nation apparently of Arabia Petrea. Open and exposed for three thousand years to the air of heaven, and the hand of man, these sculptures are still as sharp and fresh almost as when the artist exhibited them in his pride to Rameses.

To the right, entering the open area excavated in front of the temple, you have the conquest of the Shorii, to the left the submission of the Cushites. Everything bespeaks the desperate resistance of the former, the tame cowardice of the latter. On the right wall, Rameses, alike victorious on foot and in his war chariot, attacks the Shorii, kills their chief in single combat, and drives them to the fortifications of their town; his son, the heir of Egypt, storms the walls, and presents his prisoners bound to his father, who, in the last compartment of this sculptured history, is represented seated on his throne, reposing after his toils, the favorite lion that accompanied him in battle couched at his feet. On the left wall the Prince of Cush, his hand raised in supplication, his son and daughter at his side, is introduced by the Prince of Egypt to the mighty Rameses, throned in state: rings of gold, bags of precious stones, elephants' teeth, apes (but no peacocks), the wealth of Ethiopia, are borne after him, offerings to the conqueror; the lion, the giraffe, the bull, the gazelle, the ostrich, figure in the procession. The contempt of the Egyptians for their unwarlike neighbors may be traced here, as elsewhere, in the caricatured features of one of the tribute bearers, whose countenance bears a ludicrous resemblance to that of the monkey that precedes him in the procession.

And yet they did not yield absolutely without a blow. There is one scene of most touching interest. The Cushites have been defeated; they hurry confusedly to the woods for refuge, stumbling over the dying and the dead; but one of them has outstripped the fleetest in hopes of saving his friend's wife from the pursuers. He knew not that friend was already at his own door—but alas! faint and bleeding, wearily dragging on, his arms thrown around two of his comrades' necks, who grasp his wrists to strengthen him. He overtakes them at the moment when his friend's sister and his children recognize him. *She* stands aghast, one boy holds up his hand in horror—another covers his face, and runs to clasp his father's knees with the other; the third is running to tell his mother, who, unconscious of what awaits her, is preparing her husband's meal. But the tumult approaches—the flying Cushites, the chariot-wheels of Pharaoh and the Egyptians—fly! oh fly!—they see only, they hear only the wounded man!—a minute—and wife and husband, brother and sister, children and friend, will all be overwhelmed by the mighty torrent. A monkey has climbed to the top of a tree for refuge —there is yet time—but what are they to do with the wounded man?—'Tis too late now—they come, they come rushing—crushing through the forest— and now—let us drop the curtain.

The sculptures of the interior temple are highly interesting, and evidently allusive to the scenes of conquest sculptured without. A Shorian and an Ethiopian, the representatives I presume of their respective nations, lie at the feet of Rameses; with one hand he grasps their hair, the uplifted battle-axe gleams in the other. Forced on his knees, but those knees clinched together, the muscles rigid, the joints unyielding, the brave Arab meets with unquailing eye the glance of his conqueror, and raises his left hand firmly to ward off the blow which the Ethiopian tamely submits to. The contrast is that of courage with cowardice—personified in the relaxed limbs, uplifted but shrinking hands, and averted face of the Negro; the lips of both are moving, but you need not fancy to supply words: every limb, every gesture speaks."

This account is very eloquent, and generally very correct; but there is certainly a large draft drawn on the imagination of the reader. If the sculptures were intended to represent any well-known story, we could easily, from our knowledge of the tale, invest the different personages with their peculiar roles; but how in this particular instance his lordship is to remark particular ties of relationship— that one female figure is the wife of a friend of one of the parties, and that another is the sister—I am at a loss to guess; and still more incomprehensible is it, how he can define that one of the flying figures is animated with the hope of warning a friend's wife of her danger. The sculptures are, no doubt, extremely expressive, but this is making them perform functions hardly within their compass, and somewhat resembling the marvellous effects of the reliefs worked by the god Vulcan on the shield of Achilles. Those who had the privilege of being shown this godlike handiwork, were said to see the ambuscade of armed men by the river's brink; then come the cattle, accompanied by shepherds piping before them to the water; then out rushes, to slay and plunder, the same band of ambushed marauders; then, to resist them, the sitting citizens mount their horses, and gallop to the fray. Such are the wonders of art in the days of Troy; but we must remember that the workman is a god, who can do strange things; whereas the workman of Beit Wellee is only a mortal craftsman, although unquestionably a very able one.

Having passed the best part of the day in examining all these details, we were glad to get on board again, and escape from the intolerable heat, which of late has been unusually fierce. Next morning we were passing through the bold craggy scenery of Tafa, where monstrous masses of granite rise in islands or detached rocks in the river's bed, some of them lying low, like great antediluvian fossil reptiles basking in the water, others springing into lofty peaks, round which a brood of eagles were floating almost motionless. The old royal sire was sitting on one of these lofty eminences looking lazily down, as we swept with a brisk song by the base of his craggy fortress. We tried with a rifle shot to interrupt his reverie, but as the ball whistled by him, he contemptuously raised one wing for a moment, and then resumed his meditations. Our glasses showed him to be a splendid fellow. We made a more successful aim at a vulture, one of Pharaoh's hens as they call them, that was feeding on the shore; but as the boy who had been sent for milk in the small boat went to pick him up, he was forestalled by a Nubian, who carried him off eagerly. We marvelled for what purpose; "to eat him, of course," was the reply; and the crew, although they refused such savory meat, did not seem at all astonished at their countrymen relishing such a foul, disgusting bird. They certainly are the dirtiest feeders going. Cranes, cormorants, pelicans, lizards, everything in short, except pig's flesh, being gratefully received. Whenever we gave them mutton, it seemed almost a shame to waste such good, and in Nubia scarce meat, on such omnivorous beings; it was, as the eastern saying has it, "like rubbing rats' heads with jasmine oil."

Different people, however, are of different opinions, and as to the variety in tastes, old Herodotus tells us one of his pleasant chatty stories. Darius the Persian king, he says, sent for some of the Greeks who were at his court, and asked them what they would take to eat their own fathers. They replied, that no reward whatever would tempt them. He then summoned an Indian tribe who were accustomed to eat their parents, and asked them, in the presence of the Greeks, what they would take to burn with fire their deceased relatives,—οἱ δὲ ἀμβώσαντες μεγὰ εὐφημέειν, μιν ἐκέλευον, they cried aloud with horror, and begged of him to speak reverentially on such subjects.

I am sorry to remark that we have of late had a

good deal of reason to be dissatisfied with our Barabra crew; instead of the willingness, activity, and readiness to oblige, which marked their conduct at first starting from Cairo, they have been, since their return to their own country, dissatisfied and lazy, and craving for presents. Indeed on more than one occasion, they seemed much inclined to disobedience and even to revolt, which broke forth partially a few days later. My companion, who was in the small boat shooting, had reason to find fault with the man who was with him, for direct refusal to carry out his orders, and was obliged to take the law into his own hands. On his return to the *dahabiah*, one of the offender's fellow-villagers (who was always disposed to be disagreeable), although not concerned in any way with the present affair, adopted a very bullying attitude, and was evidently doing his best to create a disturbance among the other men, but found himself in one minute, to his great surprise, literally kicked out of the vessel and his clothes thrown after him. It was most ludicrous to see his rage and despair. After running as if for his life, up the bank until well out of reach, he first of all vowed implacable vengeance; he then, in the name of the Prophet, invoked the crew to see him justified, but at last in the evening sneaked down and begged pardon most submissively, entreating that we would at all events take him on as far as Philæ. We were, however, unforgiving, and after getting rid of the most unruly spirit, every thing went on smoothly enough, till our arrival at Assouan.

We were at this time not more than thirty miles from the confines of Egypt, and were in hopes of reaching Philæ by morning. But we little knew what was before us. The north wind, which had baffled our descent so long, now swelled into a regular gale, and we were nearly swamped in crossing the river to see some remains at Gertasee. Several pretty columns still standing allured us over. They formed originally part of a larger building, but there is no cartouche or inscription on them to commemorate the builder. They are, however, from their appearance, comparatively modern. Adjoining this structure are extensive sandstone quarries, with inscriptions of the time of the later Cæsars in honor of the goddess Isis, who was probably the patron deity of the temple. A short distance to the south, there is a wide square enclosure built of huge blocks of stone, with a portal on the north side of it, and which now forms a portion of the Nubian village of Gertasee. At Wady Tafa there are also several of these enclosures, the use of which seems to be doubtful, whether they were built for military or religious purposes.

Well indeed was the neighbourhood of Gertasee fixed upon our memories, for during three mortal days we were unable to make any progress whatsoever. Shortness of provisions, and total want of sugar and vegetables, were to us discomfort enough; but the emptiness of the tobacco-pouch was to my servant and the dragoman, downright misfortune. We were idle, moreover, and there was nothing to shoot. The birds disliked the drifting sand, the sickly looking sun, and the crashing branches of the palms as much as we did, and would not come forth. We almost despaired of ever getting out of Nubia. Then came across us thoughts of the Grecian host of old, windbound at Aulis, and "how the sauntering chiefs," like ourselves, "whelmed that daily, daily scene with their deep Ionian curses."

> εὖτ' ἀπλοίᾳ κεναγγεῖ βαρυ—
> νόντ' Ἀχαϊκὸς λεώς,
> Χαλκίδος πέραν ἔχων παλιρρό-
> θοις ἐν Αὐλίδος τόποις.
> πνοαὶ δ' ἀπὸ Στρύμονος μολοῦσαι
> κακόσχολοι, νήστιδες, δύσορμοι
> βροτῶν ἄλαι,
> νεῶν τε καὶ πεισμάτων ἀφειδεῖς
> παλιμμήκη χρόνον τιθεῖσαι
> τρίβῳ κατέξαινον ἄνθος Ἀργείων.—ÆSCH. *Ag.* 181.

> What time by windbound stress detained,
> Their strength dried up, their vessels drained,
> The people of the Achæans waned,
> In weariness bowed low,
> Right over against Chalcis shore,
> Where Aulis tides with rush and roar
> Alternate ebb and flow.—BLEW.

Our situation, indeed, seemed hopeless; for some god or goddess whom we had neglected in our libations at Abou Simbel to propitiate, had determined to pay us out. But in our case there was no prophet Calchas to propose a sacrifice so awful, that the bare mention of it would have made us strike the ground with our gunstocks. On the evening of the third day, however, a victim that made the wind to cease ($\pi\alpha\upsilon\sigma\acute{\alpha}\nu\epsilon\mu o\varsigma\ \theta\upsilon\sigma\acute{\iota}\alpha$) turned up. The insurgent Omar was sacrificed by being kicked out of the boat. The offended deities were appeased, and a lull came on. Profiting by it we hurried as fast as oar could dip, and on the following dawn we saw the morning sun shine calmly and pleasantly on terraced Philæ.

There can be no two views more dissimilar than the approaches to this island from the north and from the south, from the Cataracts and from Nubia. From the north it is a surprise. As you emerge from the austere and ponderous masses of granite crags, piled as if by Titans in their war with heaven, the stately architecture of the island starts up as unexpected and undreamt of, as the Castle of St. John to the eyes of brave Sir Vaux in the days of Merlin and magic spells:—

> 'Tis no deceit! distinctly clear
> Crenell and parapet appear,
> With battled walls, and buttress fast,
> And airy flanking towers, that cast
>   Their shadows on the stream.
>   *Bridal of Triermain.*

But coming from the south you are not unprepared for its graceful presence; you have not been doing fierce battle with a roaring turbid river, or struggling through a gloomy narrow pass that looks as if it would overwhelm your tiny bark, but you have gently swept to the wild tune of an Arab song, along reaches of smooth water, to that almost lake-like expanse where the Nile curves round Philæ, and lingers, and lingers, and dallies ere it takes its plunge into the land of Egypt. Mr. Stanley truly observes, " Art and nature are here unique, the rocks and river (of which you might see the like elsewhere) are wholly unlike Egypt, as the square towers, the devious perspective, and the sculptured walls, are wholly unlike anything else except Egypt." But I do not agree with the same writer, that the dead walls hardly emerge sufficiently from the sand and mud cottages that enclose them round, and the palms are not sufficiently numerous to relieve the bare and mean appearance which the rest of the island presents. I do not think this criticism applies to the view of Philæ from your boat, either as you ascend or descend; the line of sight only catches the salient points, the lofty columns of the hypæthral temple, the massive propylæa, the stonework of the quays, and the pillars of the corridors. It is not till you are moored on the eastern side of the island, that its defects are visible.

And now for a whole day's exploring among the

remains on the Holy Isle. What Delos, birthplace of Apollo, was to the Greeks; what Iona, refuge of the saints, was in our Western Islands to the early Christian converts; what Mecca now is to the Mahommedan, who five times each day bows his head in prayer towards the sacred city: such was Philæ, tomb of Osiris, to the Egyptian. His most awful asseveration was the solemn oath by the name too sacred to mention, "By him that sleeps in Philæ!"

Always endeavouring to extract a signification from words unknown to them, the Greeks, with that appreciation of natural beauty that made them christen their landing-place in Sicily "the lovely shore" (καλὴ ἀκτή), chose to convert the Egyptian word Pilak, "the frontier," into Philæ—the feminine plural—φίλαι ἀκταί perhaps, the "dear shores," as Byron speaks of Venice—

> Nor yet forget how Venice once was *dear*,
> The pleasant place of all festivity,
> The revel of the earth, the masque of Italy.

The Arabs, too, associate the island with their ideas of all the luxury and fascination that natural beauty can impart. They call it Anas-el-Wojood, and have some legend of its being built by some mighty king of old, as a retreat for the prince, his eldest son. Thus Egyptian, Greek, Arab, and Howadgi, all vie to do it honor.

But now let us land, and, proceeding to the

southern point, endeavour to form some idea of the whole. The island altogether contains about fifty acres of land, and originally every yard was occupied by terrace, quay, or building. Much of the site of the old structures is now covered by the mud remains of a deserted Nubian village, but from this point, as you look northwards, with your back to the solid parapet of cut stone that banks up the island from the water, the view is extremely grand, —innumerable pillars with as many varying capitals support galleries and corridors; to the right, the graceful columns of the hypæthral temple spring lightly from their massive base; and straight in front, the huge and heavy propylæa of the great temple fall like a portcullis, and until we mount their summit, bar the rest of the island from the sight. All the remains that we now see are of Ptolemaic date, with Roman additions and embellishments; but the names of the Pharaohs are graven on the cliffs around, and we know that their magnificence was lavished here, before the invading bands of Persian Ochus swept in their hatred of all idolatry but their own, the old temples and sanctuaries to the ground. "The buildings, therefore, that have risen from the Pharaonic ruins, are so comparatively modern that they in no way illustrate, except so far as copying, the religion of the ancient Egyptians. The earliest, indeed the only Egyptian name that occurs, is Nectanebus, an Egyptian prince who revolted against the later Persian kings. All the rest are the Grecian Ptolemies, and of these the chief is Ptolemy Physcon, or the Fat, so called because he became so bloated by luxurious living that he measured six feet round, and who proposed to Cornelia, mother of the Gracchi. But in this very part of its modern origin there is a peculiar interest. It is an attempt, like our own in Gothic architecture, to revive a style and forms which had belonged to ages far-away. The Ptolemies, here as in many other places, were trying 'to throw themselves' into Egyptian worship, following in the steps of Alexander, son of Ammon. In many ways this appears:—First, there is much for show without real use—one fine side chapel, perhaps the finest of the group, built for the sake of its terrace towards the river, the main entrance to the temple being in fact no entrance at all; then there is the want of symmetry, which more or less always distinguishes the Egyptian architecture, but which is here carried to a ridiculous excess—no perspective is carried consistently through—the sides of the same court are of different styles, no one gateway is in the same line with another. Lastly, there is the curious sight of sculptures contemporary with the finest works of Greek art and carved under Grecian kings, as rude as some of those under the earliest Pharaohs, to be in keeping with Egyptian architecture, and to preserve the ancient type, like the mediæval figures in painted windows, and the illegible inscriptions round the arches of some modern English churches. And not only are the forms but the subjects imitated, long after all meaning had passed away, and this not only in the religious figures of Isis and other gods. There is something ludicrously grotesque in colossal bas-reliefs of kings seizing innumerable captives by the hair of the head, as in the ancient sculptures of Rameses—kings who reigned at a time when all conquests had ceased, and who had, perhaps, never stirred out of the palaces and libraries of Alexandria."[1]

In spite, however, of these inconsistencies, it is difficult to conceive a grander spot than Philæ, even in the days of these imitative Ptolemies. The whole island rose from the Nile in quays of mighty blocks of stone, down which swept to the water's edge, staircases and terrace upon terrace. Where ruins and mud hovels now form foils and unsightly edifices, were spacious approaches, all of masonry, to chapels and temples; here flanked by granite sphinxes, or lions, and here running through pillared corridors. Then, unmutilated, rose the lordly propylæa; then came courts, and in them noble columns with capitals in gayest colours, supporting massive ceilings adorned with subjects of mythology, which remain unfaded till this day; stone staircases descended into subterranean chambers, now blocked up with rubbish, and the habitations of

[1] Mr. Stanley.

bats and reptiles, but not less elaborate than the structures reared above them. And when processions of priests in robes girt up and leopard-skin attire, bore the sacred bark of Isis to the temple of the goddess, and the emblems and devices of strange deities to their respective shrines; when the bray of trumpets and the clash of brazen instruments were borne over the waters, and the frankincense and smoke of morn and evening sacrifice curled upwards in the pure and cloudless air; then, indeed, Philæ must have been goodly to behold, though the crown of Upper and Lower Egypt, the imperial insignia of Thothmes and Amunoph and Rameses, had been wrested by the Macedonian sword from their degenerate race, to adorn the brow of Physcon the Fat, Euergetes, or Cleopatra.

Starting from the southern point of the island, you advance through the corridors with the innumerable pillars that I have already referred to. These galleries rise perpendicularly from the river, and looking through the openings, you perceive the island of Biggeh opposite to you, with its ruined temple of Athor. At the end of these galleries are the great propylæa of the temple of Isis, covered with inscriptions in different languages, chiefly Greek. On the right-hand side of the entrance to the court through the propylæa, is the record of the French conquest of Egypt, as follows:—

L'AN 6 DE LA RÉPUBLIQUE
LE 13 MESSIDOR,
UNE ARMÉE FRANÇAISE COMMANDÉE
PAR BUONAPARTE EST DESCENDUE
D'ALEXANDRIE.
L'ARMÉE AYANT MIS VINGT JOURS
APRÈS LES MAMMELOUKS EN FUITE
AUX PYRAMIDES
DESAIX COMMANDANT LA
PREMIERE DIVISION, LES A
POURSUIVIS AU DELÀ DES
CATARACTES, OU IL EST ARRIVÉ
LE 13 VENTOSE DE L'AN 7.
LES GÉNÉRAUX DE BRIGADE
DAOUST, FRIAND, ET BELLIARD.
DONNEBIT CHEF DE L'ÉTAT MAJOR
LATOURNERIE COMM^{dt} L'ARTILLERIE
EPPHER CHEF DE LA 21me LÉGERE
LE 13 VENTOSE, AN 7 DE LA RÉPUBLIQUE
LE 3 MARS AN DE J^s CHst 1799.
GRAVÉ PAR CASTEX SCULPTEUR.

In the middle of this inscription is another, in Russian characters, which I could only copy as accurately as possible:—

1852. Аазаревв ура Россія!!!
АЛЕКСАН
АР3.

"Lazareff. Hurra for Russia! Alexander."

Mr. Lazareff intimated that Alexander had avenged the Mamelukes.

I may remark, that the word Buonaparte in the fourth line of the inscription is almost entirely erased, but it still can be made out; and some one has painted above it in white letters this dignified rebuke to its mutilators, "Une page d'histoire ne doit pas être salie." There are also several other inscriptions, apparently comments and retorts arising from the French one, but so entirely defaced as to be illegible.

On entering the court from the propylæa, the first thing that strikes the eye are the magnificent columns that form the portico of the temple. They are twelve in number—four in front, and three deep. These capitals are various, some resembling the lotus-flower, others the papyrus; in fact, all are different, but painted with the most brilliant colours—light, and dark blue, and green, predominating. But for the hosts of sparrows that infest the temple, I have little doubt that even to this day, more than 2000 years since the painter was employed in these decorations, the tints on the capitals and ceilings would have been as brilliant as the first hour they were laid on; even now one is astonished at their freshness and beauty, and would gladly hail young Ion to come bounding into the temple with bent bow and arrows, to drive out these irreverent destroyers of colors so graceful to the visitor, and of drawings so interesting to the antiquarian.

>   ―― πτηνῶν ἀγέλας
>   αἳ βλάπτουσιν
> σέμν' ἀναθήματα τόξοισιν ἐμοῖς
> φυγάδας θήσομεν—
> Αὐδῶ μὴ χρίμπτειν θριγκοῖς
> μηδ' εἰς χρυσήρεις οἴκους.—EURIPID. ION.

These drawings seem to have reference to the antagonism of Typhon and Osiris—the spirit of evil and the spirit of good. Typhon, his implacable foe and murderer, is here represented by no means attractively. He appears as a grim monster sitting erect on his hind legs, which are bent under him from the hock, like those of a terrier; his pear-shaped stomach trails before him on the ground; long flabby breasts hang from his chest; his hand is a claw resting on some kind of weapon; his head is half of a dog, half of a crocodile; his little sharp ears are laid back viciously; his enormous jaws are grinning full of fierce teeth; and from his back depends a long tail, which he drags on the ground behind him. This is the Egyptian conception of the evil one, and certainly the expression, "as ugly as sin," could not be applied to a more hideous monster.

On both sides of the court are chambers more or less decorated, and underground communications which I did not venture to explore. On passing through the portico into the shrine of the temple, we mounted a flight of stone stairs leading to the roof, in order to inspect a small but very remarkable chamber, which is supposed to contain scenes referring to the death and sepulture of Osiris. First, you see the figure lying in the agonies of death, with mourning females at the head and feet; then two females are bandaging the defunct into the form of a mummy; then four men carry away the corpse on a bier; in the next tablet a priest lays out the corpse; in the fifth compartment it is lying in a coffin; in the sixth it is invested with a dog's head; and at the head and foot are two figures with dogs' heads in the attitude of adoration. There is another engraving here too curious not to mention —that of the god Kneph, the "creative principle" ($\delta\eta\mu\iota o\upsilon\rho\gamma o\varsigma$)—moulding in the potter's vessel clay of which mankind is formed. The scriptural account of the formation of Adam (the meaning of which word is "red earth,") "and God formed man out of the dust of the ground," may be remarked in referring to this illustration of Egyptian belief.[1] But the traditions of Osiris with which Philæ is peculiarly connected, bear with them to us a most extraordinary interest. His peculiar character—his coming upon earth for the benefit of mankind, with the titles of "Manifester of Good and Truth," his being put to death by the malice of the evil one, his burial and resurrection, and his becoming judge of the dead— all these circumstances have so strange a connection

---

[1] The hieroglyphic inscription underneath this is thus read:— "Num, who forms on his wheel the divine limbs of Osiris, who is enthroned in the great hall of life."

with the main foundations of our own belief, that it is well worth while to give a very brief sketch of the Egyptian religion, derived from Sir G. Wilkinson; as it is far removed from the senseless and indiscriminate idolatry which the grotesque drawings on their tombs and temples seem to indicate.

In the belief of the Egyptians the fundamental doctrine was, the unity of the deity; but this unity was not represented, and He was known by a sentence or an idea, being, as Jamblichus says, "worshipped in silence." But the attributes of this being were represented under positive forms; and hence arose a multiplicity of gods that engendered idolatry, and caused a total misconception of the real nature of the Deity in the minds of all who were not admitted to a knowledge of the truth through the mysteries. The division of God into his attributes was in this manner:—As soon as he was thought to have any reference to his works, or to man, he ceased to be quiescent: he became an agent, and he was no longer the ONE, but distinguishable and divisible according to his supposed character, his actions, and his influence on the world. He was then the Creator, the divine Goodness (or the abstract idea of good)—Wisdom, Power, and the like; and as we speak of Him as the Almighty, the Merciful, the Everlasting, so the Egyptians gave to each of his various attributes a particular name. But they did more: they separated them; and to the unitiated they became distinct gods.

As one of these the Deity was Amun, probably the divine mind in operation, the bringer to light of the secrets of the *hidden* will; and he had a complete human form, because man was the intellectual animal, and the principal design of the divine will is in the creation. As *"the Spirit of God"* that moveth on the face of the waters, the deity was Nef, Nû, or Nûm, over whom the asp, the emblem of royalty and of the good genius, spread itself as a canopy, while he stood in his boat. At the *creation* he was Pthah; and in this character he was accompanied by the figure of Truth— a combination of it with the creative power which recalls this sentence in the Epistle of St. Jerome, "of his own will begat he us with the word of Truth." As the principle of generation, he was Khem, called "the father of his own father"—the abstract idea of father, as the goddess was that of mother, who consequently proceeded from herself. And other attributes, characters, and offices of the Deity held a rank according to their closer or more distant relation to his essence and operations.

In order to specify and convey an impression of these abstract notions to the eyes of men, it was thought necessary to distinguish them by some fixed representations; and the figures of Pthah, Osiris, Amun, Maut, Neith, and other gods and goddesses, were invented as the signs of the various attributes of the Deity. But it did not stop there: and as the subtilty of philosophical speculation entered into the original simple theory, numerous subdivisions of the divine nature were made; and at length anything which appeared to partake of or bear analogy to it, was admitted to a share of worship. Hence arose the various grades of deities; and they were known as the gods of the first, second, and third orders. But Herodotus is quite right in saying that the Egyptians gave no divine honors to heroes.

The Egyptian figures of gods were only vicarious forms, not intended to be looked upon as real personages; and no one was expected to believe that a being could exist with the head of an animal joined to a human body; but credulity will always do its work. The uneducated failed to take the same view of them, as the initiated portion of the community; and mere emblems soon assumed the importance of the divine personages to which they belonged. These abuses were the natural consequences of such representations; and experience has often shown how readily the mind may be drawn away from the most spiritual worship, to a superstitious veneration for images, whether at first intended merely to fix the attention, or to represent some legendary tale or abstract idea. The religion of the Egyptians was a pantheism rather than a polytheism; and their admitting the sun and moon to divine worship, may rather be ascribed to the following reasons, than to any admixture of Sabæism. The sun was thought to possess much of the divine influence, in its vivifying power, and its various other effects; and was not only one of the grandest works, but it was one of the direct agents of the Deity. The moon was in another similar capacity, and as the regulator of time, and the messenger of heaven, was figured as the Ibis-headed Thoth, the god of letters, and the deity who registered man's actions and the events of his life. They not only attributed to the sun and moon, and to other supposed agents, a participation in the divine essence, but even stones and plants were thought to have some portion of it; and certain peculiarities were often discovered in the habits or appearance of animals, which were supposed to bear a resemblance to the divine character. Even a king was sometimes represented making offerings to another figure of himself in the temples, signifying that his human did homage to his divine nature.

They also represented the Deity under different names and characters. Isis, from the number of her titles, was called "Myrionymus," or "of the thousand names." A god or goddess was also worshipped as residing in a particular place, or as gifted with some particular quality: like the Minerva Polias, and various Minervas, the several Venuses, the Jupiters, and others; and modern custom has made a variety of Madonnas from the one Virgin.

Certain cities and districts were appropriated to certain gods, who were the chief deities of the place; and while Amun had his principal temple at Thebes, Memphis was the great city of Pthah, as Heliopolis of Ré, or the sun, and other cities of other divinities—no two neighboring districts or chief cities being given to the same god. But, although Amun was the great god of Thebes, as Pthah was of Memphis, it is not to be supposed that their separate worship originated in two parts of Egypt, or that the religions of the upper and lower country were once distinct, and afterwards united into one. They were members of the same pantheon.

"A balance of power," as of honor, was thus established for the principal gods: minor deities being satisfied with towns of minor importance; other divinities shared the honors of the sanctuary; and different triads or single gods were admitted to a post in the various temples. Thus Pthah had a suitable position in a Theban adytum; Amun and Nef, or the triads of Thebes and the Cataracts, of which they were respectively the first persons, were figured on the temples at Memphis; and none were necessarily excluded, provided room could be found for them, except purely local deities. Those of a neighboring town were readily admitted to a place among the contemplar gods; it was at least a neighborly compliment, and it suited the convenience of the priests quite as much as of the gods themselves. Many minor divine beings, whose worship was ordained for some particular object, and certain emblems or sacred animals, were admitted into one, and excluded in another place. Thus the reverence for the crocodile, encouraged in some inland towns that the canals might be properly cleared and kept up, was found unnecessary in places by the river's side, where he was probably held in abhorrence; and the same animal which was highly regarded in one district, was a symbol of evil in another.

The chamber which has originated this somewhat long digression was so peculiarly clean, so well swept and garnished, that I asked a poor old civil Nubian, who had accompanied me, the cause of such unusual neatness. He informed me that a European had taken up his abode in this chamber, and lived here for about three weeks the year before; and in this warm country, it would be difficult to obtain better, or cooler, or more retired quarters. Some French wag has thought to be amusing by writing on the passage in huge chalk letters, "Hotel de l'Europe. Appartements garnis."

The Nubian I have just mentioned was an example of the ferocity of the thorns which I have already described. About eleven months previous to our visit, by some accident, one of them had entered the palm of his hand, and fixed itself there in the muscle. There was no appearance of any sore, but the hand was bent double, and perfectly useless. When I was giving him some trifle for his extreme unobtrusiveness, as well as readiness to show us anything we were likely to miss seeing, he said, very much unlike his other countrymen, that his object in accompanying us was not *buckshish*, but that, if we could do anything for his hand, he would be amply paid. He said, that independently of its loss, he felt at night as if fire was in it. Our limited knowledge of the healing art could only recommend incessant poulticing. It is a sad thing to a traveller not to have even a superficial knowledge of medicine. The amount of good that he could do, the weight of sorrow that he could dispel, by understanding simple cases, exceeds belief; and there is no character that enables a man to travel in such security, and with so much attention, as that of Tabib, or physician. It is a passport better than a hundred firmans of the Padishah.

We next proceeded to the northern extremity of the island, and found it everywhere covered with the remains of buildings; while from the edge of the river sprung the palms that seem to grow at the ruins' feet. We then worked round to the eastern side, where stands the beautiful hypæthral temple, which forms one of the most conspicuous objects on the island. It is about fifty feet square; the opposite sides are formed by five columns each, and the others by two pilasters, between which are the entrances. The capitals of the columns are extremely rich, and the cornice above them graceful and simple. The intercolumniations are built up to nearly two thirds of the height, which gives it a singular effect. It is also of the age of the Ptolemies, and is one of the best preserved as well as the lightest and most elegant monuments in Egypt. The interior of it is, like all the other buildings of Philæ, covered with inscriptions and names of visitors ancient and modern. One, from its "caligraphic" execution, and ornamental scroll round it, attracted my attention.

N. PEARCE,
FIVE MONTHS FROM ADDWAR IN ABYSSINIA,
AFTER BEING IN THAT COUNTRY
FOURTEEN YEARS IN THE SERVICE OF
THE EARL OF MOUNT NORRIS AND H. SALT, ESQ.
MARCH 31, 1819.

The story of this man is curious. He was in the year 1804 a sailor on board the *Antelope*, a vessel that had been placed by Lord Wellesley, then Governor-General of India, at the disposal of Lord Valentia, to explore the Red Sea and coasts of Abyssinia. During the stay of that vessel at Mocha, many of her crew, induced by the temptations of the local authorities, ran away from the ship. Among these was Pearce. He subsequently wrote to Lord Valentia to request a Bible, which his lordship sent, together with a letter expostulating with him on the criminality of his proceedings. Either the Bible or the letter convinced him of his misconduct, for some time afterwards he begged forgiveness, which was granted, and he was taken by Mr. Salt in his expedition to Abyssinia. After remaining in that country fourteen years, he returned to Mr. Salt's service; but not finding him at Cairo, he made his way up the river in search of him, and it was then that he inscribed that account of himself on the temple at Philæ.

Our American cousins also, as the newspapers call them, have left memorials of their visits in profusion; one, however, I specially selected from that "proud throng" as a particular illustration of propriety, good taste, and wit :—

JUDGE LYNCH WAS HERE MARCH, 1854,
AND WAS SORRY THAT
CLEOPATRA WAS NOT AT HOME.

But the day is now beginning to decline, and though I turn with regret to the little chamber on the summit of the temple, and would willingly pitch my carpet there, and give at least another day to these remains, yet the reis has announced that it would be well before dark to move down towards the mouth of the cataract. Our anxiety to leave Nubia, whence we thought we never should escape, the weary dreary days of tempest we had of late endured, and the contemplation of Egypt's fleshpots which we sighed for—all these considerations banished the wish for a more protracted stay at Philæ. Therefore let us mount the lofty propylæa ere we depart, and take one general view over the whole island and the adjacent scenery. Looking *up* the stream, before you are the colonnades and covered galleries flanking the river. On your right is the Nubian village in the island of Biggeh, and its ruined temple. The water-side is gay this evening. Men are passing to and fro from one island to another, riding on palm trunks; women walk down the bank bearing water-jars so stately on their heads; and a parliament of ancients is sitting in a circle, looking gravely at the goings-on, and sending forth little blue jets of tobacco smoke from their chibouques. To the left, Arabia's gritty mountains, palm-fringed, have closed in upon the river, and the declining sun's rays from the west are playing over the white tomb of a *santon*, or holy man, perched on the hill's brow. And now farewell to the south and to the past. Let us look northward over the island, and to the future. Two ponderous rocks of granite, apt consorts, rise before you, on and yet apart from the main land, graved with the name and titles of King Psammitichus. A broad and smooth expanse of sand between the granite hillocks leads to Assouan. A few donkeys are all that are now to be seen on it; but it was once the royal road to Philæ, and Pharaohs and Ptolemies and Proconsuls have traversed it, bearing gifts and offerings to the holy island. The river, after sweeping round and forming the lake in which Philæ sleeps, turns to the west; but the strife of elements does not yet disturb its calm repose; with us it is still dimpling and serene, for between it and the cataract a rocky barrier interposes, and shuts out from view the pause, the plunge, the struggle, and the victory.

But all these pleasant views in the cool evening breeze, and the reflections they evoke, are to come to an end; for the small boat bearing back my companion has pushed off from the main land, where he had been sketching, and a hail from the crew indicated that it was time for our start. We loosened the rope from the shores of Philæ, and that evening we lay within a few hundred yards of the cataract, which the reis declared we should positively descend early in the morning.

The early morning came, all the perishable articles were removed to the upper deck, and in due course of time the pilot and his men appeared. Our crew now surrendered the oars into the custody of the strangers, the reis on duty took the helm, and a holy man sat in the front of the raised deck telling his beads and muttering prayers for the success of the descent. Our own men stood ready with poles in case of need, and divers volunteers in the look out for *buckshish* accompanied us on one pretext or another. The descent is by a different route altogether from the ascent: this passage lies by the western bank, as the latter does by the eastern. As you mount there are several rapids to be overcome; here there are only two, but those two are very different from the others. No power of man could ever force a boat up them. They really are something like what cataracts should be; and when I spoke so very contemptuously of the whole affair in mounting, I was quite unaware of the nature of the descent.

And now here we are at the mouth of the first fall—a long narrow pass between two walls of rock, which the oars will apparently almost touch in passing. A roaring, tumbling torrent pours madly through this cleft. Our boat seems to hesitate ere she takes the plunge; her stern rests on the smooth treacherous summit of the fall—her bow is hanging over it. Down, down she goes as if to strike the rocky bottom. The Nubians shout furiously as the wave hits the poor *Flea* a blow that makes her quiver, but the wave is dashed into spray which flies all over us. Amid this shouting and turbulent crew there is one man silent. The cataract reis grasps the tiller with an iron grasp; his eye, keen like that of one of the eagles of his own cliffs, is fixed on the seething race, and a rock at its tail on which we must inevitably strike. The rowers sit with oars poised and ready for the last exertion—and now it comes. Our boat, madly charging downward, reeling through the surge, and quivering with the blows of each successive plunge, is within a yard or two of the rock, borne apparently sheer upon it by the irresistible current—now is the time. With a shout from the reis high above the Babel of voices, and a gesture of his hand, the oars dash into the water; for an instant there is a struggle with the angry river, but the boat answers the call of the helmsman, her bow turns to the right, the stern just grates against the threatening rock, and the worst is over. The rowers from below now look pleasantly at the reis and the reis's friends, and the holy man above; the reis, the reis's friends, and the holy man, look pleasantly upon us; and we in return look benignantly upon all. The soft infection spreads—the word *buckshish* is gently murmured from every mouth, the holy man intersperses it in his prayers—it rises into a regular chorus, not merely of simple *buckshish*, but of " Buckshish kateer kateer"—Immense, inordinate *buckshish*—implying that the least expectation is that the whole population of the cataract should be fed and clothed, and tipped too, at our expense. Our dragoman is taken aside, and whispered that this reis got one thing from one boat, and another reis another thing; but his teeth are chattering with fear, and the supplications fall unheeded on his ear, for the other cataract is at hand, and now with a shout, a plunge, and a cloud of spray, the last obstacle is surmounted, and we run under the steep bank to disgorge our friends, who have reasons of their own for not entering Assouan. It now remains to satisfy the claimants. We first pay the stipulated sum, then give an extra *buckshish* of a few dollars; but that is not the "bucksheesh kateer" expected, and implied by our silence. The dragoman is entreated to tell us of the lovely presents always given on these occasions: how new turbans, tarbooshes, and handkerchiefs, were distributed (a most abominable lie), by the owner of the very boat who went up with us, on his return some days previous to our descent. One black head after another was thrust into the cabin, but we were inexorable. We knew we had paid liberally, and would not encourage this system of pillage. "Would we not give them any little gift at parting?" they piteously said, "just as a remembrance of our visit; medicine, anything, in short." We were touched by this last appeal and handed to them with the gravity of Æsculapius two jars of potted shrimps, desiring them to use the inestimable gifts whenever any stomach was out of order in the neighborhood of the cataracts. The compound was so inexpressibly odious, that it could not fail to work an emetic and a cure. They received the boon with a general thanksgiving. The reis explained to his merry men, the wondrous properties of these mystic vessels; the compositor's name and direction, stamped upon them, added much to the effect; and the last we saw of the reises and the holy man, was their bearing the vases of the *elixir vitæ* in solemn procession along the hill, their attendants skipping like young kids for joy before them. Our own sailors now resumed the oars; in a few minutes we were gliding by Elephantine, and then moored upon the strand of Assouan.

The country of Nubia that we have just escaped from, occupies above 220 miles as the river runs, from the northern boundary of Assouan (the ancient Syene) to Wady Halfa. Although called by the Arabs, by the simple name of "the land of the Barabra," it is in fact occupied by two distinct people, of different appearance and of different language. The Kenoos, or Kensee tribe, inhabit the north as far as Derr; thence to the Second Cataract the Nooba tribe intervene, when the Kenoos is again resumed. One is much surprised at Assouan to leave at once the Arab character and complexion, and to come upon a people almost Negro in color and appearance. The crisp hair, flat nose, and heavy lip, denote clearly a race of African origin; but on proceeding further to the south, contrary to all expectations, these distinctions disappear, and the natives become as fair as, and very much resembling, the Egyptians.

The derivation of the word Nubia is from the old Egyptian word, Nub—Gold—signifying the "land of gold." Hence was derived Canopus, from the god Nubei, probably pronounced Gnubei. In scripture Nubia is called Nub, but Ezekiel xxx. 5, seems to have spelt it Gnub,[1] although in our translation it is written Chub.

Our sailors took great pleasure in teaching us their language, which is remarkably melodious, so

[1] I am disposed to distrust the accuracy of this observation, which is derived from Bunsen's *Egypt's Place in Universal History*.

much so as to resemble in sound, Italian. It forms the most striking contrast to the accumulation of consonants and the harsh guttural sounds of Arabic. There does not appear to be the slightest similarity or accordance with any Asiatic language, whether Arabic or ancient Egyptian, in its grammatical forms, although it has borrowed and adopted from the Arabic a considerable number of its words. It is, doubtless, a purely African language, brought in by an African tribe from the south-west, who established themselves on the confines of Egypt.

There is also no doubt that in former times this portion of the valley of the Nile was far more prolific than at present—the bed of the river is considerably lower, and its inundation no longer extends the blessings of fertility to tracts of land now covered with sand, but once, as excavations have proved, of the same rich alluvial soil as the lower country of Egypt. It is in fact at this moment on the high shelving banks of the river that the cultivation, generally speaking, extends. They are planted with bearded wheat, beans, chickpea, and lupins; but wherever a small patch of soil exists over which the west wind has not poured its sand-drifts, you will find the poor Nubian struggling day and night in contest with the desert. The banks are generally so high that it would require too much manual labour for the employment of the Shadoof, but the Sakias during the whole twenty-four hours groan and creak as they struggle to give life to little patches of doura, cotton, castor-oil, and rice. As you sail along you see, wherever irrigation can be effected, a low shed shaded with melons, vine, or palm leaf, with a deep open well below it. Round and round the cow or buffalo treads its weary path, as the wheel revolves raising some score of earthen pitchers, which discharge their contents into little channels and then sink down in search of more. A Nubian sits on the shaft and keeps the cattle moving, and a chaff, generally more vigorous than polite, passes between him and the crew. The date-palm is, however, the chief resource to supply the wants of the country, and by exportation to pay the taxes, which are heavy and oppressive. Mr. Taylor mentions that the Sakias are assessed at 300 piastres each by the year, something more than £3, for they go in taxation by the statute and not the mercantile piastre. This is in lieu of the ground-tax which the Egyptians pay.

Although the sum is not large absolutely, it is nevertheless a heavy impost on these poor people, who have hardly any outlet for their produce, or other means of obtaining a livelihood than by the cultivation of the soil, as may be easily imagined from the fact of there not being a single manufactory of any article or even a shop in all Nubia. No tax can well be conceived more injurious than that which has the direct tendency to throw land into desert; but the manner of levying it, which Mr. Taylor is not aware of, is still more atrocious.

If the owner of one Sakia is unable to pay the tax, the owners of the others in the vicinity are obliged to make good the deficiency; and it constantly happens that where one proprietor decamps, the whole neighborhood decamps after him, as each successive default would fall with redoubled severity on those that remained to confront the tax-gatherer.

The country is no doubt better governed under Egyptian rule than formerly under its own native chiefs. They were not one whit less burdensome to the peasant, and he is at all events spared intestine wars, robbery, and bloodshed. But wherever a Turk governs there is sure to be bribery and spoliation, and the regular taxation, heavy as it is, is not all that weighs down and pauperizes the Nubian. The result is that they endeavour, in spite of government enactments and pains and penalties, to escape from their own villages to Cairo, where their known honesty procures them situations and good wages; but still their heart, like that of the Swiss, is always with their homes, and the great object of their life is to accumulate enough to enable them to return to their village, rent a Sakia of their own, have funds sufficient to be taxed and fleeced as their progenitors were before them, and then creak, creak, buzz, buzz, grunt, grunt, for the remainder of their existence.

To give some idea of the consequences of the irregular and illicit taxation imposed by the governors of districts for their own use and benefit,

Mr. Taylor, in describing the plains of Dongola, once so fertile, but now almost wild and abandoned, explains the causes thus. He says:— "Sakias are here taxed at 475 piastres each, notwithstanding the sum fixed by government is only 300. The remainder goes into the private treasury of the governor. For this reason many persons, unable to pay the tax, emigrate into Kordofan or elsewhere. This may account for the frequent tracts of the finest soil which are abandoned. I passed," he adds, "many fine fields given up to halfeh grass. From Handak to El Orda is two days' journey. The country presents the same aspect of desolation and ruin, as that in the neighborhood of Old Dongola,—untenanted villages line the road during nearly the whole distance. The face of the country is level, and there is no mountain to be seen on either bank of the Nile. It is a melancholy, deserted region, showing only palms growing wildly and rankly along the river, fields covered with halfeh, water-courses broken down, Sakias dismantled, and everywhere dwellings in ruin. Here and there a few inhabitants still lingered, tending their fields of stunted cotton, or watering some patches of green wheat."

In spite, however, of their grievances and oppressions, the Nubians are a bold, independent race—they have never been reduced to slavery by any of their conquerors, and have shown on more than one occasion the greatest gallantry and determination in resisting the disciplined troops of the Pacha of Egypt. They are unquestionably fine men, with a free, erect carriage, and may have many estimable qualities, but their greedy begging propensities held out very little inducement to cultivate a closer acquaintance. Judging from our own crew, I should have inclined to consider them averse to work, and indolent; but their incessant labour to till their little plots entirely relieves them from the imputation. They are notorious for their *esprit de pays*, and always messed together apart from the Arab sailors in our boat; and I remarked as a very amiable trait in their character, that if we gave to any one in particular, biscuits or pigeons, or anything in the eating way, he always shared it with his companions, and would even put aside a portion for any absentee. I may add that I found them most good humoured, although latterly we had remarked a disposition to neglect orders, indeed even to disobey them. As we went up the river, not a boat descended from Assouan that was not hailed by them; and if other Nubians were on board, there resulted a shouting match, much to our annoyance, of inquiries after all the Mohammeds, Omars, and Alis in the neighborhood of the cataracts,—how they were, their families and relatives; and, as each man had his own circle of acquaintance to inquire about, the disturbance continued as long as there was a chance of a reply. In going down, the nuisance became still more intolerable, as it went on at night, and the most animated query and reply used to be kept up with his fellow-countrymen working at the Sakias by our reis, who was the chief offender, so much so that we were forced, in order to get some sleep, to threaten condign punishment if the nocturnal clamour was continued. The Arabs in our boat had none of the affection of clanship, but, although coming from villages in the same vicinity, troubled themselves very little about the health and fortunes o their friends and relatives.

There did not appear to be any great cordiality between the Arab and Nubian sailors. My dragoman was very spiteful too, and said sarcastic things about Nubia and the Nubians, looking down on them as rude, ignorant barbarians, quite out of the pale of Egyptian refinement and civilization. Our old cook also did not love them well. His culinary art was but little exerted during our month in their country, and he felt his character to be lowered by the scantiness of his bill of fare. They chaffed him too unmercifully on all occasions, which he considered the height of presumption, but he paid them out on arriving at Assouan, by performing a war dance, brandishing his pipe instead of a battle-axe over the heads of imaginary Barabra, after the manner of Rameses the Great, calling their country the abode of starvation, and themselves animals no better than pigs. They attempted a few faint pleasantries in return, but old Hassaneen's " foot was now again on his native heath," and he settled them at once by comparing them to lizards, who carry their tails cockily enough, but trail their bellies on the ground—alluding to their sauciness and beggarly condition. It was the shout of laughter on the beach accompanying these observations that aroused our inquiries into the nature of the conversation.

It is, however, in the condition of the women that the greatest change is apparent, on passing the Egyptian boundary. They also partake of the free character of the men, and there is none of that half-concealment of the features which the Arab Fellah woman considers it right to practise. On the contrary, they never shrinked from approaching our boat, and would have been quite ready to talk and extract something either by way of barter or *buckshish*, could we have mutually understood one another. At Assouan our excellent second reis brought his wife and child on board, where she sat very contentedly until we lent her the boat to depart to the other side; nor did the other sailors have the slightest objection to bring their unveiled wives and their children (of whom they seemed devotedly fond) to the shore by the boat's side, and sit with them there for hours; they would have been only too proud to have invited them on deck, but for reasons connected with fleas and other tormentors, we ungallantly but peremptorily refused them admittance.

With all this outward liberty, from the accounts both of books and from what I heard even from Arabs, there are no women who less abuse it than the Nubian. They are in the aggregate remarkable for their modesty. It is true that they run a fearful risk in loving not wisely but too well, for death in the case of a married woman always accompanies discovery. Our Nubian lad, Mohammed, was engaged to be married as soon as he returned from this trip. Unlike the Arabs, who are averse to enter into any explanation about their family affairs, or to allude in any way to the inmates of the hareem, we found our sailors quite ready and willing to chat, laugh, and answer all questions on the subject of their womenkind. Mohammed, one evening coming home from an expedition, gave us a full account of all proceedings appertaining to marriage in his country. He said, that the young people had constant opportunities of seeing each other, and that, as in his case, attachments were formed from mutual appreciation, and not, as with the generality of Arabs, among whom, especially in cities, the bridegroom never sets eyes on the bride until after the nuptial ceremony. On obtaining the young lady's affection the next step is to apply to her parents in due form. A certain sum of money is demanded by them, and protracted negotiations ensue before the amount is fixed. The engagement is now settled, and until the marriage takes place, the future bride remains at her father's house, and it is strict etiquette that she and her husband who is to be should under no circumstances meet before the wedding day. If he pays her relations a visit, she always conceals herself or is sent away during the time of his stay. Some considerable interval very often elapses between the betrothal and the bridal; in the case of our Mahommed, nearly eight months were passed since his honorable proposals were accepted. His case was one of many: he had not got the money to make the preliminary settlements, and had to make a trip or two to earn the amount, together with the presents to the lady that follow afterwards. During this period the expense of maintenance falls upon the future husband. In Mohammed's case the settlements were not heavy— 150 piastres, or about £1. 7s.; and this, he said, was about the ordinary tarif. Of this sum 100 piastres, or two-thirds, are handed over at once to the bride's parents, the other third is reserved for the wife in case of divorce, when it is assigned to her. The newly married couple generally reside with the girl's parents until the first child is born, when they either remove to the village of the man, or else, by the aid of some mud and a few palm branches, set up an establishment of their own. I asked Mohammed if he was at all jealous of his betrothed during so long an absence. He said it was not his business to be jealous, that operation of the mind devolved on the parents of the young lady. It was their honor, not his, that was at stake, and they would take very good care there should be no cause for jealousy. We then inquired what took place, if after marriage the lady preferred another to her legitimate lord. He very significantly drew his hand across his throat, and told us that the erring wife, even if caught by her husband with her lover, would not receive her punishment from him. She would be brought before her parents; they would judge her offence, and if it were proved, a ghastly female corpse with throat cut from ear to ear would ere many days be drifted upon a Nile sandbank for the benefit of vultures and hyenas. "But as regards the wicked lover," said we, "what is done with him?" "O! nothing at all," said Mohammed, "he generally leaves the village, but he is neither obliged to pay damages, nor does the injured husband consider it necessary to invite him to single combat. He goes upon his road rejoicing."

Hereupon we took the opportunity, as Englishmen always consider themselves bound to do, to spread abroad in all lands, and among all people, the beauty, consistency, and wisdom of our social system in these respects. I informed the astonished Himmed, through the equally astonished dragoman, that in our country, our injured honor did not require such a fearful expiation, but that by bringing the matter before the cadi, a sum of money for the injury received was poured like oil and wine into our gaping wounds, and instantly cured them; that sometimes the injured husband took a different course, and, although ignorant of pistol practice, allowed the skilful lover to fire at him till death ensued; and that that was also an excellent remedy for wounded honor; and then I explained to them, how that, being a highly virtuous and moral people, we printed an account of all these transactions, omitting no detail however contaminating and indecent, and laid it on the tables of our wives and daughters, that the mature virtue of the one, and the early ingenuousness of the others, might have the full advantage of remaining unsullied after the constant perusal of such incidents; and that, although made perfectly aware by the mishaps of others of the best mode to escape detection, they should prove the excellence of their principles by resisting the same seductions that made others fall —and be found out; for without temptation the virtue of withstanding it cannot be. The Nubian and Arab Mohammed were both greatly edified by this exposition, said we were a wonderful people, inscrutably wise, but would evidently have quoted Sosie had they ever read Molière's *Amphitryon*:—

> Tout cela va le mieux du monde,
> Mais enfin coupons au discours.
> Sur cettes affaires toujours
> Le meilleur est de ne rien dire.

In the neighborhood of the cataracts some of

the Nubian girls are strikingly pretty—slight and delicate forms, soft gentle eyes, rich rosy lips, and brilliant teeth, hands over which glass bracelets pass which would not contain our children's wrists, little feet to match, and rounded graceful arms. Such are the charms which are not diminished by their glossy black complexions.

> Their hue is of that dark red dye
> That fringes oft a thunder sky,
> Their hands palmetto baskets bear,
> And cotton fillets bind their hair.
> Slim is their form, their mien is shy;
> To earth they bend the humbled eye,
> And fold their arms, and suppliant kneel,
> Bucksheesh Howaga! their appeal.
> *Bridal of Triermain (slightly altered).*

I have cautiously used the word "some" in referring to these beauties, for they are certainly the exceptions and not the rule. The little wenches seem to know the style of good looks that pleases the European's eye, and are generally successful in extracting the piastres which their dirty, dusty, unkempt brethren fail to elicit.

My companion during my explorations of Philæ was engaged in sketching on the opposite bank; and when he returned in the evening it was clear that his heart was burnt into kabobs by one of these damsels. He had been annoyed, he said, by the usual torment of beggars whom he had dispersed with stones, and was quietly resuming his work when a Nubian girl came and sat on the bank at a little distance. She would have shared the fate of the rest, but as she made no observations, his wrath was appeased, and looking up he saw that she was strikingly pretty. This discovery gave, no doubt, a very beneficent expression to his countenance, for, by degrees, she ventured nearer and nearer, until at last her curiosity conquered her fears, and she sat down by his side, watching the sketching and coloring with the greatest delight; and at last, pointing with her little finger to all the objects as they were entered on the sketch. She apparently found my friend so little of the fierce monster that Europeans are supposed to be, that she remained with him all the time he was sketching, held with him a most animated but incomprehensible conversation, and drove away all intruders who thought they might follow her example, and approach the stranger. Mr. K. spoke in such raptures of her gentle winning ways, soft voice, soft eyes, soft skin, brilliant teeth, little hands, running through the whole catalogue of female points, that I was greatly afraid his sketch (which by the way was not half finished, although there was plenty of time nominally employed in it) would require another day or two to complete, and that I should have to wait at Assouan in the interim. I therefore ventured to put to him two questions. Did she smell very unpleasantly of castor-oil? and, secondly, Did she ask for *buckshish?* And to both of these questions, to my astonishment, I received a bold and decided negative. It was true, he added, that she did receive all he had in his pocket; fortunately there was no gold, but it was accepted in a manner that showed it was only not to pain him by a refusal. The inquiry about the castor-oil was most legitimate, for the odours arising from that cosmetic are insupportable, and unfortunately it constitutes the pommade, macassar, and bear's grease of Nubia. Poor old Herodotus, too, suffered from its ill flavour; he calls it δυσώδης—" bad smelling," and remarks on the quantity of the trees planted to produce the oil with which in his day, as now, the natives smeared themselves. The women's hair is dressed in narrow plaits, which hang the same length all round the face, and make the head look something like a new black mop. Plunge this into an oil-jar, and you will have an excellent idea of the appearance of a Nubian dame " en grande tenue," with the oil flowing over her cheeks and shoulders, even unto the skirt of her garment.

My companion's good sense and regard for his family fortunately interfered, and prevented the delay which a matrimonial alliance with this charming and "superior young person" would have entailed; nor did he object, as I was much afraid he might, to our leaving Assouan the same afternoon that we arrived. We had some difficulty to manage this, for we had three new sailors to engage, and a cabin-boy in lieu of Master Nisnas, who had grown sulky and disobedient in consequence of our preference for "Himmed." In a fit of jealousy he declared it was high time for him to get circumcised, become a man, and earn men's wages; we therefore very readily left him behind at his village to organise the ceremony, and provided ourselves with a very good little fellow as a substitute. Then came the leave-taking: one man wanted to dine with his wife, another to see his sister, a third to leave some of his earnings at home, a fourth had a sick mother; in short, as Hubert very justly observed, "Ils sont comme les poules qui couvent; ils ne peuvent pas quitter leurs œufs." However, we got a scratch team together, and being promised faithfully by the others that they would rejoin us as we advanced, we slipped away from Assouan on the evening of the 7th of March.

END OF VOL. I.

www.ingramcontent.com/pod-product-compliance
Lightning Source LLC
Chambersburg PA
CBHW081912170426
43200CB00014B/2711